PEARSON
Education

In an increasingly competitive world, it is quality
of thinking that gives an edge – an idea that opens new
doors, a technique that solves a problem, or an insight
that simply helps make sense of it all.

We work with leading authors in the fields of
management and finance to bring cutting-edge thinking
and best learning practice to a global market.

Under a range of leading imprints, including
Financial Times Prentice Hall, we create world-class
print publications and electronic products giving readers
knowledge and understanding which can then be
applied, whether studying or at work.

For other Pearson Education publications, visit
www.pearsoned.co.uk

Research Methods for Leisure and Tourism

A Practical Guide

SECOND EDITION

A. J. Veal

Prentice Hall
FINANCIAL TIMES

An imprint of **Pearson Education**

Harlow, England • London • New York • Boston • San Francisco • Toronto • Sydney • Singapore • Hong Kong
Tokyo • Seoul • Taipei • New Delhi • Cape Town • Madrid • Mexico City • Amsterdam • Munich • Paris • Milan

ILAM
Institute of Leisure and
Amenity Management

Pearson Education Limited
Edinburgh Gate
Harlow
Essex CM20 2JE
England

and Associated Companies throughout the world

Visit us on the World Wide Web at:
http://www.pearsoned.co.uk

First published in Great Britain 1992
Second edition published 1997

© Longman Group UK Limited 1992
© Pearson Education Limited 1997

The right of A. J. Veal to be identified as Author
of this Work has been asserted by him in accordance
with the Copyright, Designs and Patents Act 1988.

ISBN 0 273 62052 5

British Library Cataloguing in Publication Data
A CIP catalogue record for this book can be obtained from the British Library

15 14
08 07 06 05

Typeset by Phoenix Photosetting, Chatham, Kent
Printed and bound in Great Britain by Bell & Bain Ltd., Glasgow

The Publishers' policy is to use paper manufactured from sustainable forests.

CONTENTS

LIST OF FIGURES

LIST OF TABLES

LIST OF CASE STUDIES

FOREWORD

Recent years have seen the expansion of leisure services throughout Britain, whether they are provided by institutions in the public, commercial or voluntary sectors. Such leisure facilities and services are now recognised as of critical significance in the changing social and economic structure of contemporary Britain: this was acknowledged by the government through the establishment of a Department of National Heritage led by a minister of cabinet rank. The effectiveness of such provision, however, lies in the hands of leisure officers and managers and it is clear that there is a need to ensure the highest level of professional support for leisure services.

The Institute of Leisure and Amenity Management (ILAM) is in the forefront of developing and promoting schemes of professional education and training leading to qualifications and increasing the competence of personnel in the leisure industry. The 1980s and the early 1990s saw the ILAM Certificate and Diploma faced with hundreds of examination applicants. At present there is the establishment of Industrial Lead Bodies with the identification of competencies in the form of National Vocational Qualifications (NVQs) and Scottish Vocational Qualifications (SVQs) on at least four levels. Further consideration is being given to levels 5 and 6. These professional qualifications are designed to ensure that leisure managers and their supporting personnel have a sound base of education and training to enable the competent day-to-day operation of leisure facilities and opportunities. Similarly there is a concern to ensure a thorough knowledge and understanding of the disciplines and skills appropriate to managers in the leisure business.

The aim of this series is not only to provide texts which will cover constituent elements of the earlier ILAM syllabus but also to provide a base of knowledge and examples that will allow leisure professionals to update and improve their practice and managerial skills while ensuring the competent operation of their junior staff. In that sense the series will be relevant to ILAM courses, Higher National Diploma and Degree qualifications, and will also act as a reference source for trainee professionals and personnel entrusted with the development of the NVQ and SVQ framework.

Each volume deals with a different aspect of professional activity in the leisure fields. The texts can therefore be used on an individual basis to enhance skills, competence and understanding in specific aspects of the day-to-day responsibilities of leisure managers. More significantly, however, taken together, the volumes in this series will constitute an integrated support system for professional development which will enhance the efficiency of individual managers and the effectiveness of the service they provide.

This text aims to provide the leisure manager or student with a practical insight into research methods that are relevant to the study of, and/or the management of, leisure and tourism. The book will allow those who wish to utilise research methods to do so with a confidence underpinned by the experience of the growing body of research studies into leisure and tourism that has accumulated in recent years. No less importantly, it will facilitate an understanding for both students and managers of how best to exploit, in an informed way, the research findings of others that they come across in their studies and/or day-to-day work.

The book's starting point is to provide a firm foundation of understanding of research and its relevance to leisure and tourism. Previous studies are reviewed and different approaches to research examined and a synoptic perspective provided of the 'research process', including the relationship between research management and project design. The book continues with a step-by-step examination of different methods; how to get the most out of existing sources; the role of observation techniques; and the potential contribution of quantitative and qualitative techniques. A practical guide is then provided to some of the key elements of utilising questionnaire surveys; the variety of techniques that are available; questionnaire design and the principles of sampling.

The book concludes with the critical issue of how best to get the most from research investigations, first, by examining how to analyse research data and, second, by providing guidelines on how to prepare and present a research report.

Whatever the reader's perspective – whether a potential research investigator or a practitioner wishing to benefit from the fruits of research – this book will illuminate the symbiotic relationship between research and the effective management of leisure and tourism.

Brian S. Duffield
Series Editor

PREFACE

The first edition of *Research Methods for Leisure and Tourism* was published in mid-1992. This second edition updates the book by the inclusion of references to material published since 1992 and changing the chapter on SPSS (the Statistical Package for the Social Sciences) from the DOS to the Windows version of the package. In addition a chapter on statistics has been added, and a chapter on research practice which includes, among other things, an extended treatment of the issue of research ethics. A number of other changes have been made in the light of my own and others' experience in using the book in teaching undergraduate and graduate students.

The aims of the book remain: to provide a 'how to do it' text and to offer an understanding of how research findings are generated in order to assist students and practising managers to become knowledgeable consumers of the research of others.

The first edition of the book was entirely British in orientation, and that emphasis remains; however, the widespread use of the book in Australia has prompted the inclusion of some Australian reference material, particularly in Chapter 6.

A. J. Veal, Sydney, June 1997

CHAPTER 1

Introduction: what, why and who?

INTRODUCTION

Information, knowledge and understanding concerning the natural, social and economic environment have become the very basis of contemporary societies and economies. An understanding of how information and knowledge are generated and utilised and an ability to contribute to that information and knowledge base through research can therefore be seen as key skills for managers in any industry sector and a key component of the education of the modern professional. The purpose of this book is to provide an introduction to the world of social research in the context of leisure and tourism, both as industries and fields of academic inquiry. The aim is to provide a guide to the conduct of research, a critical understanding of existing research and an appreciation of the role of research in the policy-making, planning and management processes of the leisure and tourism industries. Research is, however, not just a set of disembodied skills; it exists and is practised in a variety of social, political and economic contexts. This first chapter therefore addresses the preliminary questions of what research is, why it is done and who does it.

The focus of the book is leisure and tourism. Research methodology can be seen as universal, but various fields of research have developed their own methodological emphases and bodies of experience. For example, in some fields laboratory experiments are the norm, while in others social surveys are more common. A specialised text such as this therefore reflects the traditions and practices in its field and draws attention to examples of relevant applications of methods and the particular problems and issues which arise in such applications. The field of leisure and tourism is a large one, encompassing a wide range of individual and collective human activity. It is an area fraught with problems of definition – for example, in some settings the word *recreation* is used synonymously with *leisure*, while in others recreation is seen as a distinct and limited part of leisure or even separate from leisure. In some countries the term *free time* is used in preference to the word leisure. In some definitions *tourism* includes *business travel*, while in others such travel is excluded. In some definitions *day-trips* are included, while in others they are excluded. The aim in this book is to be *inclusive* rather than *exclusive*. Leisure is taken to encompass such activities as: recreation; play; games; involvement in sport and the arts, either as spectator or audience or as participant; the use of the electronic and printed media; live entertainment; hobbies; socialising; drinking; gambling; sightseeing; visiting parks, coast and countryside; do-it-yourself; arts and craft activity; home-based and non-home-based activity; commercial and non-commercially based activity; and doing nothing in particular. Tourism is seen primarily as a leisure activity involving travel away from a person's normal place of residence, but also as encompassing, in some cases, such activities as business travel, attending conventions and visiting friends and relatives. Since the book covers leisure *and* tourism, day-tripping is included, whether or not it is viewed as part of tourism. Leisure and tourism are seen as activities engaged in by individuals and groups, but also as service industries which involve public sector, non-profit and commercial organisations.

WHAT?

What is research? The sociologist Norbert Elias defined research in terms of its aims, as shown in Figure 1.1. Discovery – making known something previously unknown – could cover a number of activities, for instance the work of journalists or detectives. Elias, however, also indicates that research is a tool of 'science' and that its purpose is to 'advance human knowledge' – features which distinguish research from other investigatory activities.

Figure 1.1   What is research?

> The aim, as far as I can see, is the same in all sciences. Put simply and cursorily, the aim is to make known something previously unknown to human beings. It is to advance human knowledge, to make it more certain or better fitting . . . The aim is . . . discovery.
> (Elias, 1986, p. 20.)

Scientific research is research which is conducted within the rules and conventions of science. This means that it is based on logic and reason and the systematic examination of evidence. Ideally, within the scientific model, it should be possible for research to be *replicated* by the same or different researchers and for similar conclusions to emerge (although this is not always possible or practicable). It should also contribute to a cumulative body of knowledge about a field or topic. This 'model' of scientific research applies most aptly in the physical or natural sciences, such as physics or chemistry. In the area of *social science*, which deals with people as social beings and as communities, the scientific model must be adapted and modified, and in some cases largely abandoned.

Social science research is carried out using the methods and traditions of social science. Social science differs from the physical or natural sciences in that it deals with people and their social behaviour, and people are less predictable than non-human phenomena. People can be aware of the research being conducted about them and are not therefore purely passive subjects; they can react to the results of research and change their behaviour accordingly. The social world is constantly changing, so it is rarely possible to replicate research at different times or in different places and obtain similar results.

Elias' term *discovery* can be seen as, first, the process of *finding out*. But to 'advance human knowledge, to make it more certain or better fitting' requires more than just the accumulation of information. It is also necessary, second, to provide *explanation* – to explain *why* things are as they are. In this book, we are also concerned with a third function of research, namely *evaluating* – that is judging the success or value of policies or programmes. Three types of research can be identified corresponding to these three functions, as shown in Figure 1.2. In some cases particular research projects concentrate on only one of these, but often two or more of the approaches are included in the same project.

Figure 1.2   Types of research

- **Descriptive research** – finding out, describing what is

- **Explanatory research** – explaining *how* or *why* things are as they are (and using this to predict)

- **Evaluative research** – evaluation of policies and programmes

Descriptive research is very common in the leisure and tourism area. This is partly because leisure and tourism are relatively new fields of study and there is a need to *map the territory*. Much of the descriptive research in the field might therefore be described as *exploratory*: it seeks to discover, describe or map patterns of behaviour. Explanation of what is observed is often left until later or to other researchers. A second reason for the preponderance of descriptive research is that leisure and tourism phenomena are subject to constant change. For example, over time, the popularity of different leisure activities changes; the leisure preferences of different social groups (for example young people or women) change; and the relative importance of different tourism markets changes. A great deal of research effort in the field is therefore devoted to tracking basic patterns of behaviour. Although a complete understanding and explanation of these changing patterns would be preferable, the providers of leisure and tourism services must be aware of, and respond to, changing market conditions whether or not they can be fully explained or understood; they therefore rely on descriptive research to provide up-to-date information. Descriptive research is also common because there is often a separation between research projects and the policy, planning or management activity which gives rise to the commissioning of the research. So, for example, a company may commission a *market profile* study or a local council may commission a *recreation needs* study from a research team – but the actual use of the results of the research, in marketing or planning, is a separate exercise with which the research team is not involved: the research team may simply be required to produce a descriptive study.

Explanatory research moves beyond description to seek to explain the patterns and trends observed. *Why* is a particular type of activity or destination falling in popularity? *How* do particular tourism developments gain approval against the wishes of the local community? *Why* are the arts patronised by some social groups and not others? Such questions raise the thorny issue of *causality*: the aim is to be able to say, for example, that there has been an increase in A because of a corresponding fall in B. It is one thing to discover that A has increased while B has decreased; but to establish that the rise in A has been *caused* by the fall in B is often a much more demanding task. To establish causality, or the likelihood of causality, requires the researcher to be rigorous in the collection, analysis and interpretation of data. It also generally requires some sort of theoretical framework to relate the phenomenon under study to wider social, economic and political processes. The issue of causality and the role of theory in research are discussed further in later chapters.

Once causes are understood, the knowledge can be used to *predict*. This is clear enough in the physical sciences: we know that heat causes metal to expand (explanation) – therefore we know that if we apply a certain amount of heat to a bar of metal it will expand by a certain amount (prediction). In the biological and medical sciences this process is also followed, but with less precision: it can be predicted that if a certain treatment is given to patients with a certain disease then it is *likely* that a *certain proportion* will be cured. In the social sciences this approach is also used, but with even less precision. For example, economists have found that demand for goods and services, including leisure and tourism goods and services, responds to price levels so that, if the price of a product or service is reduced then sales will generally increase. But this does not always happen, because there are so many other factors involved – such as quality or the activities of competitors. Human beings make their own decisions and are far less *predictable* than non-human phenomena. Nevertheless *prediction* is a key aim of much of the research that takes place in the area of leisure and tourism.

Evaluative research arises from the need to make judgements on the success or effectiveness of policies or programmes – for example whether a particular leisure facility or programme is meeting required performance standards or whether a particular tourism promotion campaign has been cost-effective. Evaluative research is highly developed in some areas of public policy, for example education, but is less well developed in the field of leisure and tourism (Shadish *et al.*, 1991; Howell and Badmin, 1996). Again the issues facing the evaluative researcher are discussed in later chapters, particularly Chapters 3 and 14.

WHY STUDY RESEARCH?

In general

Why study research? Research and research methods might be studied for a variety of reasons, as indicated in Figure 1.3. First, it is useful to be able to

Figure 1.3   Why research?

- Understanding research reports etc.
- Academic projects
- Management tool in:
  - policy-making
  - planning
  - managing

understand and *evaluate* research reports and articles which one might come across in an academic or professional context. It is therefore advantageous to understand the basis of such reports and articles. Second, many readers of this book may engage in research in an academic environment, where research is conducted for its own sake, in the interests of the pursuit of knowledge – for example for a thesis. Third, most readers who are managers will find themselves conducting or commissioning research for professional reasons. It is therefore particularly appropriate to consider the role of research in the policy-making, planning and management process.

The role of research in policy-making, planning and management

All organisations, including those in the leisure and tourism industries, engage in policy-making, planning and managing resources to achieve their goals. A variety of terms is used in this area and the meanings of terms vary according to the context and user. In this volume these terms are used as follows:

- *policies* are considered to be the statements of principles, intentions and commitments of an organisation;
- *plans* are detailed strategies designed to implement policies in particular ways over a period of time;
- *management* is seen as being the process of implementing policies and plans.

Although planning is usually associated in the public mind with national, regional and local government bodies, it is also an activity undertaken by the private sector. Organisations such as cinema chains, holiday resort developers or sports promoters are all involved in planning, but their planning activities are less public than those of government bodies (Henry and Spink, 1990). Private organisations are usually only concerned with their own activities, but government bodies often have a wider responsibility to provide a planning framework for the activities of many public and private sector organisations. Examples of policies, plans and management activity in leisure and tourism contexts are given in Figure 1.4.

Figure 1.4 Examples of policies, plans and management

Level	Leisure centre	Tourist commission	Arts centre	National park
Policy	Maximise use by all age groups	Extend peak season	Encourage contemporary composers	Increase non-government revenue
Plan	Two-year plan to increase visits by older people by 50%	Three-year plan to increase shoulder season visits by promoting new festivals	Three-year plan to commission new work by contemporary composers	Three-year plan to implement user-pays programme
Management	Implement daily morning keep-fit sessions for older people	Choose marketing themes for festivals	Select composers and commission and produce works	Implement user-pays programme

Both policies and plans can vary enormously in detail, complexity and formality. This process is considered in more depth in specialist planning and management books (for example, Torkildsen, 1983; Howard and Crompton, 1980; Veal, 1994a). Here the process is considered only briefly, in order to examine the part played by research. The 'rational-comprehensive' process of policy-making, planning and management is often depicted diagrammatically as in Figure 1.5. Nine steps are shown, and these are discussed briefly below.

1 *Terms of reference*: The 'terms of reference' for a particular planning or management task sets out the scope and purpose of the exercise. Research can be involved right at the beginning of this process in assisting in establishing the terms of reference. For example, prior research on levels of sports participation in a community may result in a government policy initiative to do something about the level of sports participation.

2 *Environmental appraisal*: An environmental appraisal involves the gathering of a wide range of information necessary for and relevant to the task in hand. Information may relate to the organisation's internal workings or to the outside world, including actual and potential clients, and the activities of governments and competitors. Such information may be readily to hand or it may require extensive research.

3 *Mission/goals*: Statements of the mission or goals of the organisation may already be in place if the task in hand is a relatively minor one, but if it is a major undertaking, such as the development of a strategic plan for the whole organisation, then the development of statements of mission and goals may be involved. Research is unlikely to be directly involved in this stage unless it is required in the consultation process, as discussed under step 4.

4 *Consult*: Consultation with 'stakeholders' is considered vital by most organisations and, indeed, is a statutory requirement in many forms of

Figure 1.5   The planning/management process

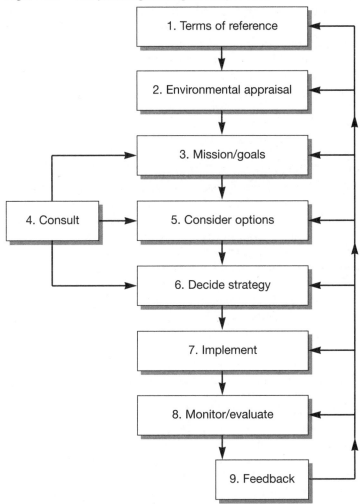

public sector planning. Stakeholders can include employees, clients, members of the public, members of boards and councils and neighbouring organisations. Clearly research can be a significant feature of such consultation.

5 *Consider options*: In order to develop a plan or strategy, consideration must be given to what policies are available, their feasibility, their likely contribution to the achievement of the organisation's goals and the best way to implement them. Research can be involved in the process of *identifying* alternative policy or planning options and also in *evaluating* them. Typical formal evaluation techniques include cost-benefit analysis, economic impact analysis and environmental and social impact analysis (*see* Shadish *et al.*, 1991; Veal, 1994a).

6 *Decide strategy*: Deciding on a strategy involves selecting a course of action from among all the options identified and taking into account the evaluative appraisals available. Even this choice process may involve a complex process requiring a research input, such as the use of the *importance-performance technique* (Martilla and James, 1977; Harper and Balmer, 1989) or *conjoint analysis* (Claxton, 1994).

7 *Implement*: Implementing a plan or strategy is the field of management. Research can be involved in day-to-day management in investigating improved ways of deploying resources and in providing continuous feed-back into the management process – for example in the form of customer surveys. However, the line between such research and the monitoring and evaluation process is difficult to draw.

8 *Monitor/evaluate*: Monitoring progress and evaluating the implementation of strategies is clearly a process with which research is likely to be involved.

9 *Feedback*: The process comes full circle with the feedback step. The data from the monitoring and evaluation step can be fed back into the planning or management cycle and can lead to a revision of any or all of the decisions previously made. The monitoring and evaluation process may report complete success, it may suggest minor changes to some of the details of the policies and plans adopted, or it could result in a fundamental re-think, going 'back to the drawing board'.

Formats

Research for leisure and tourism planning/management is presented in many forms and contexts. A number of these, as shown in Figure 1.6, are discussed briefly below. The formats are not all mutually exclusive, so that a number of them may arise in various aspects in a single research project.

Position statements are similar to the *environmental appraisals* discussed above. A position statement is a compilation of information on the current situation with regard to a topic or issue of concern, and is designed to assist decision-makers to become knowledgeable about the topic or issue and to take stock of current policies and provision. For example if a local authority wishes

Figure 1.6   Research report formats

- Position statements
- Market profiles
- Market research
- Market segmentation/lifestyle studies
- Feasibility studies
- Forecasting studies

to develop new policies for open space in an area, research should ideally be carried out to determine what open space exists, its quality and nature, existing policies, rules and regulations and levels and types of use. Such a study is called a position statement.

Market profiles are similar to position statements, but relate specifically to a *market*, particularly actual and potential consumers, but also suppliers. If an organisation wishes to start a project in a particular tourism or leisure market it will usually require a 'profile' of that market sector. How big is the market? What are its growth prospects? Who are the customers? What sub-sectors does it have? How profitable is it? Who are the current suppliers? Such a profile will usually require considerable research. A market profile can be seen as one element in the broader activity of market research.

Market research on the actual or potential market for a service can take place in advance of the service being established but also as part of the ongoing monitoring of the performance of an operation. Market research seeks to establish the scale and nature of the market (the number of people who use or are likely to use the product or service and their characteristics) and consumer requirements and attitudes (the particular requirements or tastes of users or potential users of the product or service).

Market segmentation/lifestyle studies are also referred to as *psychographic* studies. Traditionally marketers attempted to classify consumers into sub-markets or segments on the basis of characteristics such as age, sex, occupation and income. More recently they have attempted to classify people not just on the basis of such background social and economic characteristics but also on the basis of their attitudes, values and behaviour, including leisure activities and holiday behaviour. The most well-known of such studies, the *VALS* typology (Values, Attitudes and Life Styles – Mitchell, 1985), classified Americans into nine lifestyle groups: Survivor, Sustainer, Belonger, Emulator, Achiever, I-Am-Me, Experiential, Socially Conscious, and Integrated. This system has been widely used in market research, including tourism research (for example, Shih, 1986; Plog, 1994). Other lifestyle 'systems' include the *ACORN* census-based system developed in Britain (Shaw, 1984) and the Australian *Age* lifestyle typology (*The Age*, 1982).

Feasibility studies investigate not only consumer or user demands, as in a market profile, but also such aspects as the financial viability and environmental impact of proposed development or investment projects. The decision on whether or not to build a new leisure facility or launch a new tourism product is usually based on a feasibility study (Kelsey and Gray, 1986).

Leisure/recreation needs studies are a common type of research in leisure planning. These are comprehensive studies, usually carried out for local councils, examining levels of provision and use of facilities and services, levels of participation in leisure activities and views and aspirations of the population concerning leisure provision. In some cases the 'needs' study includes a leisure or recreation 'plan', which makes recommendations on future provision; in other cases the plan is a separate document.

Tourism strategies/tourism marketing plans are the tourism equivalent of the recreation needs study. Rather than a *needs* study, relating to the requirements of the local population, such studies usually involve a *demand* study, relating to the regions from which tourists are generated. In addition such studies usually consider the capacity of the local area to accommodate tourists, the quality and nature of existing and potential attractions and environmental impacts.

Forecasting studies form a key input to many plans. Such studies might provide, for example, projections of demand for a particular leisure activity or the demand for a particular type of tourist accommodation over a ten-year period. Research can be involved in predicting the likely effects of future population growth and change, the effects of changing tastes, changing levels of income or developments in technology. Leisure and tourism forecasting have become substantial fields of study in their own right (Veal, 1987; Archer, 1994).

WHO?

This book is mainly concerned with how to conduct research, but it also aims to provide an understanding of the research process which will help the reader to become a knowledgeable, critical consumer of the research carried out by others. In reading research reports and articles, it is useful to bear in mind *why* the research has been done and to a large extent this is influenced by *who* did the research and *who paid* for it to be done. Leisure and tourism research is undertaken by a wide variety of individuals and institutions, including academics and students, government and commercial research units, consultants and managers of leisure or tourism facilities and services, as listed in Figure 1.7. The respective roles of these 'actors' are discussed in turn below.

Figure 1.7 Who does research?

- Academics
- Students
- Government and commercial organisations
- Consultants
- Managers

Academics

Academics, members of the paid academic staff of academic institutions, include professors, lecturers, tutors and research staff – in American parlance 'the faculty'. In most academic institutions professors and lecturers are expected, as part of their contract of employment, to engage in both research and teaching. Typically a quarter or third of an academic's time might be devoted to research and writing. Promotion and job security depend partly (some would say mainly) on the achievement of a satisfactory track record in published research. Publication can be in various forms, including: refereed journals, un-refereed journals (such as professional magazines), books, reports/monographs (published by academic institutions or other agencies), and conference papers.

Publication of research in refereed journals is considered to be the most prestigious form in academic terms because of the element of 'peer review'. Articles submitted to such journals are assessed (refereed) on an anonymous basis by two or three experts in the field, as well as the editors. Editorial activity is overseen by a board of experts in the field. The main refereed journals in the leisure and tourism area are: *Journal of Leisure Research*, *Annals of Tourism Research*, *Leisure Sciences*, *Tourism Management*, *Leisure Studies*, *Journal of Travel Research*, *Society and Leisure*.

Some research conducted by academics requires little or no specific financial resources over and above the academic's basic salary – for example theoretical work and the many studies using students as subjects. But much research requires additional financial support, for instance, to pay full-time or part-time research assistants, to pay interviewers or a market research firm to conduct interviews, or to cover travel costs or the costs of equipment. The main sources of funding are university/college funds; government research councils; trusts/ foundations; government departments or agencies; commercial companies; and non-profit organisations.

Universities tend to use their own funds to support research which is initiated by academic staff and where the main motive is the 'advancement of knowledge'. Most universities and colleges have research funds for which members of their staff can apply. Governments usually establish organisations to fund scientific research – for example the UK Economic and Social Research Council or the Australian Research Council. Many private trusts or foundations also fund research – for example the Ford Foundation and the Leverhulme Trust. Funds may come from the world of practice – for instance from a government department or agency, from a commercial company or from a non-profit organisation such as a governing body of a sport. In this case the research will tend to be more practically orientated. Government agencies and commercial and non-profit organisations fund research to solve particular problems or to inform them about particular issues relevant to their interests.

Generally academics become involved in funded research of a practically orientated nature when their own interests coincide with those of the agency concerned. For instance an academic may be interested in ways of measuring what motivates people to engage in certain outdoor recreation activities and this could coincide with an outdoor recreation agency's need for research to assist in developing a marketing strategy. Some academics specialise in applied areas – such as marketing or planning – so they are very often in a good position to attract funding from the 'practical world'. Academics may use funds to employ one or more research assistants who may also be registered for a higher degree – usually a PhD. This leads to the second academic source of research, namely students.

Students

PhD and Masters degree students are major contributors to research. Journals periodically publish lists of theses and dissertations completed in the area (Van Doren and Stubbles, 1976; Van Doren and Solen, 1979; Jafari and Aaser, 1988). Theses from most USA and UK universities are available on microfiche. In the science area research students often work as part of a team, under the direction of a supervisor who determines what topics will be researched by individual students within a particular research programme. In the social sciences this approach is less common, with students having more freedom of choice in their selection of research topic.

PhD theses are the most significant form of student research, but research done by Masters degree and graduate diploma students and even undergraduates can be a useful contribution to knowledge. Leisure and tourism are not generally well endowed with research funds, so even, for example, a small survey conducted by a group of undergraduates on a particular leisure activity or in a particular locality, or a thorough review of an area of literature, may be of considerable use or interest to others.

Government and commercial organisations

Government and commercial organisations often have their own in-house research organisations – for example, the UK Office of Population Censuses and Surveys, the Australian Bureau of Tourism Research and the US Forest Service Experiment Stations. Commercial organisations in leisure and tourism tend to rely on consultants for their social, economic and market research, although equipment manufacturers, for instance in sport, may conduct their own scientific research for product development.

Research conducted by commercial bodies is usually confidential but that conducted by government agencies is generally available to the public. Research reports from these organisations can therefore be important sources of knowledge, especially of a more practically orientated nature. For example, in nearly every developed country some government agency takes responsibility for conducting nationwide surveys of tourism patterns and leisure participation rates (Cushman et al., 1996). This is descriptive research which no other organisation would have the resources to undertake.

Consultants

Consultants exist to offer their research and advisory services to the leisure and tourism industries. Some consultancy organisations are large, multinational companies involved in accountancy, management and property development consultancy generally, and who establish specialised units covering the leisure and/or tourism field. Examples are Coopers & Lybrand and Price Waterhouse. But there are many other, smaller, specialised organisations in the consultancy field. Some academics operate consultancy companies as a 'sideline', either because of academic interest in a particular area or to supplement incomes or both. Self-employed consultancy activity is common among practitioners who have taken early retirement from leisure or tourism industry employment.

Managers

Managers in leisure and tourism who recognise the full extent of the management process see research as very much part of their responsibilities. Managers may find themselves carrying out research on a range of types of topic (Figure 1.8). Since most of the readers of this book will be actual or trainee managers, this is a most important point to recognise.

Figure 1.8   Managers and research

- Research on customers

- Research on potential customers

- Research on staff

- Research on performance

- Research on competitors

- Research on products

Successful management depends on good information. Much information – for example sales figures – is available to the manager as a matter of routine and does not require *research*. However, the creative utilisation of such data – for example to establish market trends – may amount to research. Other types of information can only be obtained by means of specific research projects. In some areas of leisure and tourism management even the most basic information must be obtained by research. For example, while managers of theatres or resorts routinely receive information on the level of use of their facilities from sales figures or bookings, this is not the case for the manager of an urban park or a beach. To gain information on the number of users of this type of facility it is necessary to conduct a specific data-gathering exercise. Such data gathering may not be very sophisticated and some would say that it does not qualify as *research*, being just part of the management information system, but in the sense that it involves *finding out*, and sometimes *explaining*, it qualifies as research for the purposes of this book.

Most managers need to carry out, or commission, research if they want information on their users or customers – for example where they come from (the 'catchment area' of the facility) or their socio-economic characteristics. Research is also a way of finding out customers' evaluations of the facility or service. It might be argued that managers do not themselves need research skills since they can always commission consultants to carry out research. However, managers will be better able to commission good research and evaluate the results if they are familiar with the research process themselves. It is also the case that few managers in leisure and tourism work in an ideal world where funds exist to commission all the research they would like; often the only way managers can get research done is to do it themselves.

THE RELEVANCE OF PUBLISHED RESEARCH TO PLANNING AND MANAGEMENT

Who does research is important because it affects the nature of the research conducted and hence has a large impact on what constitutes the *body of knowledge* which students of leisure and tourism must absorb and which leisure and tourism managers draw on.

Academic research and publication is, to a large extent, a 'closed system'. Academics referee other academics' book proposals for commercial publishers; they are the editors of the refereed journals and serve on their editorial advisory boards and referee panels. They therefore determine what research is acceptable for publication. Practitioners therefore very often find published 'academic' research irrelevant to their needs. This is hardly surprising since much of it is not designed specifically for the practitioner but is intended for the academic world. The student in training to become a professional practitioner in the leisure or tourism field should not therefore be surprised to find that much of the scholarly writing available on leisure and tourism is not suitable for direct practical application to policy, planning and management. This does not mean that it is irrelevant, but simply that it does not necessarily focus explicitly on immediate practical problems.

Some research arises from academic interest and some arises from immediate problems being faced by the providers of leisure or tourism services. Much published academic research tends to be governed by the concerns of the various theoretical disciplines, such as sociology, economics or psychology, which may or may not coincide with the day-to-day concerns of the leisure or tourism industries. In fact part of the role of academic research is to 'stand apart' from the rest of the world and provide disinterested analysis, which may be critical and may not be seen as particularly supportive by those working in the industry. However, what some see as overly critical and unhelpful, or just plain irrelevant, others may see as insightful and constructive. There are nevertheless applied disciplines which focus specifically on aspects of the policy, planning and management process, such as planning, management, marketing or financial management. While academic research in these areas can also be critical rather than immediately instrumental, it is more likely to be driven by the sorts of issues which concern the industry. In each of these theoretical and applied disciplines there is a distinctive body of leisure and tourism research. In addition there is research which draws on more than one discipline (multi-disciplinary) and research which occupies a niche somewhere between two or more disciplines (inter-disciplinary). Further, in the areas of *leisure studies* and *tourism studies*, there is research which recognises no disciplinary allegiance. The disciplinary aspects of leisure and tourism research are examined in Chapter 2.

QUESTIONS AND EXERCISES

1 What is the difference between research and journalism?

2 Choose a leisure or tourism organisation with which you are familiar and outline ways in which it might use research to pursue its objectives.

3 Choose a leisure or tourism organisation and investigate its research activities. What proportion of its budget does it devote to research? What research has it carried out? How are the results of the research used, by the organisation or others?

4 Take an edition of a leisure or tourism journal, such as *Leisure Studies* or *Annals of Tourism Research*, and ascertain, for each article: why the research was conducted; how it was funded; and who or what organisations are likely to benefit from the research and how.

5 Repeat exercise 4, but using an edition of a journal outside the leisure/tourism field, for example a sociology journal or a physics journal.

6 Using the same journal edition as in 4 above, examine each article and determine whether the research is descriptive, explanatory or evaluative.

FURTHER READING

For discussions of leisure research generally, *see*: Jackson and Burton (1989).

For a review of tourism research methods, *see*: Smith (1989) for a quantitative, geographical approach; Ryan (1995) for coverage of similar ground to this book; Dann, Nash and Pearce (1988) and Pearce and Butler (1993) for a number of methodological papers and, for a mine of information on all aspect of tourism research, *see* the comprehensive collection of papers edited by Ritchie and Goeldner (1994).

On leisure and tourism forecasting, *see*: Archer (1994); Veal (1987, 1994a); Kelly (1987a); Martin and Mason (annual); Henley Centre for Forecasting (quarterly).

On the role of research in planning, *see*: Kelsey and Gray (1986); Marriott (1987); Veal (1994a).

For the conduct of feasibility studies, *see*: Kelsey and Gray (1986).

On psychographics/lifestyle, *see*: Wells (1974); Veal (1989a, 1993a); Chisnall (1991).

On evaluative research, *see*: Henderson and Bialeschki (1995); Pollard (1987); Shadish *et al.* (1991); Howell and Badmin (1996).

CHAPTER 2

Approaches to leisure and tourism research

INTRODUCTION

This chapter examines the traditions of a number of academic disciplines and their approaches to leisure and tourism research, including sociology, economics, geography, psychology, social psychology, history and philosophy. In addition some cross-disciplinary dimensions of research are discussed, including such aspects as: theoretical and applied research; induction and deduction; descriptive and explanatory research; experimental and non-experimental methods; positivist and interpretive approaches; quantitative and qualitative methods; primary and secondary data and self-reported and observed data. The aim of the chapter is to familiarise the reader with a range of disciplines and paradigms within which leisure and tourism research is conducted.

THE DISCIPLINARY TRADITIONS OF LEISURE AND TOURISM RESEARCH

The bulk of published leisure and tourism research has arisen, not from the explicit demands of the leisure and tourism industries, but from the interests of academics who generally owe allegiance to a particular discipline. While this statement is broadly true of both leisure and tourism research it is probably more true of the former than the latter. Here we examine briefly the contributions made to leisure and tourism research by a number of the most significant of these disciplines.

Disciplines are characterised by the particular aspect or dimension of the universe with which they are concerned, as well as by the techniques they use for research and the theories which they develop for explanation. Figure 2.1 provides a very simple representation of the social world within which leisure and tourism exist, and which may assist in placing the various disciplinary approaches into perspective. It consists of five main elements:

- *people*
- *organisations*
- *services/facilities/attractions*
- the *linkages* between these three, and
- the physical *environment* within which everything takes place

Figure 2.1 A leisure/tourism studies framework

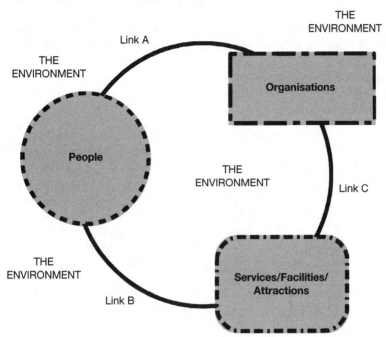

The linkages between people, organisations and services/facilities/attractions consist of processes such as:

- Link A – market research and political activity
- Link B – marketing, buying, selling, employing, visiting or using
- Link C – planning and investment

The (physical) environment is all-pervasive and affects and is affected by all of the other elements in various ways. The boxes enclosing the elements are deliberately depicted with dotted lines to suggest that the elements should not be seen as hermetically sealed – indeed, organisations are of course made up of people and services/facilities/attractions are managed and/or provided by people, so most people play a role in, and move between, more than one of the elements of the system.

Disciplines vary in terms of their primary focus of attention within this system.

1 Psychology and social psychology are focused primarily on the *people* element, with some concerns with links A and B.
2 Political science is concerned mainly with *organisations*, and with link A.
3 History can cover the whole system; much of historical research has also had the same focus as political science.
4 Economics is concerned with the whole system, with different sub-disciplines (for example, micro-economics, macro-economics) focusing on different parts.

5 Sociology is concerned primarily with *people* and with Link A and with *organisations*.
6 Applied disciplines, such as planning, management and marketing, are based in organisations, then move along links A and C to the other elements of the system.
7 Geography's basis is the *environment*.
8 Comprehensive systems of thought, such as Marxism or liberalism, encompass the whole system.

While much of this may seem fairly obvious, it is not always made explicit in the disciplinary literature, so that research is often criticised unfairly for ignoring phenomena which are outside its disciplinary scope.

It is of course impossible to gain a full appreciation of the research contribution and methods of any discipline without understanding the discipline as a whole: an academic discipline is after all defined by its body of research. The student of leisure or tourism faces the daunting challenge of having to grasp the essence of a wide range of disciplinary contributions to the field. The discussions below, which relate to the academic disciplines of sociology, geography, economics, psychology and social psychology, history and anthropology, political science and philosophy are therefore inevitably somewhat superficial, but references to more detailed reviews are given in the guide to further reading.

Sociology

Why do men tend to play sport more than women? Why do middle class, more highly educated, people make greater use of arts facilities and outdoor recreation areas than other groups? To what extent do people freely choose their leisure activities and holidays and to what extent is their choice limited by economic and social constraints or commercial manipulation? Who is involved and who is excluded when major decisions are made on leisure or tourism investment in local areas? Why do some groups in society engage in leisure activities which are viewed as 'deviant' or 'anti-social' by others and how do such activities come to be viewed as deviant or anti-social? These are the sorts of questions which sociological research attempts to answer.

Leisure

Sociologists have arguably been the most significant contributors to the field of leisure studies, but less significantly to the specific field of tourism studies. Much of the early research, and some current research, which appears to be 'sociological' has, however, not been carried out by sociologists trained in the discipline. This is true, for example, of many of the major leisure participation and tourism surveys which provide much of the basic factual information about patterns of participation (Cushman *et al.*, 1996). Much *apparently* sociological research might more aptly be called *social* research, since it is often somewhat pragmatic, lacking the theoretical framework which many formally trained sociologists would like to see.

Sociology is concerned with explaining or understanding social behaviour – particularly the behaviour of groups or classes of people. Early survey evidence on leisure participation from the 1960s showed that leisure behaviour exhibited a number of uniform features across the whole of society (for example, the importance of home-based leisure) but that aspects of leisure (for example engagement in the arts or sport) varied considerably between different groups in the community, depending on such social characteristics as family status, age, gender, educational level and ethnic group. Early researchers pursued the idea that if only they could identify sufficient of these characteristics they would be able to develop a *model* of leisure behaviour which could be used to predict the patterns of participation of different social groups. The research approach was *quantitative*, being highly statistical and concerned primarily with predicting numbers of participants and visits. It generally involved the construction of mathematical *models* of human behaviour (Christensen, 1988), with regression equations representing the relationships between leisure participation and causal variables, such as age, gender and income. The research can be seen as part of the *functionalist* tradition in sociology, which is based on the premise that elements in social systems can be studied in terms of the structure of the system and the functioning of its various interacting elements. Most of the high profile early American research was in the structure-functionalist mode, much of it of the quantitative/modelling type. The highly quantitative approach held less sway in Britain where, for example, Parker's (1971) influential work on the relationships between work and leisure, while being empirically based, was not markedly quantitative, and early survey work was generally descriptive (for example, BTA/Keele University, 1967; Sillitoe, 1969).

The modelling/prediction approach was eventually rejected by many sociologists, mainly because it did not work well in its own terms. In America, as Kelly (1980) has pointed out, the models did not perform well, although in Britain more success was obtained (Settle, 1977; Veal, 1987, pp. 152–4). But the main concern of sociologists was that the approach lacked a framework of sociological theory: it was too pragmatic and it asked the wrong questions. Methodologically it was challenged by those sociologists who were not 'quantitatively' orientated but instead believed in the power of theoretical reasoning and in the value of qualitative evidence from small groups of 'real people' rather than statistical evidence from large numbers of 'abstract' people. They were also less interested in 'predicting' behaviour than in 'explaining' it. They wanted to know not just *what* people did with their leisure time but *why* – what leisure meant to them, and so on. In Britain Rhona and Robert Rapoport epitomised this shift, while in the USA it was championed by Kelly (1983). The Rapoports indicated the new trend with their book, *Leisure and the Family Life Cycle* (1975), which was based on in-depth interviews with only about 30 people altogether; and in which detailed case studies of the motivations and feelings of individuals were reported. In fact the research moves into the area of social psychology.

In the 1980s the research traditions which had developed up to that point were attacked from a critical, neo-Marxist standpoint – typified by Clarke and Critcher's *The Devil Makes Work* (1985). On one hand this work relied on broader, often historically based, analysis of society and on the other hand it relied heavily on the findings of the *ethnographic* style of research emerging from the area of *cultural studies* and involving in-depth interaction with usually small groups of individuals – such as youth gangs, ethnic groups and young mothers. The intellectual sweep of the neo-Marxists was broader than that of their predecessors, even though the contemporary empirical basis was, in some senses, a narrow one.

The neo-Marxist research introduced the *agency/structure* debate into leisure studies – that is the question of the extent to which individuals are free *agents*, exercising free choice in their lives, including their leisure lives, and the extent to which such choice is constrained and manipulated by the capitalist, economic and political *structure*, which is beyond the control of the individual (Rojek, 1989). Further, it raised questions about the role of the state in contemporary society, in particular whether the leisure services provided by the state should be seen as providing for people's needs in response to democratic demands or whether the state should be viewed as merely a tool of the capitalist system, providing it with an acceptable 'human face' through the provision of necessary, but unprofitable, services. This led to a considerable growth in research on the state and public policy in leisure (Coalter, 1988, 1990; Henry, 1993; Bramham *et al.*, 1993). Explicit critiques of the neo-Marxist approach have been few (Moorhouse, 1989; Veal, 1989a), but it has nevertheless become unfashionable in the 1990s, with the decline of Marxism as a political force in the world.

In the United States the neo-Marxist approach was not embraced by mainstream sociological leisure research, the major development in the 1980s being John Kelly's (1987a, 1994) *existential* and *symbolic interaction* approach, in which leisure is seen as a process of negotiation by the individual in the context of personal, social, community and professional relationships, commitments and ties.

The 1980s also saw an attack on existing leisure research by *feminist* sociologists, who noted that much of the empirical work to date had been based on samples of men and, in focusing on aspects such as occupation and work/leisure relationships, had ignored the day-to-day experience of women and their traditional responsibilities for child care and unpaid domestic work. Further, in focusing on 'choice' in leisure, the research had ignored the power relationships in society which limited or negated the range of choice for some groups, including women (Deem, 1986; Wimbush and Talbot, 1988; Henderson *et al.*, 1989; Green *et al.*, 1990; Scraton, 1994). In general the empirical research underpinning the feminist contribution was qualitative in nature, concerned as it was to explore meanings and experiences of leisure among women.

The critical perspective in the sociology of leisure has, in recent years, been assumed by the idea of *postmodernism* (Rojek, 1995), the cultural equivalent of post-industrialism. The *modern* era of western civilisation dates from the eighteenth and nineteenth centuries when science, rationality and the idea of *human progress* displaced traditional, largely religion-dominated, values. Postmodernists argue that western societies – and indeed other parts of the world – are entering a new era, when values are becoming uncertain and the modern idea of progress no longer seems valid; the basis of modern economies and contemporary culture is becoming dominated by the ephemeral, fast-moving world of the electronic communications media and the cultural 'products' which they purvey. One implication of this is a shift in the focus of the sociology of leisure to examine popular cultural forms, such as television (O'Connor and Boyle, 1993) and the world of Disney (Rojek, 1993), although there is also a tendency to add the term 'postmodern' to research on a wide variety of more mundane topics, such as the fun run (Wilson, 1995), rock climbing (Morgan, 1994) and social history (Seaton, 1994). The effect of these tendencies is to move parts of leisure sociology closer to a humanities approach, in which *the text*, or cultural artefact, rather than people, becomes the empirical focus and *cultural criticism* and *hermeneutics* (the interpretation of texts) are the research techniques deployed (for example, Hultsman and Harper, 1992).

Space precludes examination of a number of other developments in the sociology of leisure, including Robert Stebbins' idea of *serious leisure* (Stebbins, 1992), the potential of *figurational sociology*, as propounded by Elias and Dunning (1986; *see* Maguire, 1988), the revisiting of *play* as a focus for research and theorising (Hamilton-Smith, 1994; Rojek, 1995, ch. 9) and the concept of *lifestyle* (Veal, 1993a).

The culmination of this brief history of the sociology of leisure is that the field is now characterised by a wide range of *social* or *sociological* research conducted within what Rojek (1985) refers to as *multi-paradigmatic rivalry* – that is alternative, competing traditions, with different ways of looking at the world. In addition an enormous range of research approaches is now deployed by sociologists studying leisure: quantitative methods are still used (see any edition of the American *Journal of Leisure Research*); major surveys continue to be conducted (mainly for government/policy purposes); and a variety of qualitative and experimental methods are also used. In short, anything goes.

Tourism

It is notable that, although leisure encompasses the major tourism activity of 'going on holiday', the general leisure literature rarely refers specifically to tourism or going on holiday. A further oddity in the leisure/tourism research tradition is that a great deal of North American research on leisure, which is concerned primarily with outdoor recreation, in fact involves studies of people who are staying away from home, often camping, while visiting major attractions such as national parks. So a great deal of what is recognised as *recreation research* in North America could in fact equally be seen as *tourism research* – but this is rarely, if ever, acknowledged. So research on the *sociology of tourism* is conventionally seen as separate from research on the *sociology of leisure*.

Dann and Cohen (1991) point out that there is 'no single sociology of tourism', instead 'there have been several attempts to understand sociologically different aspects of tourism, departing from a number of theoretical perspectives' (p. 157). They indicate that leisure is only one of the contexts in which tourism is studied; it is also viewed in the context of the sociology of migration and in the context of research on travel. Tourism research has been driven by private industry demands to a greater extent than leisure research; as a result tourism research is characterised by a predominance of economic and marketing and related psychological research, rather than sociological research. Indeed, John Urry has remarked that: 'There is relatively little substance to the sociology of tourism' (Urry, 1990, p. 7).

Cohen (1984) divides sociological research on tourism into four 'issue areas': the tourist; relations between tourists and locals; the structure and functioning of the tourist system; and the social and environmental consequences of tourism. Reflecting the situation in leisure research, he concludes:

> While a variety of often intriguing conceptual and theoretical approaches for studying the complex and manifold touristic phenomena have emerged, none has yet withstood rigorous empirical testing; while field-studies have proliferated, many lack an explicit, theoretical orientation and hence contribute little to theory building (Cohen, 1984, p. 388).

MacCannell's (1976) seminal work on tourism as a 'quest for authenticity' linked tourism research to the area of *semiotics*, involving the study of symbols and signs, and this is reflected in Urry's (1990) *The Tourist Gaze*. Such studies focus on tourism involving travel to strange places to 'see things', as opposed to the mass of tourism which is domestic and quasi-domestic (for example trips by northern Europeans to the Costa Del Sol) and involves going somewhere for 'sand, sea and sun'. The emergence of postmodern perspectives in sociology has affected tourism research as it has leisure research generally. The implications for research involve a similar shift towards areas previously the preserve of the humanities, as discussed in Chapter 9.

The main focus of empirical research in the sociology of tourism has been on the social interaction between tourists and host communities and its effects (*see* Ryan, 1991 for summary). In recent years there has also been a tendency to move away from consideration of the phenomenon of mass tourism and to examine the behaviour patterns and motivations of smaller, more specialised groups, engaged in 'special interest' tourism, centring on such developments as 'eco-tourism' and activity-based holidays (*see* Weiler and Hall, 1992).

Geography

What is the relationship between where people live, their access to leisure facilities and their patterns of leisure participation? How do people's perceptions of and appreciation of different landscapes affect their leisure travel behaviour?

How are the leisure and tourism trips of the population of a region accommodated and distributed within the region? How do people make use of outdoor recreation areas? How do they view crowding and congestion? What is the capacity of various environments to absorb visitors? These are the sorts of questions which geographical leisure and tourism research addresses.

Geographers have been very prominent in leisure research (Coppock, 1982) and have not generally restricted their interests to the formal confines of their discipline. For example, the Tourism and Recreation Research Unit of Edinburgh University was a creation of the Geography Department of that university and was at the forefront of the development of the modelling techniques discussed under sociology above (Coppock and Duffield, 1975). 'Social modelling' was extended to 'spatial modelling' with the aim of predicting not just levels of participation in activities in general, but levels of trips to particular recreation sites. This research was based on data gathered by interview surveys of the population in general and the users of particular recreation sites.

Of course geographers can be expected to be concerned primarily with spatial and environmental issues and also with large-scale natural and man-made phenomena such as the coastline, wilderness and human settlement patterns. Geography has indeed contributed a great deal of insight into these aspects of leisure research. Thus, for example, a considerable amount of research has been completed on the catchment areas of different kinds of leisure facilities – that is, surveys which ask people how far they travel to use facilities and which therefore establish the area that the facilities serve (Cowling *et al.*, 1983). Much of this research also included tourism sites. Traditionally geographers have focused on recreation in 'green' areas, such as urban and national parks (for example, Pigram, 1983), but the text by Williams, entitled *Outdoor Recreation and the Urban Environment* (1995) indicates the contemporary range of the geographer's interest, covering environments as diverse as the domestic garden, urban thoroughfares, children's playgrounds, parks and sports facilities.

Tourism is of course quintessentially a geographical phenomenon and geography has made major contributions to research in that field (Mitchell, 1985; Smith, 1983; Pearce, 1987; Mitchell and Murphy, 1991), including studies of travel patterns and their modelling using the 'gravity model', tourism/recreation carrying capacity studies and regional development studies.

Geographers have been at the forefront of various types of observational research (Burch, 1964; TRRU, 1983). In particular they have demonstrated the use of aerial photography in examining the spatial distribution of recreational resources and utilisation and they have examined the way visitors make use of dispersed sites such as parks (Van der Zande, 1985; Glyptis, 1981a). Geographers have linked the concept of lifestyle with census information to create 'lifestyle maps' based on the common social characteristics of neighbourhoods, such characteristics being closely associated with leisure behaviour (Bickmore *et al.*, 1980; Shaw, 1984). A mixture of geography and psychological research has been responsible for a large amount of research on 'landscape perception' – that is what it is that people find attractive about different kinds of landscape (Patmore, 1983, p. 212).

Economics

How do increases in incomes affect leisure expenditure and behaviour? How can an annual subsidy of £10 million to an opera company or a sports centre be justified? What is the impact in terms of business turnover and jobs, of an event such as the Olympic Games? How significant is tourism, the arts or sport, in the economy? How will a change in the exchange rate affect international tourist arrivals? These are the sorts of question which economic research on leisure and tourism attempts to answer.

Economics is the discipline concerned with the 'allocation of scarce resources between competing ends' – that is with what is produced by a society and with the distribution of what is produced – who gets what. Since leisure and tourism products and services now account for between 20 and 30 per cent of consumer spending in modern western societies, the economics of leisure and tourism is of increasing importance. Most of the economics of leisure is, however, concerned with the public sector, where the free market forces with which economics is so concerned are constrained or inoperative (Veal, 1989a). In the case of tourism, economists have drawn largely on macro-economics, that part of economics which is concerned with economies as a whole, including levels of economic output, multipliers, unemployment, international trade and so on.

The major focus of research in the economics of leisure has been on the public sector, particularly rural outdoor recreation and the arts. One of the major concerns of this area of research has been the economic valuation of the recreational, natural and aesthetic values of public recreation lands and wildernesses or of arts facilities, where entrance is often free or subsidised. In such situations information on users' willingness to pay is not immediately available as a measure of their evaluation of the experience, as it is, say, with a commercial facility such as Disneyland. This therefore has spawned a great deal of research on 'cost-benefit analysis' – ways of measuring both the full costs and the full benefits to society of these publicly provided facilities.

As governments moved to the right in the 1980s and began to examine critically many areas of public enterprise with a view to expenditure cuts or privatisation, there was a burst of 'economic impact' studies – in which economists were engaged to establish the economic significance of the arts (Myerscough, 1988) or sport (Henley Centre for Forecasting, 1986; DASETT, 1988a, 1988b). The general political/economic environment has also stimulated some research on the effects of pricing on demand (Coalter, 1993; Gratton and Taylor, 1995).

Another distinct area of the economic study of leisure has been the work on the economics of professional sport. Professional sport is a 'peculiar' – and fascinating – industry sector to economists because of the nature of competition, which is unlike that in other industries (Cairns et al., 1986).

Of a more practical bent is the work of forecasters such as Martin and Mason (annual) and the Henley Centre for Forecasting (quarterly), who produce regular forecasts of consumer expenditure on leisure products and services as a service to the leisure industries. Demand forecasting has been a major focus of tourism research (Eadington and Redman, 1991). In most countries, at least one organisation exists to produce forecasts of domestic and overseas tourist trips and such forecasts are often based on primarily economic models (Archer, 1994).

In terms of research techniques, economists have tended to use similar methods to those used by other social scientists, including household and site interviews, but they tend to have access to more government-collected data, for example on consumer expenditure, and tend to make use of quantitative methods, such as regression.

Psychology and social psychology

What satisfactions do people obtain from their leisure? How do people's perceptions of tourist destinations affect their decision to travel? What motivates people to engage in one form of leisure activity rather than another? How do people's relationships with family and friends affect their leisure behaviour? These are the sorts of question which psychological and social psychological research addresses.

In discussing sociological research, we have already referred to the work of the Rapoports and Kelly as being social-psychological in nature, based as it is on attempts to understand the underlying motivations of individuals as well as their social interactions.

Ingham (1986) has reviewed the contributions of psychology to leisure research and classifies the body of work into four main categories: motivation and needs ('why individuals do what they do'), satisfactions (the idea that 'particular types of leisure behaviour and experience lead to differential levels of satisfaction'), leisure as a state of mind (including Csikszentmihalyi's (1990) concept of 'flow'), and individual differences (including gender, age, personality and cultural differences). The field is divided into two general approaches, the 'experiential' approach of Neulinger and Csikszentmihalyi and the broader approach dealing with reported motivations, satisfactions and attributions typified by the work of Iso-Ahola. Ingham points out that:

> By far the majority of psychological research has relied on the use of self-report questionnaire-derived data. ... Alternative methodological approaches are relatively rare: these could include detailed case studies, direct physiological recording, open-ended self-reporting, field experimentation, and careful observation and analysis of behaviour in different settings (Ingham, 1986, p. 258).

In the second part of his review Ingham commends for the future the socio-psychological work of Kelly (1983), which involves viewing leisure as a medium in which individuals develop their identities, styles and social roles.

In the area of tourism Pearce and Stringer (1991) divide psychological research into five types: physiological and ergonomic (for example, jet-lag and travellers' health problems); cognition (for example, the use of maps and tourists' 'mindfulness' of areas visited); individual differences approaches (for example, relationships between personality types and types of touristic experience sought, and links with motivation, psychographics and need); social psychology (including intra-individual, inter-individual and group processes); and environmental studies (for example, perception of crowding). Pearce and Stringer argue that the psychology of tourism is not well developed but that 'In the absence of a broad psychological thrust in tourism, geographers, sociologists, and leisure and recreation researchers are doing much work which at heart is psychological' (p. 150).

Pearce's text, *The Ulysses Factor* (1988) includes a diverse collection of papers on visitor behaviour and attitudes in a variety of settings, including theme parks, museums, and natural environments. Ryan's (1995) *Researching Tourist Satisfaction* considers the psychology of the tourist from a market research point of view. In his theoretical review he reveals that research on tourist attitudes and satisfaction draws extensively on the same psychological basis as leisure research, including Maslow, Csikszentmihayli and Iso-Ahola.

History and anthropology

What are the historical roots of the practices, attitudes and institutions involved in contemporary leisure and tourism? To what extent has leisure time increased since pre-industrial times? How is change constrained by the effects of past actions and events? Historians, in addressing such questions, have been influential in the development of leisure research. For instance, Huizinga's classic work on play, *Homo Ludens* (1955), is largely historical and Young and Willmott's study of *The Symmetrical Family* (1973) has a firm base in historical analysis, as has Clarke and Critcher's *The Devil Makes Work* (1985). Historians and theorists have produced histories of leisure, particularly in the nineteenth century (Cunningham, 1980; Bailey, 1978), which show how leisure has been an integral part of the development of the cultures and economies of western capitalist societies. In fact one of the claims of the 1980s critics of earlier leisure research was that it was ahistorical, or at least that its view of history was naive.

A comprehensive history of leisure has, however, yet to be written. The available historical writing tends to jump from ancient Greece, with a brief dalliance in medieval Europe to observe the concept of 'carnival' as described by Bahktin (*see* Rojek, 1985, p. 85), to the industrial revolution in Europe. There is little material, in the English language literature, on history outside of Europe and North America. And there is virtually no reference to periods before the first millennium BC, even though it is clear that most leisure forms, such as music, dance, art, sport, gambling and drinking, have their origins in pre-history. By and large, anthropology has been ignored in leisure research, despite the wealth of leisure or play related material in works such as Sahlin's *Stone Age Economics* (1972).

Most textbooks on tourism (for example, Burkart and Medlik, 1981) provide a historical overview of the development of travel and tourism. Tourism is traced back to classical Greek and Roman times, to the emergence of the 'grand tour' in Europe in the seventeenth and eighteenth centuries and the development of spas and resorts. In Britain historical research has addressed some of the theoretical issues on social structure and change which have been addressed by sociologists (Urry, 1990), but in America studies have tended to be more descriptive case studies (Towner and Wall, 1991).

Some attention has been given to the anthropology of tourism in a historical sense (Nash and Smith, 1991), taking the history of tourism back beyond the classical period, but the 'anthropology of tourism' is also seen as a more contemporary phenomenon, drawing on the particular research approaches of anthropology in the study of (often clashing) inter-cultural relationships which arise as a result of tourism (Graburn and Moore, 1994).

While reviews of the contributions of history to leisure and tourism research tend not to discuss techniques, in fact one of the major contributions of historical analysis is to illustrate the use of secondary data sources, such as diaries, official records and reports, and newspaper reports. Anthropological research methods, however, emerge through such areas as 'cultural studies' in the form of *ethnographical* methods, which are discussed in Chapter 8 on qualitative methods.

Political science

Despite the importance of public policy matters in leisure and tourism, the political dimension of the subject was neglected for many years. More recently, important contributions have been made to rectify this by Bramham and Henry (1985), Wilson (1988) and Coalter (1990) in relation to leisure generally, and by Richter (1994) and Hall (1994) in relation to tourism. While leisure studies research has focused on the relationships between political ideology and leisure policy, in tourism the focus is less ideological and more to do with the role of tourism in political behaviour (Matthews and Richter, 1991).

Philosophy

Histories of leisure in standard textbooks often begin with 'classical' views and definitions of leisure as propounded particularly by such classical Greek philosophers as Aristotle. Murphy's (1974) textbook, *Concepts of Leisure*, is typical of this genre and has long been a standard. One of the most famous essays on leisure was by the philosopher Bertrand Russell, entitled *In Praise of Idleness* (1935). The most comprehensive review of the relationship between philosophy and leisure is by Dare, Welton and Coe (1987), which ranges from Aristotle to Sartre via Kant, Marx and many others.

APPROACHES AND DIMENSIONS

A number of alternative approaches to and dimensions of leisure and tourism research cut across the disciplines; some of them, as listed in Figure 2.2, are

Figure 2.2 Approaches, dimensions and issues

- Theoretical/applied
- Induction/deduction
- Empirical/non-empirical
- Positivist/interpretive
- Experimental/non-experimental
- Primary/secondary data analysis
- Self-reported/observed
- Qualitative/quantitative
- Validity and reliability

discussed here in the form of dichotomies. These are terms and ideas which recur in the literature and discourses on research so that a basic understanding of them is necessary if the literature and the discourses are to be understood.

Theoretical and applied research

Theoretical research seeks to draw general conclusions about the phenomena being studied. Some research, however, is less universal in its scope: it seeks not necessarily to create wholly *new* knowledge about the world but to apply existing theoretical knowledge to particular problems or issues. This form of research is known as *applied research*, which is research designed to find solutions to problems which arise in particular policy, planning or management situations.

Induction and deduction

It has been noted that research involves finding out and explaining. *Finding out* might be called the 'what?' of research – what is happening? What is the situation? *Explaining* might be called the 'how?' and the 'why?' of research – how do things happen? Why do they happen the way they do? What are the causes of different phenomena?

Finding out involves description and it involves gathering information. Explaining involves attempting to understand that information: it goes beyond the descriptive. Research methods can facilitate both these processes: describing and explaining. Description and explanation can be seen as part of a circular model of research as illustrated in Figure 2.3. The research process can work in two ways:

Figure 2.3   Circular model of the research process

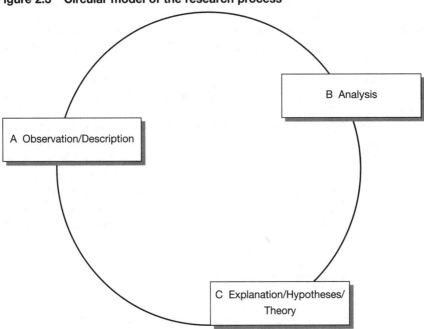

Source: based on Williamson *et al.*, 1982, p. 7.

1 *Inductive*
   ● begin at point A, *observation/description*
   ● proceed to point B, *analysis*
   ● arrive at point C, *explanation*

2 *Deductive*
   ● begin at point C, with a *hypothesis*
   ● proceed to point A, *observation/description*, gathering data to test the hypothesis
   ● proceed to point B, *analysis*, to test the hypothesis against the data

A *hypothesis* is a proposition about how something might work or behave – an explanation which may or may not be supported by data, or possibly by more detailed or rigorous argument. A hypothesis may arise from informal observation and experience of the researcher or from examination of the existing literature. The term *theory* is also included at point C since, when more elaborate hypotheses or a number of interrelated hypotheses are involved, the term theory may be used. A theory can be similar to a hypothesis, in being propositional, or it may have been subjected to empirical validation – that is testing against data.

A research project may involve a single circuit or a number of circuits of the process, possibly in both directions. If the research process begins with description, at point A, and moves from there to explanation, the process is described as *inductive*. The explanation is *induced* from the data – the data come first and the explanation later. If the process starts at point C then it is seen as *deductive*; it involves *deduction*, where the process is based on prior logical reasoning. Case studies 2.1 and 2.2 at the end of this chapter illustrate these ideas using a hypothetical example on the relative popularity of two leisure activities.

In practice data are rarely collected without some explanatory model in mind – otherwise how would we know what data to collect? So there is always an element of deduction in any research. And it is not possible to develop hypotheses and theories without at least some initial information on the subject in hand, however informally obtained; so there is always an element of induction. Thus most research is partly inductive and partly deductive.

Whether hypotheses or theories containing the explanation are put forward at the start of a research project or arise as a result of data analysis, they represent the key creative part of the research process. Data collection and analysis can be fairly mechanical but interpretation of data and the development of explanations require at least creativity and, at best, inspiration!

Descriptive and explanatory research

In Chapter 1 the difference between descriptive and explanatory research was discussed and it is appropriate to raise the issue again here. *Descriptive* research aims to describe, as far as possible, what is. The focus is not on explanation. *Explaining* the patterns in observed or reported data usually involves establishing that one phenomenon is caused by another. For example, descriptive research might show that a tourism destination is losing market share. Explanatory research would seek to establish whether this was caused by, for example, price movements or ineffective marketing. This raises the question of *causality*: whether A is caused by B. Labovitz and Hagedorn (1971) state that there are 'at least four widely accepted scientific criteria for establishing causality. These criteria are association, time priority, nonspurious relation and rationale' (p. 4).

Association is a 'necessary condition for a causal relation' – that is, A and B must be associated in some way – for example, A increases when B decreases.

> There are two characteristics of an association that generally strengthen the conclusion that one variable is at least a partial cause of another. The first is magnitude, which refers to the size or strength of the association. . . . The second . . . is consistency. If the relation persists from one study to the next under a variety of conditions, confidence in the causal nature of the relation is increased' (Labovitz and Hagedorn, 1971, p. 5).

Time priority means that for A to be the cause of B then A must take place before B.

Non-spurious relationships are defined as associations between two variables that 'cannot be explained by a third variable' (p. 9). This means that it must be established that there is no third factor, C, which is affecting both A and B.

Rationale means that statistical or other purely empirical evidence is not enough; the conclusion that A causes B is not justified simply on the basis of an observed relation; it should be supported by some plausible, theoretical or logical explanation to suggest how it happens.

These matters are taken up again in Chapters 3 and 14.

Empirical and non-empirical research

In empirical research conclusions are based on data, or specifically collected information. But there is another type of research which is equally, if not more, important, but which makes no explicit or formal reference to data as such. This is research which results from thinking and reading and contemplation. It is the research which develops ideas, hypotheses and theories.

A review of the contents of one or two editions of the main leisure or tourism journals will reveal the existence of both sorts of research – and the contributions which each can make. While the empirical studies provide some of the 'building blocks' of a great deal of research and knowledge, non-empirical contributions are needed to review and refine ideas and to place the empirical work in context. A book like this inevitably devotes more space to empirical methods, because they involve more explicit, technical processes which can be described and 'taught'. It cannot however be too strongly stressed that a good review of the literature or a thoughtful piece of writing arising from deep, insightful, inspirational thinking about a subject can be worth a thousand, unthinking, surveys!

Positivist and interpretive approaches

The positivist/interpretive dichotomy is related to, but distinct from, the empirical/non-empirical dichotomy. It is primarily a reference to sociological schools of thought or traditions. *Positivism* is a framework of research, similar to that adopted by the natural scientist, in which the researcher sees people as phenomena to be studied from the outside, with behaviour to be explained on the basis of facts and observations gathered by the researcher, using theories and models developed by researchers. Some sociologists are highly suspicious of such attempts to translate natural science approaches into the social sciences (Rojek, 1989, p. 70). They believe that it is dangerous to draw conclusions about the causes and motivations of human behaviour on the basis of the type of evidence used in the natural sciences. In fact, Giddens has pointed out that the term *positivist* 'has become one of opprobrium, and has been used so broadly and vaguely as a weapon of critical attack . . . that it has lost any claim to an accepted and standard meaning' (1974, p. 2).

The *interpretive* model places more reliance on the people being studied to provide their own explanation of their situation or behaviour. The interpretive researcher therefore tries to 'get inside' the minds of subjects and see the world from their point of view. This of course suggests a more flexible approach to data collection, usually involving qualitative methods and generally an inductive approach.

It is common to refer to the positivist approach as 'dominant' in leisure studies in particular. In the 1990s, with the wide range of methodological approaches evident in published research, particularly outside North America, this is hard to substantiate (Veal, 1994b). In fact, it is notable that the numerous calls by American writers for an end to the alleged dominance of positivist methods and for the adoption of more interpretive leisure research are often published in journals published outside of the USA and make little or no reference to the substantial body of methodologically heterogeneous non-American leisure research, or to each other (for example, Godbey and Scott, 1990; Howe, 1991; Hultsman and Harper, 1992; Glancy, 1993; Hemingway, 1995).

Experimental and non-experimental methods

The popular image of the scientist is someone in a white coat in a laboratory, conducting experiments. The experimental method of research involves the scientist attempting to control the environment of the subject of the research and measuring the effects of controlled change. Knowledge progresses on the basis that, in a controlled experimental situation, any change in A must have been brought about by a change in B because everything except A and B were held constant. The researcher therefore aims to produce conditions such that the research will fulfil the requirements for causality discussed above.

In the world of human beings, with which the social scientist deals, there is much less scope for experiment than in the world of inanimate objects or animals with which natural scientists deal. Some situations do exist where experimentation with human beings in the field of leisure or tourism can take place. For instance it is possible to experiment with variations in children's play equipment; it is possible to conduct experiments with willing subjects; and it is possible to experiment in management situations, for instance by varying prices or advertising strategies in relation to leisure or tourism services. But many areas of interest to the leisure or tourism researcher are not susceptible to controlled experiment.

For instance the researcher interested in the effect of level of income on behaviour cannot take a group of people and vary their incomes in order to study the effects of income on leisure participation or tourism behaviour – it would be difficult to find people on executive salaries willing voluntarily to spend a year living on a student grant in the interests of research! Alternatively, unlike the scientist experimenting with rats, it is not possible to find two groups of humans identical in every respect except for their level of income. Even more fundamentally, it is of course not possible to vary people's social class or race. In order to study these phenomena it is necessary to use *non-experimental* methods, that is it is necessary to study differences between people as they exist.

So, for example, in order to study the effects of income on leisure participation patterns or touristic behaviour it is necessary to gather information on the leisure and travel behaviour patterns of groups of people with different levels of income. But people differ in all sorts of ways, some of which may be related to their level of income and some not. For example, two people with identical income levels can differ markedly in terms of their personalities, their family situation, their physical health and so on. So, in comparing the behaviour of two groups of people, it is difficult to be sure which differences arise as a result of income differences and which as a result of other differences. The results of the research are therefore likely to be less clear-cut than in the case of the controlled experiment.

Some areas within the broad field of leisure and tourism do lend themselves to experimental research: these are the areas which are closest to the natural sciences, namely psychology and the human movement aspect of sports research. Thus in the case of psychological research, it is possible to set up experiments in which people are subject to 'stimuli' – for example, the viewing of photographs or video – and to study their reactions. In the case of human movement, subjects can be asked to engage in particular forms of physical exercise and their physical and psychological reactions can be measured. Although some of the techniques and approaches described in this book are applicable to experimental as much as non-experimental research, in general the experimental method is not dealt with here.

Primary and secondary data

In planning a research project it is advisable to consider whether it is necessary to go to the expense of collecting new information (*primary* data, where the researcher is the first user) or whether existing data (*secondary* data, where the researcher is the secondary user) will do the job. Sometimes existing information is in the form of research already completed on the topic or a related topic. A fundamental part of any research project is therefore to scour the existing published – and unpublished – sources of information for related research. Existing research might not obviate the originally proposed research, but it may provide interesting ideas and points of comparison with the proposed research.

Even if the research project is to be based mainly on new information it will usually be necessary also to make use of other, existing, information – such as official government statistics or financial records from a leisure or tourism facility or service. Such information is generally referred to as *secondary data*, as opposed to the *primary data*, which is the new data to be collected in the proposed research. The topic of secondary data is dealt with in Chapter 6.

Self-reported and observed data

The best, and often the only, sources of information about individuals' leisure or tourism behaviour or attitudes are individuals' own reports about themselves. Much leisure and tourism research therefore involves asking people about their past behaviour, attitudes and aspirations, generally using interviews.

There are some disadvantages to this approach, mainly that the researcher is never sure just how honest or accurate people are in responding to questions. In some instances people may deliberately or unwittingly distort or 'bend' the truth – for instance in understating the amount of alcohol they drink or over-stating the amount of exercise they take. In other instances they may have problems of recall – for instance in remembering just how much money they spent on a recreational or holiday trip some months ago.

The alternative to relying on people to tell the researcher what they do, is for the researcher to use an alternative source of evidence. For instance, to find out how children use a playground or how adults make use of a resort area or a park it would probably be better to watch them than to try to ask them about it. Patterns of movement and crowding can be observed. Sometimes people leave behind evidence of their behaviour – for instance the most popular exhibits at a museum will be the ones where the carpet is most worn, and the most used beaches are likely to be those where the most litter is dumped. Generally these techniques are referred to as *observational* or *unobtrusive* techniques and are dealt with in Chapter 7.

Qualitative and quantitative research

Much leisure and tourism research involves the collection, analysis and presentation of statistical information. Sometimes the information is innately quantitative – for instance the numbers of people engaging in a list of leisure activities in a year, the number of tourists visiting a particular holiday area or the average income of a group of people. Sometimes the information is qualitative in nature but is presented in quantitative form – for instance numerical 'scores' calculated from asking people to indicate levels of satisfaction with different services, where the scores range from 1, meaning 'very satisfied', to 5, meaning 'very dissatisfied'.

The *quantitative* approach to research involves statistical analysis. It relies on numerical evidence to draw conclusions or to test hypotheses. To be sure of the reliability of the results it is often necessary to study relatively large numbers of people and to use computers to analyse the data. The data can be derived from questionnaire surveys, from observation involving counts or from secondary sources.

In fact there can be said to be two approaches to quantitative research, which we will refer to as type A and type B research. Type A research makes use of statistical methods and tests, as outlined in Chapter 14. Type B research is also based on numerical data, but makes little or no use of statistical tests: its most sophisticated statistical measure is usually the percentage. Type B research is very common in the British tradition of leisure and tourism research. For example, in reading the British journal *Leisure Studies*, it is notable that, whereas there are many articles which present numerical information, very few utilise statistical tests and techniques, such as chi-square tests, *t*-tests, analysis of variance, correlation or regression. This is in marked contrast to the leading American journal, *Journal of Leisure Research*, where most articles which include numerical data make use of such tests. Type B research is more informal than type A and is closer in approach to qualitative methods.

The *qualitative* approach to research is generally not concerned with numbers. It involves gathering a great deal of information about a small number of people rather than a limited amount of information about a large number of people. The information collected is generally not presentable in numerical form. It is used when a full and rounded understanding of the leisure or tourist behaviour and situation of a few individuals, however 'unrepresentative' they may be, is required, rather than a limited understanding of a large, 'representative' group.

The methods used to gather qualitative information include observation, informal and in-depth interviewing and participant observation. Research studying groups of people using non-quantitative, anthropological approaches, is referred to as ethnographic research or ethnographic fieldwork. Such methods were initially developed by anthropologists, but have been adapted by sociologists for use in their work. Qualitative methods are considered in Chapter 8.

While the debate between protagonists of qualitative and quantitative research can become somewhat partisan, it is now widely accepted that the two approaches complement one another. Thus quantitative research is often based on initial qualitative work. It is even possible that the two approaches are moving closer together, as computers are now being used to analyse qualitative data (Fielding and Lee, 1991).

Validity and reliability

Validity is the extent to which the information collected by the researcher truly reflects the phenomenon being studied. Leisure and tourism research is fraught with difficulties in this area, mainly because empirical research is largely concerned with people's behaviour and with their attitudes, and for information on these the researcher is, in the main, reliant on people's own reports in the form of responses to questionnaire-based interviews and other forms of interview. These instruments are subject to a number of imperfections. Consequently, the validity of leisure and tourism data can rarely be as certain as that of data in the natural sciences. For example, data on the number of people who have participated in an activity at least once over the last month (a common type of measure used in leisure research) cover a wide range of different types of involvement with an activity, from the person who participates for two hours every day to the person who accidentally engaged in the activity just once for a few minutes. So the question of what is a *participant* can be complex. More detailed questioning to capture such complexity can be costly to undertake on a large scale.

Reliability is the extent to which research findings would be the same if the research were to be repeated at a later date or with a different sample of subjects. Again it can be seen that the model is taken from the natural sciences where, if experimental conditions are properly controlled, a repetition of an experiment should produce identical results. This is rarely the case in the social sciences, because they deal with human beings in ever-changing social situations. While a single person's report of their behaviour may be accurate, when it is aggregated with information from other people, it presents a snap-shot picture of a group of people, which is subject to change over time, as the composition of the group changes, or as *some* members of the group change their patterns of behaviour. This means that the social scientist, including the leisure and tourism researcher, must be very cautious when making general statements on the basis of empirical research. While measures can be taken to ensure a degree of generalisability, strictly speaking, any research findings relate only to the subjects involved, at the time and place the research was carried out.

CASE STUDY 2.1

Tennis vs. golf – inductive approach

Suppose a descriptive piece of research shows that more people play tennis than play golf. This is just a piece of information; we cannot explain why this is so without additional information and analysis. If the research also reveals that it costs more to play golf than to play tennis then we could offer the explanation that popularity is related to price.

However, qualitative information from the research could indicate that more people consider tennis as being fun to play than consider golf to be fun. This suggests that tennis is intrinsically more attractive than golf and its popularity is not related to price but to intrinsic enjoyment.

On the other hand, the research could indicate that there are more tennis courts available than golf courses in the particular community being studied, suggesting that, if there were more golf courses available, then golf would be more popular – implying that popularity is related to availability of facilities.

In this example, a series of possible explanations is being *induced* from the data. In its most fully developed form the explanation amounts to a theory. In this case we would be developing a theory of sports participation relating demand, supply of facilities, costs, perceived attractiveness of the activity, intrinsic satisfactions and so on.

CASE STUDY 2.2

Tennis vs. golf – deductive approach

Hypothesis 1: If sport A is more expensive to play than sport B, then sport B will be more popular.

Hypothesis 2: If more facilities are available for sport B than for sport A then sport B will be more popular.

To test these hypotheses we have to design a research project to collect information on:

(a) the relative popularity of two sports – for example, tennis and golf;
(b) the costs of participating in the two sports;
(c) the availability of facilities for the two sports.

The two hypotheses would then be tested using the data collected. In this case the research is guided from the beginning by the initial hypotheses.

QUESTIONS AND EXERCISES

1 Examine any edition of either *Leisure Studies* or *Annals of Tourism Research* and classify the articles into disciplinary areas. Contrast the key questions which each article is addressing.

2 Using the same journal as in exercise 1, determine whether the articles are: (a) empirical or non-empirical; (b) deductive or inductive; (c) positivist or interpretive.

3 Using either *Leisure Studies* or *Annals of Tourism Research*, take an edition of the journal at two-yearly intervals over 10 or 12 years and summarise the apparent change over time in the topics addressed and methods used in the articles.

4 Select one of the following topics and examine it from the point of view of three different disciplines:
(a) the impact of tourism on the host community;
(b) inequalities in sports participation;
(c) inequalities in participation in the arts;
(d) the rise of 'special interest' tourism;
(e) the effects of recreation/tourism on the environment;
(f) the role of leisure/tourism in the urban environment.

FURTHER READING

The journal *Leisure Studies* has published a number of articles which review the contributions of various disciplines to leisure research; these are by: Coppock (1982) on geography; Parry (1983) on sociology; Vickerman (1983) on economics; and Ingham (1986, 1987) on psychology. And in 1989 it published an analysis and review of the contribution of historians to leisure studies in Britain by Bailey (1989).

Books edited by Barnett (1988) and Jackson and Burton (1989) provide disciplinary reviews of leisure research in more detail than those presented above.

For a recent contribution on the sociology of leisure, *see* Jarvie and Maguire's (1994) *Sport and Leisure in Social Thought*; on cultural studies, *see* During (1993) and McRobbie (1994); and on the geography of leisure, *see* Williams (1995) *Outdoor Recreation and the Urban Environment*.

The journal *Annals of Tourism Research* devoted a special issue to tourism social sciences in 1991 (Graburn and Jafari, 1991), covering such disciplines as sociology (Dann and Cohen, 1991); geography (Mitchell and Murphy, 1991); history (Towner and Wall, 1991); psychology (Pearce and Stringer, 1991); political science (Matthews and Richter, 1991) and economics (Eadington and Redman, 1991).

Tourism research is discussed from an interdisciplinary perspective and from the point of view of sociology and psychology in Pearce and Butler (1993), while Ryan (1995) and Pearce (1982, 1988) address the psychology of tourism particularly as it affects motivation and satisfaction. Edwards (1991) discusses the reliability of tourism statistics.

For discussion of qualitative versus quantitative research *see* Kelly (1980); Henderson (1990); Borman *et al.* (1986); Godbey and Scott (1990); Kamphorst *et al.* (1984); Krenz and Sax (1986); Veal (1994b).

For a discussion of the experimental method in leisure research *see* Havitz and Sell (1991).

For a discussion of historical research methods, *see* Barzun and Graff (1985).

CHAPTER 3

Starting out: research plans and proposals

INTRODUCTION

This chapter examines the planning of research projects; the formulation of research proposals; the relationship between policy, planning and management problems, research problems and research design; and the research/consultancy tendering process. A research plan or proposal must consider how a research project is to be conducted in its entirety; consequently it involves examination of the whole research process from beginning to end. In this chapter, therefore, a certain amount of cross-referencing is required to later chapters, where elements of the process are dealt with in detail.

THE RESEARCH PROCESS

The research process can be divided into eight main elements, as shown in Figure 3.1. However, the enormous variety of approaches to research suggests that not all research projects follow precisely the same sequence of procedures. In particular, the first four elements – selecting the topic, reviewing the literature, devising a conceptual framework and deciding the key research questions – rarely happen in the direct, linear way that the numbered sequence implies. There is generally a great deal of 'to-ing and fro-ing' between the elements. Hence, in Figure 3.1, these elements are located on a circle, implying that a number of circuits may be necessary before proceeding to element 5.

To illustrate the process in operation, three case studies are appended to this chapter. Case study 3.1 is clearly explanatory research and arises from a hypothetical management problem; it seeks to find the causes of a decline in the number of visitors to a leisure or tourism facility. Case study 3.2 bridges leisure and tourism and deals with the role of the holiday as a leisure activity. It lies somewhere between descriptive and explanatory research. Case study 3.3 is evaluative in nature, and considers the relationship between a local authority's objectives for leisure services and how its performance in meeting those objectives might be assessed. The case studies cover the first six elements of the process shown in Figure 3.1. Because of space limitations they are presented in somewhat abbreviated form, but the essential process is illustrated.

Each of the elements in Figure 3.1 is now discussed in turn.

Figure 3.1   Elements of the research process

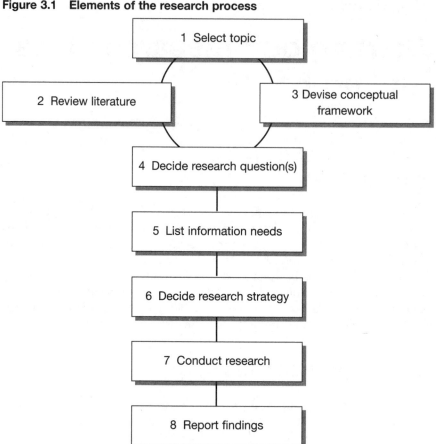

1 Select topic

How do research topics arise? They may arise from a range of sources. As illustrated by the examples in Figure 3.2, these include: (a) the researcher's personal interests; (b) issues identified in the literature; (c) a policy or management problem; (d) an issue of social concern; or (e) a popular or media issue.

Personal interest can give rise to a research project in a number of ways. For example, the researcher may be personally involved in a sport or other leisure activity, may be a member of a particular social group, based on gender, ethnicity or occupation, or may live in a particular tourism location and so be personally aware of certain local issues or problems. Using such an interest as a focus for research has advantages and disadvantages. The advantage lies in the knowledge of the phenomenon which the researcher already has, the possibility of access to key individuals and further information, and the high level of motivation which is likely to be brought to the research. The disadvantage is that the researcher may be biased and may not be able to view the situation as 'objectively' as someone with no prior interest or knowledge. Personal interest

Figure 3.2   Examples of research topics from different sources

Source of topic	Examples of topics
a Personal interest	• a particular sport – trends • leisure access and needs of a particular ethnic or age group • tourism conflicts in a particular (home) locality • a particular professional group – its ethos, history and future
b The literature	• Does Csikszentmihalyi's (1990) idea of 'flow' apply to participation in sport X, or to tourist trips to destination Y? • How do MacCannell's (1976) ideas on 'signs' relate to 'sun sea sand sex' holidays, as opposed to sight-seeing holidays? • What is known about the leisure activity of 'taking a holiday', as opposed to the activity of choosing a tourism destination?
c Policy/ management	• Why are visits to leisure facility X declining? • What market segments should be used to develop a strategy for promoting sport X, arts venue Y, or tourism destination Z? • What are the leisure needs of community X?
d Social	• The impact of growing tourism on a local environment • Leisure needs of single parents • The role of sport in a third world community
e Popular/media	• Are recreational drugs harmful? • Are city streets less safe than they used to be? • Who goes to 'rave' parties and what do they get out of them?

is generally just a starting point in selecting a topic. If the selected topic area is initially fairly broad, deciding on a *specific focus* for the research will usually depend on consideration of one or more of the other four criteria discussed below.

The literature is the most common source of ideas for academic research. A researchable idea from the literature can take a variety of forms. It may be that a certain theory or theoretical proposition has never been tested empirically, or it merits further empirical testing:

• *geographically* – for example, it has been tested in the USA but not elsewhere, or it may have been developed in relation to urban areas, but not rural areas;

• *socially* – for example, it is based on research on men and ignores women;

- *temporally* – for example, it was last tested 20 years ago and so may be out of date, or it has not been fully investigated historically;
- *contextually* – for example, it was developed in another area of human activity but has never been applied to leisure or tourism;
- *methodologically* – for example, it was initially based on qualitative data and has not been tested quantitatively.

Clearly if the literature is to be the main source of ideas for a research topic then the first two elements of the research process – selecting a topic and reviewing the literature – are effectively combined. Identifying a topic from the literature requires a special approach to reading, in that the aim is not just to identify what the literature *says*, but also to ascertain what it does *not* say. The process of critically reviewing the literature is discussed further below under element 2, and in Chapter 5.

Policy or management topics are generally specified by a leisure or tourism organisation, but students or academics interested in policy or management issues can also identify such topics. For example, tourism forecasting is done not only by, and at the behest of, government and commercial tourism bodies but also by academics. User surveys of leisure or tourist facilities or cost-benefit analyses of programmes and projects can be conducted by interested academics as well as leisure service organisations. The difference is that the results of academic research will often be made public and will generally be presented so as to highlight their more general implications rather than the particular application to the facility or programme being studied. Research carried out by or for a commercial organisation, on the other hand, will often not be made public and the wider implications of the research may not be examined. Research sponsored by government bodies lies somewhere in between these two situations: the results of the research may be very specific, but will often not be confidential. Another difference is that academic studies are often as concerned with *methodology* as with the substantive findings of the research.

It is common for policy or management topics to be outlined by an organisation in a *brief* for a funded research or consultancy project. Research organisations – usually consultants – are invited to respond in the form of a competitive *tender* to conduct the project. This type of procedure has its own set of practices and conventions, as discussed later in this chapter, under *Briefs and tenders*.

Social concern can give rise to a wide range of research topics. For example, concern for certain deprived or neglected groups in society can lead to research on the leisure needs or behaviour of members of such groups. Concern for the environment can lead to research on the environmental impact of tourism. Often such research is closely related to policy issues, but the research may have a more limited role, seeking to highlight problems rather than necessarily to devise solutions.

Finally, a *popular issue* can inspire research that seeks to explore popular beliefs or conceptions, especially where it is suspected that these may be inaccurate. 'Popular' usually means 'as portrayed in the media'. For example this might be seen as the motivation for much research on media portrayals of such phenomena as sporting crowd violence (Cuneen and Lynch, 1988) and 'alienated youth' (Rowe, 1995, p. 4).

2 Review the literature

The process of reviewing the existing literature is sufficiently important for a complete chapter to be devoted to it in this book (Chapter 5). 'Reviewing the literature' is a somewhat academic term referring to the process of identifying and engaging with previously published research relevant to the topic of interest. The process can play a number of roles, as listed in Figure 3.3, and discussed further in Chapter 5.

Figure 3.3   Roles of the literature in research

- Entire basis of the research

- Source of ideas on topics for research

- Information on research already done by others

- Source of methodological or theoretical ideas

- Basis of comparison

- Information that is an integral/supportive part of the research

In many cases the review undertaken in the early stages of the research has to be seen as an 'interim' literature review only, since time does not always permit a thorough literature review to be completed at the start of a project. Part of the research programme itself may be to explore the literature further. Having investigated the literature as thoroughly as possible, it is usually necessary to proceed with the proposed research in the hope that all relevant material has been identified. Exploration of the literature will generally continue for the duration of the project. Researchers always run the risk of coming across some previous – or contemporaneous – publication which will completely negate or upstage their work just as they are about to complete it. But that is part of the excitement of research! In fact, unlike the situation in the natural sciences, the risk of this happening in the leisure and tourism field is minimal, since research in this area can rarely be replicated exactly. In the natural sciences research carried out in, say, California can reproduce exactly the findings of research carried out in, say, London. In leisure and tourism research however, this is not the case. A set of research procedures carried out in relation to residents of California could be expected to produce very different results from identical procedures carried out in London, or even New York, simply because leisure and tourism research is involved with unique people in varying social settings.

Where possible, attempts should be made to explore not just published research – the *literature* – but also unpublished and ongoing research. This process is very much 'hit and miss'. Knowing what research is ongoing or knowing of completed but unpublished research usually depends on having access to informal networks, although some organisations publish registers of ongoing research. Once a topic of interest has been identified it is often clear, from the literature, where the major centres for such research are located and to discover, from direct approaches or from annual reports or newsletters, what research is currently being conducted at those centres. This process can be particularly important if the topic is a 'fashionable' one. However, if this is the case, the communication networks are usually very active, which eases the process. In this respect papers from conferences and seminars are usually better sources of information on current research than books and journals, since the latter have long gestation periods, so that the research reported in them is generally based on work carried out two or more years prior to publication.

As discussed in Chapter 5, a review of the literature should be concluded with a *summary* which provides an overview of the field, its substantive and methodological merits and deficiencies or gaps, and an indication of how such conclusions are related to the research task in hand.

3 Devise conceptual framework

The development of a conceptual framework is arguably the most important part of any research project and also the most difficult. And it is the element which is the weakest in many research projects. A *conceptual framework* involves *concepts*. Concepts are general representations of the phenomena to be studied – the 'building blocks' of a study. The first column of Figure 3.4 lists some examples of concepts encountered in leisure and tourism research.

A conceptual *framework* indicates how the researcher views the concepts involved in a study – in particular the *relationships* between concepts. The concepts identified and the framework within which they are set determines the whole course of the study.

Thus the development of a conceptual framework involves four elements: (a) identification of concepts; (b) definition of concepts; (c) exploration of relationships between concepts; and (d) operationalisation of concepts – as depicted in Figure 3.5. Examination of the *relationships* between concepts is discussed further below. *Operationalisation* of concepts involves deciding how they might be measured, if quantitative in nature, or recognised or assessed, if qualitative in nature. 'Identification of concepts' is usually the starting point, but the exercise is generally *iterative* – that is, it involves going backwards and forwards, or round and round, between the various elements until a satisfactory solution is reached.

It is necessary to decide what sort of research is being conducted in order to determine how elaborate the conceptual framework needs to be – that is, it is necessary to decide whether the research is descriptive, explanatory or evaluative. *Descriptive research* rarely requires an elaborate conceptual framework, but

Figure 3.4 Concepts

Concept	Definition	Operationalisation
Leisure need	Demand for leisure activity which someone considers should be met	*Felt need* – what individuals feel they require, discoverable by asking people questions *Expressed need* – demands which are actively expressed; measured by visits, waiting lists, etc. *Normative need* – as assessed by a panel of experts, using a variety of methods *Comparative need* – level of requirements determined by comparisons with others
Tourism demand	Total level of tourist visitation in a given area in a given period of time	Visitor bed-nights per annum in region X
Social class	Socio-economic or political position of a group of people in society	Combination of: person's occupation (or occupation of main bread-winner of household), income, education level, occupation of parents
Efficiency	Level of output per unit of input	e.g. for a public leisure facility: net subsidy per visit
Attitude	Person's feelings towards something/someone	Response (agree strongly, agree, disagree, etc.) to a number of statements on a given topic
Market for a product/ service	Demand for a product in a given area or community over a given time period	Current (and potential/future) annual purchases of the product in various price ranges and categories, in money and volume terms, by residents of area X

Figure 3.5   Development of conceptual framework

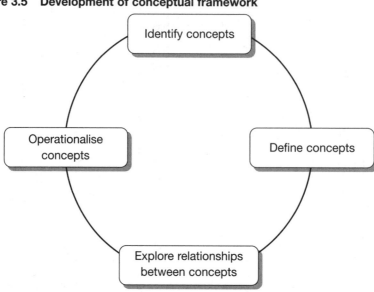

clear definitions of the concepts involved are required. In some cases this can nevertheless be a considerable undertaking, for example when the descriptive task is to decide people's time use and a taxonomy and associated coding system must devised for every conceivable form of leisure and non-leisure activity (*see* Burton, 1971), or when the task is to gather data on the many types of tourist expenditure and activity (Frechtling, 1994, p. 374). Both *explanatory* and *evaluative* research call for a well-developed conceptual framework which forms the basis for the explanation or evaluation work required from the research.

The key element for most research is therefore the exploration of relationships between concepts. One approach to this is to use the device of a *concept map*, sometimes referred to as a *mind map*. Concept mapping can be seen as a form of visual 'brainstorming' and can be done alone or as part of a group exercise. The idea is to write down, on a piece of paper or a board or flip-chart, all the concepts which appear to be relevant to a topic, in any order which they come to mind. Then begin to group the concepts and indicate linkages between them. Case studies 3.1, 3.2 and 3.3 present finalised versions of simple concept maps. All three are simple in format and are presented to demonstrate an approach in general terms. In each case more detailed concept maps could be developed, breaking down various general concepts into their constituent parts.

In this discussion the term *conceptual framework* has been used to cover a wide range of research situations. Thus such a term can be used in applied research when the framework adopted might relate to such activities as planning or marketing. In such cases, ideas for conceptual frameworks may be found in the planning or marketing literature. When the research is more academically orientated, the term *theoretical framework* might equally well be used (*see* Veal, 1995).

A theoretical framework might also be called a *model*, particularly when the research is quantitative in nature. For example, in Case study 3.2, one aspect of the relationship between holiday-taking and a person's social and economic circumstances could be expressed in quantitative modelling terms as follows:

The level of holiday-taking (H) of a particular group is positively related to the average level of income (I) of the group.

This would then be expressed in the form of an equation:

$$H = a + bI$$

By studying various groups with different levels of income and holiday-taking patterns, research would then seek to find values for the 'parameters' a and b, so that the level of holiday-taking of a particular group could be predicted once the average income of that group was known. The technicalities of this process are not pursued further here, but are touched on again in Chapter 14, where the technique of regression is discussed.

4 Decide research question(s)

In some cases the research *topic* selected by the researcher is quite specific from the beginning and the literature review and conceptual framework are the process by which the specific issue is placed in the context of existing knowledge. In other cases the topic is initially quite vague: it is an area of interest without a specific focus. In such cases the literature review and process of developing a conceptual framework help to focus the topic and determine what exactly should be researched. In both cases it is desirable to focus the research on one or more very specific questions which can be answered by the research.

In most situations the idea of *primary* and *subsidiary* questions is helpful. The subsidiary questions are necessary steps towards answering the primary question. This idea is illustrated in the case studies.

In the natural sciences and in some areas of the social sciences it is more customary, at this stage, to state *hypotheses* to be tested. A *hypothesis* is a statement or proposition which can be tested by reference to empirical study. Thus, for example, a *research question* might be expressed in the form: what is the relationship between holiday-taking and income? A *hypothesis* dealing with the same topic might be expressed as: there is a positive relationship between holiday-taking and level of income. In the latter case the hypothesis may be shown to be true or false as a result of empirical research. The *question* format lends itself to descriptive and inductive research, while the *hypothesis* format is more appropriate for explanatory and deductive research.

5 List information needs

The research question(s) and the conceptual framework should give rise to a list of information needs. Again the case studies provide illustrations of such lists. At this stage the information is expressed in general terms: for example, 'perceived characteristics of a holiday' or 'user perceptions of the museum'. Just how the information might be collected is not yet determined. No item should appear on the list unless it is related to the research question(s) and the conceptual framework.

6 Decide research strategy

Development of a *research strategy* involves making decisions on a number of aspects of the research process, as listed in Figure 3.6.

Figure 3.6   Research strategy

1 Project elements

2 Information gathering techniques to be used

3 Data analysis techniques

4 Budget

5 Timetable

Project elements

Often a research project will involve a number of different elements, or 'sub-projects' – for example, gathering of primary and secondary data or data-gathering in different locations or in different time periods.

Information-gathering techniques to be used

It is at this stage that alternative information-gathering techniques are considered. While the *operationalisation of concepts* process may have indicated certain types of information source, it is here that the detail is determined. For each item of information listed under element 5, a range of sources may be possible. Judgement is required to determine just what techniques to use, particularly in the light of time and resources available, or likely to be made available.

A further review of the literature can be valuable at this stage, concentrating particularly on techniques used by previous researchers, and asking such questions as: have their chosen methods been shown to be limiting or even misguided? What lessons can be learned from past errors?

The range of information-gathering methods most likely to be considered at this stage are those covered in the following chapters of this book, namely:

● utilisation of existing information, including published and unpublished research and secondary data (Chapters 5 and 6);
● observation (Chapter 7);

- qualitative methods: including ethnographic methods, participant observation, informal and in-depth interviews, group interviews or focus groups (Chapter 8);
- questionnaire-based surveys: including household face-to-face surveys, street surveys, telephone surveys, user/site surveys, postal surveys (Chapters 9–10).

These individual techniques are not discussed further here since they are covered in general terms in Chapter 4 and in detail in subsequent chapters, as indicated.

Where the process of information-gathering involves going out into the 'field' – for instance to conduct interviews or to undertake observation – the planning of *fieldwork* needs to be considered. In experimental research the proposed programme of *experiments* would be considered here. If the proposed research does not involve primary data collection then this will not be a consideration. Where extensive data collection is involved, the organisation of fieldwork may be complex, involving recruitment and training of field staff (for example, interviewers), obtaining of permissions, including ethics committee clearance in universities, and organisation of data processing and analysis. These matters are discussed in more detail in Chapter 11.

Approach to data analysis

Data analysis may be simple and straightforward and may follow fairly logically from the type of information-collection technique to be used. This is particularly so when the research is descriptive in nature. In some cases, however, the analysis of data may be complex, and thought needs to be given to the time and the skills which will be required to undertake the analysis. Consideration must be given to the format of the data which will be collected and just how analysis of the data will answer the research questions posed. The planned analysis procedures have implications for data collection. For example, Case study 3.2 involves comparing holiday-takers and non-holiday-takers, implying that an adequate sample of the two groups would need to be involved and ways would need to be found to compare their characteristics, patterns of holiday-taking, local leisure participation and perceptions. Where qualitative data are to be collected, for example, using in-depth interviews, thought must be given to how the results of the interviews will be analysed. Details of analysis methods which are appropriate and possible for different data-collection techniques are discussed in subsequent chapters, but it must be borne in mind that, when planning a project, full consideration should be given not only to the *collection* of data but also to their *analysis*.

Budget and timetable

In some situations key aspects of the budget and timetable are fixed. For example a student may have available only her or his own labour and no other resources and may be required to submit a report by a specified date. Similarly, research consultancies usually have an upper budgetary limit and a fixed completion date. In other situations, for example, when seeking a grant for research from a grant-giving body, or permission to conduct an 'in-house' project, the proposer of the research is called upon to recommend both budget and timetable. Whatever the situation, the task is never easy, since there is rarely enough time or money available to conduct the ideal research project, so compromises invariably have to be made. Again the details of budgeting and timetabling are not discussed here, but are covered in Chapter 11 on research practice.

7 Conduct research

Actually conducting the research is what the rest of the book is about, and again, some details of practical matters are covered in Chapter 11 on research practice. However, it cannot be stressed enough that good research will rarely result if care is not taken over the preparatory processes discussed in this chapter. In a more positive vein, good preparation can ease the rest of the research process considerably. Inexperienced researchers often move too rapidly from stage 1, selecting the topic, to stage 7, conducting the research. This can result in the collection of data which are of doubtful use and the researcher being presented with a problem of making sense of information which has been laboriously collected but does not fit into any framework. If the above process is followed then every item of information collected should have a purpose, since it will have been collected to answer specific questions. This does not of course mean that the unexpected will not happen and 'serendipitous' findings may not arise, but at least the core structure of the research should be 'under control'.

8 Report findings

The question of the writing up of research results is not discussed in detail here because the whole of the final chapter of the book is devoted to this topic. Unlike the actual conduct of the research, which inexperienced researchers invariably rush into too quickly, the writing up of results is usually delayed too long, so that insufficient time is left to complete it satisfactorily. An outline of the research process, as presented here, can itself be part of the problem, in that it implies that the writing-up process comes right at the end. In fact, the writing of a research report can begin almost as soon as the project begins, since all the early stages, such as the review of the literature and the development of the conceptual framework, can be written up as the project progresses.

RESEARCH PROPOSALS

Research proposals of two broad kinds are discussed here. The first is the *self-generated* research proposal of the sort prepared by academics seeking funds for a research project of their own devising or by students seeking approval for research for a project or thesis on a topic of their own choosing. The second is the *responsive* proposal prepared by consultants responding to research briefs prepared by potential clients. Students can also be required to prepare responsive proposals when they conduct projects for real or hypothetical clients. Planners and managers seeking 'in-house' resources to conduct research fall somewhere between the two types of proposal described.

In each case the proposal is a written document, which may or may not have to be supported by a 'live' presentation, and which must be convincing to the person or persons who will decide whether the research should go ahead. The writer of a research proposal is faced with the difficult task of convincing the decision-makers of the value of the research; the valuable and original insights which they will bring to the project; and their personal capability to conduct the research. In some cases the decision-making person or persons will be experts in the field, while in other cases they may be non-experts, so care must be taken to ensure that the proposal is understandable to all concerned. Clarity of expression and succinctness are often the key qualities looked for in these situations.

Self-generated research proposals

Academic research proposals, for student theses/projects or for academics seeking funding, not only have to describe what research is to be done and how, but also must provide a rationale for the choice of topic. The topic and its treatment must be seen to be appropriate, in terms of scale and complexity, to the particular level of project involved, be it an undergraduate project, a PhD thesis or a funded project involving a team of researchers over a number of years.

In general the academic research proposal must cover the material dealt with in this chapter. In some cases considerable preliminary work will already have been completed before the proposal is submitted. This could apply in the case of a PhD proposal or a proposal from an experienced academic who has been working in a particular field for a number of years. In such cases, the proposal may present considerable completed work on elements 1 to 6 of the research process as discussed above, funding being sought only to conduct the fieldwork part of the research and write up the results – elements 7 and 8. In other cases little more than the selection of the topic may have been completed and the proposal outlines a programme to undertake elements 2 to 8. Some proposals contain a preliminary review of the literature with a proposal to undertake more as part of the project. Some proposals are very clear about the conceptual framework to be used; in other cases just speculative ideas are presented. While bearing in mind, therefore, that there can be substantial differences between proposals of various types, the checklist in Figure 3.7 is offered as a guide to the contents of a proposal.

Figure 3.7   Research proposal checklist: self-generated research

1 Background and justification for selection of topic.

2 (Preliminary) review of the literature.

3 Conceptual or theoretical framework.

4 Statement of research problems and questions and/or hypotheses.

5 Outline of data requirements and overall research strategy. Division of project into elements, stages and tasks.

6 Details of information-collection methods:

- types of information collection
- sample or subject selection methods – measures to ensure quality
- justification of sample sizes (where appropriate)
- data/information to be generated by each method.

7 Details of data analysis methods.

8 Timetable (N.B. some tasks will be concurrent):

- preparatory work
- ethics approval if required
- fieldwork: data-collection tasks
- analysis
- draft report or thesis
- feedback on draft
- final report or thesis presentation.

9 Budget, where applicable: costing of each element, stage and task:

- project staff costs (n days at £x per day)
- permissible overheads
- fieldwork or data collection costs
- additional items, e.g. travel, printing, telephone, postage.

10 Report or thesis chapter outline or indication of number and type of publications.

11 Resources, skills and experience available (necessary when seeking funds):

- researcher(s) – curricula vitae, especially experience relevant to the proposed project
- availability of computers, equipment, library resources, etc.

Responsive proposals: briefs and tenders

A *brief* is an outline of the research which an organisation wishes to be undertaken. Consultants wishing to be considered to undertake the project must submit a written proposal or 'tender'. Usually briefs are prepared by an organisation with a view to a number of consultants competing to obtain the contract to do the research. In some cases potential consultants are first asked, possibly through an advertisement, to indicate their 'expression of interest' in the project; this will involve a short statement of the consultants' capabilities, their experience in the field and staff available. In some cases public bodies maintain a register of accredited consultants with particular interests and capabilities, who may be invited to tender for particular projects. In the light of such statements of interest or information in the register, a 'shortlist' of consultants is sent the full brief and invited to submit a detailed tender. Successful tenders are not usually selected on the basis of price alone (the budget is in any case often a fixed sum) but on the quality of the submitted proposal and the 'track record' of the consultants.

Briefs vary in the amount of detail they give. Sometimes they are very detailed, leaving little scope for consultants to express any individuality in their proposals. In other cases they are very limited and leave a great deal of scope to consultants to indicate proposed methods and approaches. Client organisations which are experienced in commissioning research can produce briefs which are clear and 'ready to roll'. In other situations it is necessary to clarify the client's meanings and intentions. For example a client might ask for a study of the 'leisure needs' of a community, in which case it would be necessary to clarify what the client means by 'leisure' – for example, whether they wish to include home-based leisure, holidays, entertainment, restaurants and nightclubs. If a client asks for the 'effectiveness' of a programme to be assessed it may be necessary to clarify whether a statement of objectives or a list of performance criteria for the programme already exists, or whether that must be developed as part of the research.

Paradoxically, problems can arise when client organisations are over-specific about their research requirements. For example an organisation may ask for a 'user survey' or 'visitor survey' to be conducted. It is not easy to decide what should be included in such a survey without information on the management or policy questions which the data are intended to answer. Is the organisation concerned about declining attendances? Is it wanting to change its 'marketing mix'? Is it concerned about the particular mix of clientele being attracted? Is it concerned about future trends in demand? It would be preferable in such a situation for the client to indicate the nature of the management problem and leave the researcher to determine the most suitable research approach to take, which might or might not include a survey.

Sometimes there is a hidden agenda which the researcher would do well to become familiar with before embarking on the research. For example, research can sometimes be used as a means to defuse or delay difficult management decisions in an organisation. An example would be where a leisure or tourism service may be suffering declining attendances because of poor maintenance of facilities and poor staff attitudes to customers. This is very clear to anyone who walks in the door, but the management decides to commission a 'market study', in the hope that the answer to their problem can be found 'out there' in the market, when in fact the problem is very much 'in there', and their money might be better spent on improving maintenance and staff training than on research!

A situation where the client's requirements may seem vague is when the research is not related to immediate policy needs but to possible future needs or is simply to satisfy curiosity. For example, a manager of a leisure or tourism facility may commission a user survey (perhaps because there is spare money in the current year's budget) without having any specific policy or management problems in mind. In that case the research will need to specify hypothetical or potential policy or management issues and match the data specifications to them.

What should a proposal contain? The first and golden principle is that it should *address the brief*. It is likely that the brief will have been discussed at great length in the commissioning organisation; every aspect of the brief is likely to be of importance to some individual or section in the organisation, so every aspect of the brief should be considered in the proposal. So, for example, if the brief lists, say, four objectives, the proposal must indicate how each of the four objectives will be met. A proposal must therefore indicate clearly:

- what is to be done
- how it is to be done
- when it will be done
- what it will cost
- who will do it

A typical proposal might include elements as shown in Figure 3.8.

It can be helpful to present aspects of the proposal in diagrammatic form, particularly the conceptual approach, the various stages or elements of the project and the timetable. Examples of the latter are shown in Figures 3.9 and 3.10. There are computer programs, such as *Microsoft Project* and *ABC Flowcharter* which can assist in the organisation of complex projects and their graphical presentation.

Figure 3.8   Research proposal checklist: responsive research

1   Brief summary of key aspects of the proposal, including any unique approach and particular skills or experience of the consultants.

2   Re-statement of the key aspects of the brief.

3   Interpretation of key concepts in the brief.

4   Overall 'approach' to the problem(s).

5   Division of project into elements, stages and tasks – related to structure of brief.

6   Information-collection methods:

   - information-collection tasks
   - sampling methods, where appropriate – measures to ensure data quality
   - sample sizes, where appropriate
   - information to be generated by each method used.

7   Timetable (N.B. some tasks will be concurrent):

   - meetings with clients
   - other meetings with interested parties
   - preparatory work
   - fieldwork: data collection
   - analysis
   - draft report
   - feedback on draft
   - final report.

8   Budget: costing of each element, stage and task:

   - project staff costs (n days at £x per day: gross costs, including normal office overheads and support)
   - fieldwork and data-collection costs
   - additional items: e.g. travel, printing
   - report preparation costs, if significant (e.g. multiple copies required).

9   Chapter outline of report and, if appropriate, details of other proposed reporting formats: e.g. interim reports, working papers, articles.

10   Resources available:

   - project and supervisory staff: curricula vitae, especially experience relevant to the proposed project
   - support staff, back-up resources, organisation capability, experience.

Figure 3.9 Example of research programme diagrammatic representation

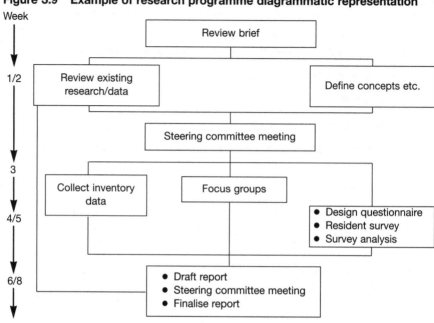

Figure 3.10 Example of research project timetable

Week	1	2	3	4	5	6	7	8
Review literature	▓	▓	▓					
Secondary data analysis			▓	▓	▓			
Conduct survey				▓	▓			
Analyse survey						▓		
Focus groups			▓					
Meetings with clients	✪			✪		✪		✪
Write up report				▓			▓	▓

Case studies of research project planning

Note: These case studies are designed to illustrate approaches to project planning. They are necessarily brief. In practice project proposals will tend to be more discursive and to explore issues in more detail.

CASE STUDY 3.1

Facility use

1 Topic

The topic has been presented by the management of a museum. Attendances have been declining over a number of years and the management would like to know why.

2 Literature review

The literature to be reviewed covers museums and leisure/tourism facility management generally. There is an extensive literature on museum visitors and part of the proposed research will therefore involve a detailed examination of this literature. At this planning stage two sources have been drawn on to provide a starting point for the study.

- Loomis (1987, pp. 71–4) lists 18 questions which might form a 'basic' museum visitor survey;
- Bennett and Frow (1991) show that gallery and museum users are overwhelmingly drawn from the more highly educated, higher income social groups, suggesting that attendance and non-attendance at such facilities may be something to do with class, education or income.

Museums are, however, just one type of leisure facility. Therefore general texts on the management of leisure facilities, such as Torkildsen's *Guides to Leisure Management* (1993), may offer ideas on how to research the problem of declining attendances. Torkildsen offers two perspectives which might be used in this study: the idea of *customer focus* in leisure management and the overall approach to services *marketing*.

The *customer service* focus suggests that falling attendances may be the result of a lack of attention to the quality of experience of current users. Torkildsen offers examples of 'flow charts' of the visitor experience in leisure facilities, indicating the aspects of management which impinge on each stage, from the individual's initial decision to visit to leaving the facility. Such a flow chart could be developed for museum visitors and visits and could be used as a framework for questioning museum visitors about their visit experiences.

Marketing offers a broader framework of study. It opens up the possibility that, in order to reverse declining visitor numbers, it may be necessary to consider not just the quality of delivery of current services but changes in the nature of the service being offered. Torkildsen offers some 42 'practical marketing hints for a leisure facility'. The first few of these offer an agenda for research upon which an effective marketing strategy may be built. They focus on: defining exactly 'what business you are *really* in'; knowing your customers and potential customers (including demographic and socio-economic trends in the market *catchment area*); and knowing your competitors.

This suggests three broad-ranging studies: (1) a study to establish clearly the goals of the museum owners or managers (what business are they in?); (2) a study of current *visitors* and their *experiences*; (3) a study of *former visitors* and their experiences of visiting the museum; (4) a study of *non-visitors* to the museum and their perceptions of the museum. It is assumed that a clear strategic plan exists which covers study (1); the proposal below therefore concentrates on studies (2)–(4).

3 Conceptual framework

A comparison between the perceptions and/or experiences and socio-demographic characteristics of the three visitor and non-visitor groups may provide insights into reasons for falling attendances. The basic concepts involved and their relationships, based primarily on the discussion arising from the review of Torkildsen's ideas, are presented in the concept map.

Concept	Definition	Operationalisation
Customer	Current and potential visitors to the museum	(a) Current customers = visitors in current year (b) Former customers = persons who last visited more than 12 months ago, but live within main catchment area (c) Non-customer = persons who have never visited, but live within main catchment area
Catchment area	Geographical area from which visitors travel	Area from which 70% of users come – can include residential and tourist accommodation
Visitor experience	Visitor evaluation of visit	Visitor evaluation (e.g. on scale of 1–5) of each stage of the visit, as defined by a checklist based on a Torkildsen-style analysis of stages of the visit (e.g. obtaining information; transport; parking; ticket-buying; displays; toilets; cafe; shop; staff assistance; cleanliness)
Non-visitor perception	Former and non-customer perception of museum	As for visitor evaluation
Visitor/non-visitor characteristics	Socio-economic and dem-ographic characteristics	Age, occupation, education, whether a parent

4 Research questions

Major question
4.1 Why are attendances at the museum falling?

Subsidiary questions
4.2 How is the experience of visiting the museum seen and evaluated by current visitors?

4.3 How is the experience of visiting the museum seen and evaluated by former visitors? (reasons for ceasing to visit)

4.4 How do non-visitors perceive the museum? (negative, positive?)

4.5 How are questions 4.2–4.4 affected by the socio-demographic characteristics of the three groups?

4.6 What is the catchment area of the museum? (defines search area for non-visitors)

4.7 What are the demographic trends in the museum's catchment area?

Concept map

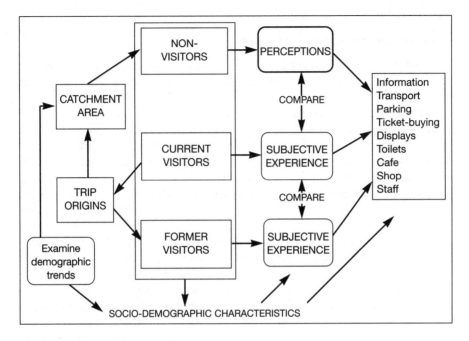

5 Information needs

Group	Information			
	Museum visit experience	Place of residence	Perception of museum	Socio-demographic characteritics
Current visitors	✔	✔		✔
Former visitors	✔	✔		✔
Non-visitors			✔	✔
Residents of catchment area				✔

6 Research strategy

6.1 Conduct survey of current visitors – seek information as in 5. Use place of residence to identify catchment area.

6.2 Conduct community household survey within catchment area – and identify non-visitors and former visitors. Seek information, as in 5.

6.3 Examine trends in demographic, social and economic characteristics of local community (from census), compared with visitor characteristics.

CASE STUDY 3.2

The holiday as leisure

1 Introduction and review of literature

The topic is: the role of the holiday in the leisure repertoire of the individual. This topic arises from an examination of the literature on the sociology of both leisure and tourism.

The sociology of leisure literature is represented in this review by the work of Parker (1976), Roberts (1978), Rapoport and Rapoport (1975), Clarke and Critcher (1985), Rojek (1995) and Driver et al. (1991). In general, an examination of these works reveals that the sociology of leisure has been largely focused on the leisure needs and demands of individuals in particular communities or social groups. Thus, for example, well-known writers have analysed the needs of individuals in their work, family and educational setting (Parker, 1976, pp. 65–102; Roberts, 1978, pp. 93–124), their life-cycle situation (Rapoport and Rapoport, 1975) and in relation to their personal satisfactions (Kelly and Godbey, 1992, pp. 195-326). A broader type of leisure sociology seeks to situate leisure in the social, economic and cultural fabric of the nation state (Roberts, 1978, pp. 41–92; Clarke and Critcher, 1985; Rojek, 1995). Research on the benefits of leisure to the individual (Driver et al., 1991) is concerned particularly with the question of equity: who has access to leisure time and resources and who does not? Which socio-economic groups participate and which do not? While leisure includes holiday-taking, the sociology of leisure literature rarely refers to holiday-taking explicitly; it might be said, therefore, that the sociology of leisure is concerned with leisure in the local community: what might be referred to as *local leisure*.

The approach in the sociology of tourism, represented here by Cohen (1972), MacCannell (1976), Urry (1990) and Krippendorf (1987), is generally very different. Here people are referred to as *tourists* and are seen as *consumers*, comparatively disembodied from their community of origin or other social roles. The focus of most research in the sociology of tourism is on the tourist *destination*, with tourists' geographical origins merely serving to furnish them with certain attributes, such as a certain level of income and a set of 'cultural baggage', and information on these and on demographic characteristics is required only as inputs to effective marketing. The 'five star' tourist is the main focus of attention; those who are unable to go on holiday, or can only afford to take their holidays locally, are rarely the focus of interest. For example, Cohen's (1972) seminal paper on the sociology of tourism classifies tourists as types of consumer; MacCannell (1976) is concerned with how tourists interpret tourist sites; and Urry (1990) focuses largely on the cultural impact of tourists and the tourism industry on host communities. The exception is Krippendorf (1987) who sets tourism in the context of leisure and everyday life. However, Krippendorf's empirical sources are limited and, being a Swiss author, he draws largely on research evidence in German which is therefore somewhat inaccessible to English-speaking readers. Of those who do *not* go on holiday, Krippendorf considers only the privileged, who do not need to go on holiday because of their non-stressful lifestyles (1987, p. 16). He therefore ignores those who are unable to go on holiday because of financial or other constraints. With the exception of this partial treatment, therefore, it appears that the tourism literature has been unconcerned with the question of equity. It has generally ignored those who are prevented from going on holiday as a result of socio-economic circumstances.

A concept which might be used to link the two areas of research is the notion of *quality of life* (Marans and Mohai, 1991). Both local leisure and tourism can be seen as contributing to a person's quality of life, and lack of opportunities for either could be seen as resulting in a poor quality of life. The question therefore arises as to what are the respective contributions of local leisure and holiday-taking to a person's quality of life and, conversely, what effect does a lack of local leisure and holiday-taking opportunities have on a person's quality of life? This issue *could* be studied at a 'macro' level, exploring the political and economic reasons for its neglect by researchers, government and industry, but, at this stage, it seems appropriate to study the phenomenon at the level of the individual.

3 Conceptual framework

The discussion suggests that quality of life is affected by a person's social and economic circumstances, by the quality of local leisure participation and by the qualities of a person's holiday experiences. These concepts are defined in the table and their inter-relationships are depicted in the concept map.

Concept	Definition	Operationalisation
Holiday	Staying overnight away from normal place of residence, for leisure purposes	Period of at least 5 days spent at least 40 km from normal place of residence, for leisure purposes
Local leisure	Leisure activity in normal place of residence	Leisure activity within 40 km of home
Qualities (of leisure/holidays)	Perceived and actual characteristics of the activity which contribute positively to a person's quality of life	Benefits such as: relaxation, relief of stress, exercise, social bonding, education, 'flow' experiences
Social/economic circumstances	Social characteristics and circumstances likely to influence or constrain leisure, e.g. age, gender, occupation, family responsibilities	Age; occupation; gender; whether partnered; whether children, if so, what age(s); income; level of education
Quality of life	To be explored in the literature as part of project	To be explored in the literature

4 Research questions

Major question

4.1   What contribution does a holiday make to a person's quality of life, compared with local leisure activity?

Concept map

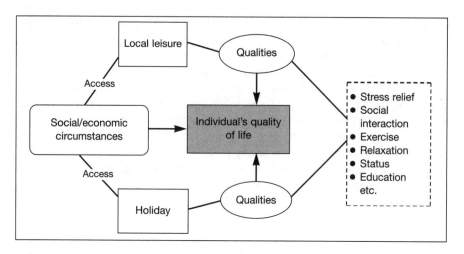

Subsidiary questions

4.2 How is 'quality of life' defined and how can it be measured?

4.3 What characteristics or qualities of local leisure contribute to a person's quality of life*?

4.4 What are the characteristics/qualities of a holiday which contribute to a person's quality of life*?

4.5 What effect does lack of a holiday have on a person's quality of life*?

4.6 Can local leisure compensate for lack of a holiday?

4.7 How are questions 4.3–4.6 perceived by the individual?

4.8 How do questions 4.3–4.7 vary with social or economic situation of the individual?

(* as defined in question 4.2)

5 Information needs

5.1 Information on 'quality of life' and its measurement.

5.2 Individual perceptions of value of leisure activities.

5.3 Individual perceptions of quality of life.

5.4 Individual perceptions of value of a holiday.

5.5 Individual perceptions of effects of lack of holiday.

5.6 Characteristics of holiday-takers and non-holiday-takers – for example, age, gender, family situation, occupation, education, health, income.

Note: As a result of information gained under item 5.1, it is likely that quality of life can be measured by subjective assessment by the individual and possibly by 'objective' measures, such as health or levels of stress. The proposed project concentrates on subjective assessment only.

6 Research strategy

6.1 Review literature on quality of life.

6.2 Conduct in-depth interviews to explore items 5.2–5.5.

6.3 Taking account of the results of item 6.2, conduct a questionnaire survey in a local community, seeking a 50/50 quota of:

- people who have been on holiday (5 days or more, 40+ km) in the last year;
- people who have not been on holiday (5 days or more, 40+ km) in the last year.

The questionnaire survey is to collect information from the two groups addressing items 5.2–5.6 by asking questions on:

- local leisure activities undertaken
- perceived characteristics of leisure and their contribution to quality of life
- perceived characteristics of the holiday and its contribution to quality of life
- perceived consequences for quality of life of not going on holiday
- social/economic characteristics: age, gender, family situation, occupation, income

Compare perceptions of people who have and people who have not been on holiday and groups in varying social/economic situations.

CASE STUDY 3.3

Evaluating public recreation services

1 Topic

The topic is the evaluation of the performance of a public leisure or recreation service, such as that which might be provided by a local authority.

2 Review of literature

Hatry and Dunn (1971) give an example of how concepts can be isolated from a set of objectives for a public recreation service. Their suggested objectives for a public recreation service are:

> Recreation services should provide for all citizens, to the extent practicable, a variety of adequate, year-round leisure opportunities which are accessible, safe, physically attractive, and provide enjoyable experiences. They should, to the maximum extent, contribute to the mental and physical health of the community, to its economic and social well-being and permit outlets that will help decrease incidents of antisocial behaviour such as crime and delinquency (Hatry and Dunn, 1971, p. 13).

Other literature will be examined in the course of the proposed study, but meanwhile, from this statement a number of concepts, which constitute criteria for effectiveness, can be isolated:

(a) adequacy

(b) enjoyableness

(c) accessibility

(d) (un)crowdedness

(e) variety

(f) safety

(g) physical attractiveness

(h) crime avoidance

(i) health

(j) economic well-being

3 Conceptual framework

The ten factors nominated by Hatry and Dunn provide the basis for the research. Five of these (c, d, e, f and g) can be seen as service qualities, which should affect attendance levels (Effect 1). High attendance levels should lead to high community impacts (Effect 2), as measured by factors h, i and j, and high criteria satisfaction (a and b). The concepts are defined in the table and their suggested relationships are depicted in the concept map.

Concept	Definition	Operationalisation
(a) Adequacy of service	Services which meet community demand; provision of access to all	Level of attendance; number of participants and non-participants; persons living within x minutes and y km of facilities; crowdedness indices (waiting times, ratios of use to capacity, user perceptions)
(b) Enjoyableness	Providing pleasure for users/participants	Level of attendance; number of participants and non-participants; citizen satisfaction
(c) Accessibility	Facilities within x minutes and y km travelling for all of the community	Persons living within x minutes and y km of facilities
(d) (Un)crowdedness	Facilities not perceived as crowded by users	Crowdedness indices (waiting times, ratios of use to capacity, user perceptions)
(e) Variety	Range of different activities on offer	Number of different activities catered for
(f) Safety	Accident-free environment	Number of accidents p.a.
(g) Physical attractiveness	Facilities which appear attractive to users and interested non-users (e.g. neighbours)	Index of facility attractiveness (user and non-user perceptions), especially re parks and open space
(h) Crime avoidance	Services which help reduce crime by providing creative outlets for energies	Reported crime rates in community
(i) Health promotion	Facilities/services which promote health (e.g. through exercise)	Community health/illness measures
(j) Economic well-being	Facilities/services which contribute to economic well-being (e.g. jobs, income, etc.)	Business income; jobs; property values

Concept map

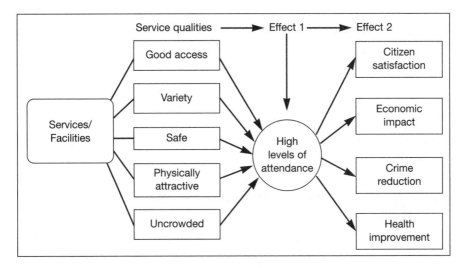

4 Research questions

Main question
4.1   To what extent is the authority achieving its goals in recreation provision?

Subsidiary questions
4.2   To what extent is the authority achieving its goals with regard to: (a) adequacy;
(b) enjoyableness; (c) accessibility; (d) (un)crowdedness; (e) variety; (f) safety;
(g) physical attractiveness; (h) crime avoidance; (i) health; (j) economic well-
being?

5 Information requirements

In this case the information requirements are clearly listed in the 'operationalisation'
column in point 3 above.

6 Research strategy

6.1   Gather all available data on attendance levels; relate to census of population to
estimate numbers of users and non-users (a).

6.2   Plot all facilities on map and use census data to indicate populations living
within y km and x minutes travel (b).

6.3   Undertake study of waiting times and crowding in all facilities (d).

6.4   Gather information on range of programmes/activities offered (e).

6.5   Conduct community/household survey and/or user surveys on citizen satisfaction with services and perceptions of facility attractiveness (a, b).

6.6   Collect data on crime rates (h).

6.7   Collect data on community health and use of services (possible survey/study on
fitness) (i).

6.8 Economic study: collect data on new business investment, job, property values. Possible survey of businesses (j).

On an annual basis, or some other suitable cycle, compare the above with past values and/or set targets.

QUESTIONS AND EXERCISES

1 Select three articles from an issue of a leisure or tourism journal and identify the basis of their choice of research topic.

2 Select any article from a copy of a leisure or tourism journal and: (a) identify the key concepts used in the article; and (b) draw a simple concept map to show how the concepts are related.

3 Draw a concept map for a possible research project on either: (a) the effects of American culture on British leisure; or (b) the effects of the ageing of the population on trends in tourism in western countries.

4 Write a case study, similar in structure and length to Case studies 3.1, 3.2 and 3.3, on a topic of your own choice.

FURTHER READING

The best reading material for this chapter would be examples of successful research grant applications and proposals written in response to tenders.

For a discussion of approaches to tourism research *see* Pizam (1994) and Ryan (1995); and for a discussion of concepts in tourism, *see* Chadwick (1994).

On selection of a research topic, *see* Howard and Sharp (1983, ch. 2).

Most general and specific research methods texts deal with the stages in the research process, for example, Kidder (1981); Kraus and Allen (1987); Williamson *et al.* (1982); Burgess (1982); Hudson (1988); Kelsey and Gray (1986); Frank Small and Associates (1988).

For examples of conceptual frameworks in leisure studies, *see* Veal (1995); Brandenburg *et al.* (1982); Marans and Mohai (1991); and, in tourism, *see* Echtner and Ritchie (1993); Witt and Wright (1992).

On concept mapping, *see* Howell and Badmin (1966, pp. 243–50) and Buzan (1995).

CHAPTER 4

The range of research methods

INTRODUCTION: HORSES FOR COURSES

This chapter examines in broad terms the range of alternative research methods and criteria for the use of particular methods, as an introduction to the techniques to be covered in more detail in subsequent chapters. The roles of scholarship and research are discussed, together with the idea of 'just thinking', and the use of existing literature, secondary data, observation, qualitative methods and questionnaire-based surveys is introduced. The qualitative–quantitative debate is also considered.

Choosing appropriate research methods or techniques is clearly vital. In this book the principle is espoused that every technique has its place; the important thing is for the researcher to be aware of the limitations of any particular method and not to make claims which cannot be justified on the basis of the methods used. There has been much debate in recent years, especially in the sociological literature, about appropriate methods for leisure and tourism research, particularly concerning the relative merits of qualitative as opposed to quantitative methods (for example, Rojek, 1989; Henderson, 1990; Kelly, 1980). The commentaries have often been very partisan in tone, as if there were a contest in progress between the two approaches and some sort of conspiracy at work to maintain quantitative methods as the dominant research mode in leisure studies. While this domination may be apparent in leisure studies in the United States, it is less apparent in the literature emanating from other countries (Veal, 1994b). In tourism research quantitative and qualitative research approaches seem to coexist without the apparent rivalry seen in leisure studies.

There is a tendency, in the methodological literature, for commentators to defend the methods in which they themselves are skilled. It is rare to find a researcher who is experienced in the full range of techniques discussed in this book. It is hoped that the new generation of researchers in leisure and tourism will be competent in a wide range of skills and will therefore adopt a balanced and non-partisan approach to their use. As Henderson points out in discussing qualitative versus quantitative methods:

> Ideally, a researcher who understands the array of methods available through both quantitative and qualitative approaches will be able to address the ways to best study the issues related to leisure (1990, p. 179).

It is possible for research to be conducted entirely quantitatively, entirely qualitatively, or using a mixture of both approaches (Kamphorst *et al.*, 1984). It is quite common for large-scale quantitative research to be planned on the basis of prior, exploratory, qualitative studies (Peterson, 1994).

In this book a *horses for courses* approach is adopted; techniques are not considered to be intrinsically *good* or *bad*, but are considered to be *appropriate* or *inappropriate* for the task in hand. Further, it is maintained that it is not a question of good or bad techniques which should be considered, but of good or bad *use* of techniques. The range of techniques to be examined is listed in Figure 4.1.

Figure 4.1   The range of methods

- Scholarship

- 'Just thinking'

- The use of existing literature

- Secondary data

- Observation

- Qualitative methods

- Questionnaire-based surveys

SCHOLARSHIP AND RESEARCH

Although the dividing line between *scholarship* and *research* can be difficult to draw, it is useful to consider the differences between the two. Scholarship involves being well informed about a subject and also thinking critically and creatively about the subject and the accumulated knowledge on it. Scholarship therefore involves *knowing the literature*, but also being able to synthesise it, analyse it and critically appraise it. Scholarship is traditionally practised in the role of teacher, but when the results of scholarship are published they effectively become a contribution to research. Research involves the generation of new knowledge. Traditionally this has been thought of as involving the gathering and presentation of new data – empirical research – but clearly this is not a necessary condition for something to be considered 'research'. New insights, critical or innovative ways of looking at old issues or the identification of new issues or questions – the fruits of scholarship – are also contributions to knowledge. Indeed, the development of a new framework or *paradigm* for looking at a field can be far more significant than a minor piece of empirical work using an old, outmoded paradigm.

Recognising therefore that research does not have to be empirical, the first method discussed below is *just thinking*.

JUST THINKING

There is no substitute for thinking! Creative, informed thinking about a topic can be the only process involved in the development and presentation of a piece of research, although it will usually also involve consideration of the literature, as discussed below.

But even when data collection is involved, the difference between an *acceptable* piece of research and an *exceptional* or *significant* piece of research is usually the quality of the creative thought that has gone into it. The researcher needs to be creative in identifying and posing the initial questions or issues for investigation, in conceptualising the research and developing a research strategy, in analysing data and in interpreting and presenting findings. Texts on research methods, such as this, can provide a guide to mechanical processes, but creative thought must come from within the individual researcher – in the same way that the basics of drawing can be taught but *art* comes from within the individual artist.

THE LITERATURE

There is virtually no research that can be done which would not benefit from some reference to the existing literature. For most research, such reference is essential. It is possible for a research project to consist only of a review of the literature. In comparatively new areas of study, such as leisure and tourism, especially when they are multi-disciplinary as leisure and tourism are, there is a great need for the consolidation of existing knowledge which can come from good literature reviews.

The review of the literature often plays a key role in the formulation of research projects; it indicates the state of knowledge on a topic and is a source of, or stimulator of, ideas, both substantive and methodological.

A review of the literature can be important even when it uncovers no literature on the topic of interest. To establish that *no* research has been conducted on a particular topic, especially when the topic is considered to be of some importance to the field, can be a research finding of some significance in its own right. The literature review process is discussed in detail in Chapter 5.

EXISTING INFORMATION: SECONDARY DATA

Clearly, if information is already available which will answer the research questions posed, then it would be wasteful of resources to collect new information for the purpose. As discussed in Chapter 6, large quantities of information are collected and stored by government and other organisations as routine functions of management, including sales figures and visitor numbers, income and expenditure, staffing, accident reports, crime reports, and health data. Such data are referred to as *secondary* data, because their primary use is administrative and research is only a secondary use. Even when such data are not ideal for the research at hand, they can often provide answers to some questions more quickly and at less cost than new data.

Secondary data need not be quantitative. Historians, for example, use diaries, official documents or newspaper reports as sources. In policy research such documents as the annual reports or minutes of meetings of organisations might be utilised.

In some cases data have been collected for research as opposed to administrative purposes but may not have been fully analysed, may have been analysed only in one particular way for a particular purpose, or may even not have been analysed at all. Secondary analysis of research data is a potentially fruitful, but widely neglected, activity.

OBSERVATION

The technique of observation is discussed in Chapter 7. Observation has the advantage of being unobtrusive – indeed, the techniques involved are sometimes referred to as *unobtrusive* techniques (Kellehear, 1993). Unobtrusive techniques involve gathering information about people's behaviour without their knowledge. While in some instances this may raise ethical questions (*see* Chapter 11), it clearly has advantages over techniques where the subjects are aware of the researcher's presence and may therefore modify their behaviour, or where reliance must be placed on subjects' own recall and description of their behaviour, which can be inaccurate or distorted.

Observation may be the only possible technique to use in certain situations, for example, when researching illicit activity, which people may be reluctant to talk about, or when researching the behaviour of young children (for example their play patterns) who may be too young to interview.

Observation is capable of presenting a perspective on a situation which is not apparent to the individuals involved. For example, the users of a crowded part of a recreation or tourist area may not be aware of the uncrowded areas available to them; the pattern of use of the site can only be assessed by observation. Observation is therefore an appropriate technique to use when knowledge of the presence of the researcher is likely to lead to unacceptable modification of subjects' behaviour, and when mass patterns of behaviour not apparent to individual subjects is of interest.

QUALITATIVE METHODS

Qualitative methods are discussed in detail in Chapter 8. Three particular techniques or groups of techniques are examined.

1 *Informal and in-depth interviews* usually involve relatively small numbers of individuals being interviewed at length, possibly on more than one

occasion. Relatively large amounts of information is generally collected from relatively small numbers of people. This is in contrast to questionnaire-based surveys which usually involve gathering relatively small amounts of structured information from relatively large numbers of people.

2 *Group interviews or focus groups* apply the informal/in-depth interview approach to groups of people rather than separate individuals.

3 *Participant observation* involves the researcher becoming a participant in the phenomenon being studied.

Qualitative techniques stand in contrast to quantitative techniques. The main difference between the two groups of techniques is that quantitative techniques involve numbers – quantities – whereas qualitative techniques do not. With qualitative techniques generally the information collected does not lend itself to statistical analysis and conclusions are not based on such analysis. By contrast, with quantitative techniques, the data collected are susceptible to statistical analysis and the conclusions are based on such analysis.

In consequence there is a tendency for qualitative techniques to involve the gathering of large amounts of relatively rich information about relatively few subjects and for quantitative techniques to involve the gathering of relatively small amounts of data on relatively large numbers of subjects. It should be emphasised, however, that this is just a tendency. It is possible, for example, for a quantitative research project to involve the collection of 500 items of data on only 20 people and for a qualitative research project to involve the collection of relatively little information on 200 people. The difference lies in the nature of information collected and the way it is analysed.

In what situations are qualitative techniques used? They tend to be used for the study of groups, where interaction between group members is of interest; when exploratory theory building rather than theory testing is called for; when the focus of the research is on meanings and attitudes (although these can also be studied quantitatively); and when the researcher accepts that the concepts, terms and issues must be defined by the subjects and not by the researcher in advance. Qualitative techniques are not appropriate when the aim of the research is to make general statements about large populations, especially if such statements involve quantification.

Analysis of texts

In some fields of inquiry the focus of research is textual – for example politicians' speeches or press coverage of an event. The analysis and interpretation of the content of published or unpublished texts is referred to as *content analysis* or *hermeneutics*. The technique has not traditionally been widely used in leisure and tourism studies, but with the developing linkages with cultural studies, and the widening of the scope of *text* to include a wide variety of *cultural product*, such as film and television, advertising and postcards, the technique is attracting increasing attention. Approaches to the analysis of texts are discussed in Chapter 8.

QUESTIONNAIRE-BASED SURVEYS

Questionnaire-based surveys come in a variety of forms and these are discussed in detail in Chapter 9. They are probably the most commonly used technique in leisure and tourism research. This is partly because the basic mechanics are relatively easily understood and mastered, but also because so much leisure and tourism research calls for the sorts of general, quantified statement referred to above. Thus, for example, governments want to know how many people engage in sport; managers want to know how many people are dissatisfied with a service and marketers want to know how many people are in a particular market segment. All these examples come from practical policy or management situations. The fact that they do so emphasises that most of the resources for survey research come from the public or private sector of the leisure/tourism industries. Academic papers are very often a secondary spin-off from research which has been sponsored for such specific, practical purposes.

Unlike qualitative techniques, where the researcher can begin data collection in a tentative way, can return to the subjects for additional information and can gradually build up the data and concepts and explanation, questionnaire-based surveys require researchers to be very specific about their data requirements from the beginning, since they must be committed irrevocably to a questionnaire.

A further key feature of questionnaire-based surveys is that they depend on respondents' own accounts of their behaviour, attitudes or intentions. In some situations – for example, in the study of 'deviant' behaviour or in the study of activities which are socially approved (for example, playing sport) or disapproved of (for example, smoking or drinking) – this can raise some questions about the validity of the technique, since accuracy and honesty of responses may be called into question.

Questionnaire-based surveys are used when quantified information is required concerning a specific population and when individuals' own accounts of their behaviour and/or attitudes are acceptable as a source of information.

OTHER METHODS

The range of research methods, techniques and approaches available to the researcher are legion and it is not possible to give full weight to all possibilities in a text such as this. Mention is made here of some additional techniques which arise in leisure and tourism research (see Figure 4.2) and an indication is given of how they relate to the pattern of this book.

Coupon surveys and conversion studies

In marketing research use can be made of information from the responses of the public to advertising coupons – that is where the public is invited in an

Figure 4.2   Other methods

a   Coupon surveys/conversion studies

b   *En route* surveys

c   Time-budget surveys

d   Panels

e   Longitudinal studies

f   Projective techniques

g   Media surveys

h   Case studies

i   Delphi technique

advertisement to write or telephone for information on a product. The data can be used to indicate the level of interest in the product on offer (compared with other products or with the same product in previous years) and also to indicate the geographical spread of the interested public. The question then arises as to the extent to which people who respond to such advertising actually become customers. Thus conversion studies are designed to examine the extent to which enquirers 'convert' to become customers (Woodside and Ronkainen, 1994).

En route surveys

In tourism research surveys of tourists while travelling, as opposed to home-based surveys, are sometimes referred to as *en route* surveys (Hurst, 1994). Such surveys may be conducted while the traveller is actually travelling, for example, in aeroplanes, at airports or while travelling by car (when travellers are waved into lay-bys for survey purposes with the assistance of police), or they may be contacted at their place of accommodation or while visiting attractions. In this book this type of survey is considered to be a special case of site or user surveys, as discussed in Chapter 9.

Time-budget surveys

There is a long tradition in leisure studies of investigating people's allocation of time between such categories as paid work, domestic work, sleep and leisure (Szalai, 1972). This approach to leisure research is basically a special case of the household survey and some reference is made to it in that context in Chapter 9.

Panels

Market research companies usually maintain 'panels' of individuals for some of their surveys. Panels are made up of a representative cross-section of the public who agree to be 'on call' for a series of surveys over a period of time. Often some financial reward is paid to panel members, but this cost is offset by the savings in not having to continually select and contact new samples of respondents. While managing such panels presents particular problems, the range of survey methods which can be used with panels – by telephone, by mail or by face-to-face interview – is the same as for normal one-off samples (LaPage, 1994).

Longitudinal studies

Longitudinal studies involve the same sample of individuals being interviewed periodically over a number of years. Such studies are of course expensive because of the need to keep track of the sample members over the years, and the need to have a large enough sample at the beginning to allow for the inevitable attrition to the sample over time. They are, however, ideal for studying social change and the combined effects of social change and ageing. While longitudinal studies are a recognised technique in the social sciences, there are very few examples in leisure or tourism research.

Projective techniques

Projective techniques might be termed 'what if?' techniques, in that they involve subjects responding to hypothetical – projected – situations. For example subjects might be asked to indicate how they might spend a particular sum of money if given a free choice, or how they might spend additional leisure time if it were made available, or they might be invited to respond to photographs of particular locations (Ryan, 1995, p. 124). While the technique can become elaborate and specialised, in this book it is considered to be an extension of questionnaire-based surveys and possibly of focus-group interviews.

Media surveys

Newspapers, magazines and radio and television stations often run opinion poll type surveys among their readers, listeners and viewers. At the local level the public's views on an issue may be canvassed by the inclusion of some sort of form in a newspaper, which readers may fill in and return, and radio and television stations often run 'phone in' polls on topical issues. The results of these exercises have entertainment value, but should not generally be taken seriously. This is mainly because there is no way of knowing whether either the original population (the readers, listeners or viewers who happen to read, hear or view the item) or the sample of respondents are representative of the population as a whole. In most cases they are decidedly unrepresentative, in that only those with pronounced views, one way or the other, are likely to become involved in the process.

Case studies

A case study involves the study of an example – a case – of the phenomenon being researched. The aim is to seek to understand the phenomenon by studying single examples. Cases can consist of single individuals (for example, Saunders and Turner, 1987; Rapoport and Rapoport, 1975), communities, whole countries (for example, Williams and Shaw, 1988; Bramham *et al.*, 1993), organisations and companies (for example, Harris and Leiper, 1995) or places and projects (for example, Murphy, 1991; Grahn, 1991). Often a research project using the case study method will involve a number of *contrasting* cases, but studied in a similar manner. Case studies can range from small-scale vignettes to major projects in their own right. The case study as research method can encompass any or all of the techniques discussed in this book.

Delphi technique

The Delphi technique (named after the classical Greek 'Delphic oracle') is a procedure involving the gathering and analysing of information from a panel of experts on future trends in a particular field of interest. The experts in the field (for example, leisure or tourism) complete a questionnaire indicating their views on the likelihood of certain developments taking place in future; these views are then collated and circulated to panel members for further comment, a process which might be repeated a number of times before the final results are collated. The technique is used in some areas of business and technological forecasting, and has been used to a limited extent in leisure and tourism. In this book the technique is not examined explicitly, but to some extent it involves questionnaire design and analysis, as covered in Chapters 9, 10, 13 and 14.

FURTHER READING

On the methodological debate *see*: Kelly (1980); Henderson (1990); Rojek (1989); Wilson *et al.* (1979); Borman *et al.* (1986); Krenz and Sax (1986).

On case studies, *see*: Henderson (1991, pp. 88–90); Stake (1994); Ryan (1995, pp. 115–17).

On the Delphi technique, *see*: Veal (1994a, p. 124); Moeller and Shafer (1994); Green *et al.* (1990).

For readings on particular techniques, *see* subsequent chapters.

CHAPTER 5

Reviewing the literature

INTRODUCTION: AN ESSENTIAL TASK

This chapter explains the importance, for any research project, of reviewing previous research and being aware of existing writing – the literature – on a topic. In addition the chapter indicates general sources of information on leisure and tourism studies literature, sets out the mechanics of compiling bibliographies and recording bibliographical references and considers the process of reviewing the literature.

Reviewing previous research or writing on a topic is a vital step in the research process. Leisure and tourism studies are relatively new areas of academic enquiry and are wide-ranging and multi-disciplinary in nature. Research is not so plentiful in the field that we can afford to ignore work which has already been completed by others. As indicated in Chapter 3, the literature can serve a number of functions, as indicated in Figure 5.1.

Figure 5.1 The roles of the literature in research

- The entire basis of the research

- A source of ideas on topics for research

- A source of information on research already done by others

- A source of methodological or theoretical ideas

- A source of comparison between your research and that of others

- A source of information that is an integral or supportive part of the research – e.g. vital statistical data on a local community

An important part of nearly all research is a 'review of the literature'. Identifying relevant literature is therefore a demanding but essential task. It involves a careful search for information on relevant published work and, if necessary, unpublished work; obtaining copies of relevant items and reading them; making a list of useful items to form a *bibliography*; and assessing and summarising salient aspects for the research proposal or the research report.

The aim of research of an academic nature is to add to the body of human knowledge. In western civilisations that body of knowledge is generally in written form – the literature. To presume to add to that body of knowledge it is therefore necessary to be familiar with it and to indicate precisely how the proposed or completed research relates to it. In research which is of a consultancy nature, where the *primary* aim is to use research to assist in the solution of immediate problems, a familiarity with existing knowledge in the area is still vital. Much time and valuable resources can be wasted in 'reinventing the wheel' to devise suitable methodologies to conduct a project, or in conducting projects with inadequate methodologies, when reference to existing work would have provided information on tried and tested approaches.

THE VALUE OF BIBLIOGRAPHIES

This chapter focuses on reviewing the literature in relation to planned research projects, but the development of bibliographies can be a useful exercise in itself. It might be thought that modern electronic search methods, as discussed below, have made the compilation and publication of bibliographies obsolete, but this is not the case. Electronic databases are still incomplete, especially with regard to older published material and to 'ephemeral' material, such as conference papers and reports and working papers not published by mainstream publishers. In addition, the electronic databases do not provide an evaluation of material: they rarely distinguish between a substantial research paper and a lightweight commentary with no original content. Further, until full-text databases become more widely available, electronic systems will only be able to identify items on the basis of their titles or, in some cases, keywords and abstracts. Most existing databases do not indicate, for example, whether a report on 'recreation activities' includes data on a specific activity, such as golf, or whether a report on holiday patterns mentions a specific form of holiday, such as backpacking. A great deal of useful work can therefore still be done in compiling bibliographies on specific topics, thus helping to consolidate the 'state of the art' and saving other researchers a great deal of time and trouble in searching for material.

Examples of published bibliographies in the leisure and tourism area are listed in the Further reading section at the end of the chapter and considerable scope exists for the development of similar bibliographies on other topics.

SEARCHING

Where can the researcher look for information on existing published research on a topic? In this section a number of sources are examined, as listed in Figure 5.2.

Figure 5.2   Sources of information

- Library catalogues

- Published bibliographies

- Published indexes and electronic databases

- The Internet

- General leisure and tourism books

- Reference lists

- Beyond leisure and tourism

- Browsing

- Asking

Library catalogues

Modern libraries have computerised catalogues which are accessed via terminals within the library and which can also be accessed from remote locations via the Internet. In many university and college libraries it is now possible to access the catalogues of a number of libraries, often world-wide. Searches can be made on the basis of the titles of publications or using keywords assigned to publications by the library. This can be very helpful as a starting point in establishing a bibliography. But it is *only* a starting point, particularly for the researcher with a specialist interest.

If search words such as *leisure, tourism, sport* or *the arts* are used, the typical computerised catalogue will produce an enormous number of references – in most cases far too many to be manageable. But if, for example, more specialised words such as *golf* or *backpacking* are entered, the catalogue will probably produce relatively few references, and many of these will be of a 'popular' nature, concerned with, for example, how to play golf or with biographies of Greg Norman, or backpacker guides to budget accommodation in Europe. Such material may be of interest to some researchers, but will be of little use if the researcher is interested in such aspects as levels of participation in golf, the socio-economic characteristics of golfers or trends in the numbers of backpackers. But the fact that this latter type of material is not listed by the computerised catalogue does not mean that it does not exist in the library. The catalogue search is based only on the *titles* of catalogued items and on the *keywords* which the librarian decides to include. Library catalogues generally do not contain references to:

- individual articles in journals
- individual chapters in books which are collections of readings
- individual papers in collections of conference papers

To identify these more detailed items, other sources must be used, as discussed below.

Neither can a library catalogue indicate, for instance, whether a general report on *sport* or *recreation* or *tourism* includes any reference to a specific leisure activity or a particular type of tourism. And of course the catalogue will not identify publications which, while they deal with one topic, provide an ideal methodology for studying other topics. Such material can only be identified by actually reading – or at least perusing – original texts.

Published bibliographies

Reference has already been made to the value of bibliographies on particular topics. Libraries usually have a separate section for bibliographies and it may be worth browsing in that section, especially when the topic of interest is interdisciplinary.

Published indexes and electronic databases

Published indexes are specialist listings of bibliographical material published on a regular basis by specialist libraries or research centres. Such indexes readily lend themselves to production in CD-ROM format or to being made available on the Internet. Often they are available in more than one format. An example is the most extensive and well-established index and electronic database of leisure and tourism publications:

Leisure, Recreation and Tourism Abstracts (LRTA)

LRTA has been published quarterly for over a decade by CAB International of Oxford and is sponsored by the World Leisure and Recreation Association. It has very detailed subject indexes which make searching relatively easy. LRTA is also available on CD-ROM and on-line in libraries which subscribe to the DIALOG service.

LRTA has the advantage of drawing on a much wider database than most individual libraries and it includes listings of individual journal articles and conference papers. However, it still suffers from some of the limitations of library catalogues in that it is only as good as the indexing or keywording system used. So again, for highly specialised needs, such searches may only be the starting point.

The *Travel and Tourism Index* is published quarterly and contains details of the contents of numerous tourism journals. The *Social Science Citation Index*, available in most university libraries, is a comprehensive listing of papers from thousands of social science journals, cross-referenced by author and subject. In addition, items referred to by authors in papers are themselves listed and cross-referenced, so that further writings of any cited author can be followed up. Unfortunately the major leisure and tourism journals are not included in the database, but the index nevertheless includes references to a considerable amount of leisure and tourism material.

The Internet

The Internet is rapidly becoming a source of information for researchers (Gushiken, 1996). Various organisations have set up 'home pages' on the Internet, which provide data of interest to both the researcher and the manager. Examples are given in Figure 5.3.

Figure 5.3   Internet sites

The following list is indicative only. Each of the sites provides a wealth of information, including: bibliographies, conferences, journals, ongoing research and cross-references to other sites.	
Site	**Address**
Leisure Studies Home Page	http://132.234.58.200/services/lswp/home.htm
Laboratory for Leisure, Tourism and Sport	http://playlab.uconn.edu/mylab.html
Outdoor Recreation Research	http://www.vt.edu:10021/Y/yfleung/recres.html
Sport Management Information Centre	http://www.unb.ca/web/sportmanagement
Sport Sociology	http://playlab.uconn.edu/nasss.html
World Tourism Organisation	http://www.world-tourism.org/wtich.htm
UTS On-line Bibliographies	http://www.uts.edu.au/fac/business/leisure_tourism

General leisure and tourism books

The researcher should be aware of publications which contain information on specific activities or aspects of leisure or tourism. For example, in Chapter 6, national leisure participation and tourism surveys are discussed. These surveys contain information on as many as a hundred leisure activities, on tourism flows of different types and a number of background items such as age and income. They are therefore often a source of at least some information on a topic of interest.

Many general books on leisure or tourism may have something to say on the topic of interest or may provide leads to other sources of information. Examples are, in the area of leisure:

- Cushman *et al.* (1996) *World Leisure Participation*
- Torkildsen (1983) *Leisure and Recreation Management*
- Kelly and Godbey (1992) *The Sociology of Leisure*
- Jackson and Burton (1989) *Understanding Leisure and Recreation*
- Jarvie and Maguire (1994) *Sport and Leisure in Social Thought*
- Driver *et al.* (1991) *Benefits of Leisure*
- Lynch and Veal (1996) *Australian Leisure*
- Perkins and Cushman (1993) *Leisure, Recreation and Tourism*

In the area of tourism:

- Ritchie and Goeldner (1994) *Travel, Tourism and Hospitality Research*
- Burkart and Medlik (1981) *Tourism: Past, Present and Future*
- Ryan (1995) *Researching Tourist Satisfaction*
- Leiper (1995) *Tourism Management*

Searching through such texts, using the contents pages or the index, can be a somewhat 'hit and miss' process, but can often be rewarded with leads which could not be gained in any other way. Even scanning through the contents pages of key journals, such as *Leisure Studies* or *Annals of Tourism Research*, may produce relevant material which would not be identified by conventional searches.

Reference lists

Most importantly, the lists of references in the books and articles identified in initial searches will often lead to useful material. Researchers interested in a particular topic should be constantly on the alert for sources of material on that topic in anything they are reading. Sometimes key items are encountered when they are least expected. The researcher should become a 'sniffer dog' obsessed with 'sniffing out' anything of relevance to the topic of interest. In a real-world research situation this process of identifying as much literature as possible can take months or even years. While a major effort should be made to identify material at the beginning of any research project, it will also be an ongoing exercise, throughout the course of the project.

Beyond leisure and tourism

Lateral thinking is also an aid to the literature search task. The most useful information is not always found in the most obvious places. Some commentators have remarked on how many researchers fail to look beyond immediate *leisure* or *tourism* material. Leisure and tourism are interdisciplinary areas of study, not disciplines in their own right; they do not have a set of research methods and theories uniquely their own. Much is to be gained from looking outside the immediate area of leisure or tourism studies. For example, if the research involves measurement of *attitudes* then certain *psychological* literature will be of interest; if the research involves the study of leisure or tourism *markets* then general *marketing* journals may be useful sources and if the research involves the leisure activities of the *elderly* then *gerontology* journals should be consulted.

OBTAINING COPIES OF MATERIAL

If material is not available in a particular library it can often be obtained through the *inter-library loan* service. This is a system through which loans of books and reports can be made between one library and another. In the case of journal articles the service usually involves the provision of a photocopy. In theory any item published in a particular country should be available through this system since it is connected with national copyright libraries – such as the British Lending Library in Boston Spa or the National Library in Australia – where copies of all published items must be lodged by law. Practices vary from library to library, but in academic libraries the service is often available to postgraduate students but undergraduate students may only access it through a member of academic staff.

For researchers working in metropolitan areas the other obvious source of material is specialist libraries, particularly of government agencies. For example, in London, the Sports Council and English Tourist Board libraries are major resources for leisure and tourism researchers. In metropolitan areas and some other regions there is also often a co-operative arrangement between municipal reference libraries whereby particular libraries adopt particular specialisms, so it can be useful to discover which municipal library service specialises in leisure and/or tourism.

In a number of areas the full texts of journals are beginning to be made available on CD-ROM and via the Internet. This means that copies of complete articles can be down-loaded and printed out, not just the reference. While subscriptions to these services can be expensive, and are therefore not available in all libraries, they can be more cost effective than subscriptions to printed versions of infrequently used journals. It seems likely that, in future, more and more academic publishing will be made available in such formats.

COMPILING AND MAINTAINING A BIBLIOGRAPHY

What should be done with the material once it has been identified? First, a record should be made of everything which appears to be of relevance. The researcher is strongly advised to start a card index of everything identified. This can be of use not only for the current research project but also for future reference: a personal bibliography can be built up over the years. Such record-keeping is best done on a computer, using simply a wordprocessor or a database program, which can also store keywords. This has the attraction that when there is a need to compile a bibliography on another topic in future, a start can be made from your personal bibliography by getting the computer to copy designated items into a new file. In this way the researcher only ever needs to type out a reference once! Specialist packages, such as *Endnote* and *Pro-Cite*, are now becoming available, which store reference material in a standard format, but will automatically compile bibliographies in appropriate formats to meet the requirements of different report styles and the specifications of different academic journals.

It takes only seconds to copy out the full details of a reference when it is first identified. It is advisable to have a stock of blank cards always at hand for such purposes. If this practice is adopted, hours of time and effort can be saved in not having to chase up details of references at a later date. Not only should the details be recorded accurately, as set out below, but a note should be made on the card or in the database about the availability of the material – for example, the library catalogue reference, or the fact that the item is *not* in the library, or that a photocopy has been taken.

REVIEWING THE LITERATURE

Reviewing the literature on a topic can be one of the most rewarding – and one of the most frustrating – of research tasks. It is a task where a range of skills and qualities needs to be employed – including patience, persistence, insight and lateral thinking. The review of the literature can play a number of roles in a research project, as outlined above, and this leads to a number of approaches to conducting a review, as listed in Figure 5.4.

Figure 5.4   Types of literature review

- Inclusive
- Inclusive/evaluative
- Exploratory
- Instrumental
- Content analysis/hermeneutics

Inclusive

The *inclusive* approach to reviewing the literature seeks to identify everything that has been written on a particular topic. The compilation of such a bibliography may be a significant achievement in itself, independent of any research project with which it may be connected. It becomes a resource to be drawn on in the future by others. Two bibliographies on the Olympic Games, compiled by Mallon (1984) and Burkhardt *et al.* (1995), each containing references to hundreds of items, provide examples of such inclusive bibliographies.

Inclusive/evaluative

The *inclusive/evaluative* approach takes the inclusive approach a stage further by providing a commentary on the literature in terms of its coverage and its contribution to knowledge and understanding of the topic. Examples of such reviews are the review of the tourism forecasting literature by Calantone *et al.* (1987) and a recent bibliography and review of the literature on the concept of *lifestyle* (Veal, 1993a).

One approach to this style of review involves a systematic, quantitative appraisal of the findings of a number of projects focused on the same topic. The technique, known as *meta-analysis* (Glass *et al.*, 1981), is suitable for the sort of research where findings are directly comparable from one study to another – for example when the key findings are expressed in terms of correlation and regression coefficients (*see* Chapter 14). In this approach the reported findings of the research themselves become the subject of research and the number of reported projects can become so large that it is necessary to *sample* from them in the same way that individuals are sampled for empirical research. An example is the study by Crouch and Shaw (1991) of the tourism forecasting literature.

Exploratory

The *exploratory* approach is more focused and seeks to discover existing research which might throw light on a specific research question or issue. This is very much the classic literature review which is the norm for academic research and best fits the model of the research process outlined in Chapter 3. Comprehensiveness is not as important as the focus on a particular question or issue. The skill in conducting such a review lies in keeping the question or issue in sight, while 'interrogating' the literature for ideas and insights which may help shape the research. The reviewer needs to be open to useful new ideas, but must not be side-tracked into areas which stray too far from the question or issue of interest.

Instrumental

An example of the *instrumental* approach is the brief review in Case study 3.1. Here the focus of the research is a management issue and the literature is used as a source of suitable ideas on how the research might be tackled. The criterion for selection of literature is not to present a picture of the state of knowledge on the topic, but merely to identify a useful methodology for the project in hand.

Content analysis and hermeneutics

Content analysis and *hermeneutics* are techniques which involve detailed analysis of the contents of a certain body of literature or other documentary source as *texts*. The text becomes a focus of research in its own right rather than being merely a report of research. The texts might be, for example, novels, the speeches of politicians or the contents of advertising. Content analysis tends to be quantitative, involving, for example, counting the number of occurrences of certain phrases. Hermeneutics tends to be qualitative in nature, the term being borrowed from the traditional approach to analysis and interpretation of religious texts. The essence of this approach is discussed in Chapter 8, in relation to the analysis of in-depth interview transcripts.

Reading critically and creatively

Reviewing the literature for *research* purposes involves reading the literature in a certain way. It involves being concerned as much with the methodological aspects of the research (which are not always well reported) as the substantive content. That is, it involves being concerned with *how* the conclusions are arrived at as well as with the conclusions themselves. It involves being critical – questioning rather than accepting what is being read. The task is as much to ascertain what is *not* known, as to determine what *is* known. As material is being read, a number of questions might be asked, as set out in Figure 5.5. The questions relate to both individual items and the body of literature as a whole.

Figure 5.5   Questions to ask when reviewing the literature

(a) Individual items
- What is the (empirical) basis of this research?
- How does the research relate to other research writings on the topic?
- What theoretical framework is being used?
- What geographical area does the research refer to?
- What social group(s) does the research refer to?
- When was the research carried out and is it likely still to be empirically valid?

(b) In relation to the literature as a whole
- What is the *range* of research that has been conducted?
- What *methods* have generally been used and what methods have been neglected?
- What, in summary, does the existing research tell us?
- What, in summary, does the existing research *not* tell us?
- What contradictions are there in the literature – either recognised or unrecognised by the authors concerned?
- What are the *deficiencies* in the existing research, in substantive or methodological terms?

As regards the substantive content of the literature, a major challenge for a reviewer is to find some framework to classify and analyse it. This can be similar to the development of a conceptual framework for a research project, as discussed in Chapter 3. Some sort of diagrammatic, concept-map approach, as indicated in Figure 5.6, may be helpful. Such a diagram might be devised before starting a review, or may be developed, inductively, as the review progresses.

Summarising

A review of the literature should draw *conclusions* and *implications* for the proposed research programme. It is advisable to complete a review by

Figure 5.6   Making sense of the literature

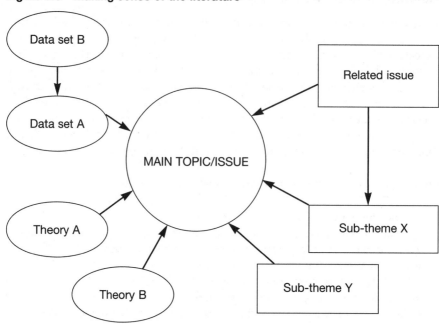

presenting a *summary* which addresses the second set of questions in Figure 5.5. This should lead logically to the research project in hand. It should be very clear to the reader just how the proposed research relates to the existing body of literature – whether it is seeking to add to it, to fill a gap, to update it, to correct or contradict some aspect, or whether it is simply using the existing literature as a source of ideas or comparison.

RECORDING REFERENCES

A number of standard or conventional formats exist for recording references to the literature. The conventions have been established by leading academic organisations and publishers. Guides are produced by organisations such as the American Psychological Association (1983) and the Australian Government Publishing Service (1994), to which the reader is referred for more detail. The formats presented here do not conform to any one standard approach but offer a style which, if followed consistently, would be acceptable in most academic contexts. In what follows, the word *text* refers to the main body of the research report or article.

The general format recommended for recording references is as shown in Figure 5.7.

In some systems the date is put at the end, but when using the *author/date* or *Harvard* system, as discussed below, the date should follow the author name.

Figure 5.7   Standard/generic reference formats

- **A book or report:**
  Author(s), Initials (Year) <u>Title of Book or Report Underlined</u>, Place of publication: Publisher.

- **An article from a periodical (journal/magazine/newspaper):**
  Author(s), Initials (Year) 'Title of article', <u>Title of Periodical Underlined</u>, Volume number, Issue number, Page numbers.

Note that the part of the reference which is *underlined* is the title which would be found in a library catalogue. Thus what is found in a library catalogue is the name of the periodical, not the title of the article, so it is the *title of the periodical* that is underlined. In the case of a chapter from a book, the title of the book is found in the catalogue, not the title of the chapter, so the *title of the book* is underlined.

<u>Underlining</u> is the typing convention for what, in printed books, would be in *italics*: so if a word processor and printer which will produce italics is available then italics can be used rather than underlining.

Note that the *publisher* of a book is not the same as the *printer* of the book; references do not need to refer to the printer. And note that it is *not* necessary to refer to the publisher in the case of periodicals.

Some examples are set out in Figure 5.8 to illustrate the principles.

REFERENCING AND REFERENCING SYSTEMS

What is the purpose of referencing? First, referencing is evidence of the writer's scholarship: it indicates that the particular research report is related to the existing body of knowledge. This is not only of importance to teachers marking student assignments or theses; it is part and parcel of the development of knowledge. Second, references enable the reader of the research report to check sources – either to verify the writer's interpretation of previous research or to follow up areas of interest.

There are two commonly used referencing systems: the 'author/date' system, sometimes referred to as the 'Harvard' system, and the 'footnote' or 'endnote' system. These two systems are discussed in turn below.

The author/date or Harvard system

Basic features

In the author/date, or 'Harvard', system, references to an item of literature are made in the text by using the author's name and the year of the publication; at

Figure 5.8 Examples of references

1 A book	Iso-Ahola, S. E. (1980) The Social Psychology of Leisure and Recreation, Dubuque, IA: Wm. C. Brown.
2 An edited book of readings	Ritchie, J. R. B and Goeldner, C. R. (eds.) (1994) Travel, Tourism, and Hospitality Research: A Handbook for Managers and Researchers, (2nd edn.) New York: John Wiley and Sons.
3 A single paper from an edited book of readings	Gunn, C. A. (1994) 'A perspective on the purpose and nature of tourism research methods', in Ritchie, J. R. B and Goeldner, C. R. (eds.) Travel, Tourism, and Hospitality Research: A Handbook for Managers and Researchers, (2nd edn.), New York: John Wiley and Sons, pp. 3–12.
4 A number of references to chapters from the same edited book (NB. The details of the main reference, Ritchie and Goeldner, only needs to be listed once. The abbreviation op. cit. stands for the Latin opere citato, meaning 'in the work cited'.	Archer, B. H. (1994) 'Demand forecasting and estimation', in Ritchie and Goeldner, op. cit., pp. 105–14. Peterson, K. I. (1994) 'Qualitative research methods for the travel and tourism industry', in Ritchie and Goeldner, op. cit., pp. 487–92. Ritchie, J. R. B and Goeldner, C. R. (eds.) (1987) Travel, Tourism, and Hospitality Research: A Handbook for Managers and Researchers, (2nd edn.), New York: John Wiley and Sons.
5 A published conference report (NB. In the example, the printed proceedings were published two years after the conference had been held)	Ruskin, H. and Sivan, A. (eds.) (1995) Leisure Education: Towards the 21st Century, Proceedings of the International Seminar of the World Leisure and Recreation Commission on Education, Jerusalem, Aug. 1993, Provo, Utah: Brigham Young University Press.
6 A published conference paper	Veal, A. J. (1995) 'Leisure studies: frameworks for analysis', in Ruskin, H. and Sivan, A. (eds.) (1995) Leisure Education: Towards the 21st Century, Proceedings of the International Seminar of the World Leisure and Recreation Commission on Education, Jerusalem, Aug. 1993, Provo, Utah: Brigham Young University Press, pp. 124–36.
7 A government agency report, authored and published by the same agency	Sports Council (1982) Sport in the Community: The Next Ten Years, London: Sports Council.
8 A government report published by the government publisher (NB. Abbreviations normally used: HMSO = Her Majesty's Stationery Office; AGPS = Australian Government Publishing Service)	In UK: Coopers & Lybrand Associates (1981) Service Provision and Pricing in Local Government, London: HMSO. In Australia: Department of the Arts, Sport, the Environment, Tourism and Territories (1989) Ideas for Australian Recreation, Canberra: AGPS.
9 A journal article	Ravenscroft, N. (1993) 'Public leisure provision and the good citizen', Leisure Studies, Vol.12, No.1, pp. 33–44. Alternative: Ravenscroft, N. (1993) 'Public leisure provision and the good citizen', Leisure Studies, 12 (1): 33–44.
10 A newspaper article with named author	Horney, A. (1996) 'Market researchers facing major hurdles', Sydney Morning Herald, 11 April, p. 26.
11 A newspaper item without a named author	Sydney Morning Herald (1996) 'Our green future', 7 June, p. 12.

the end of the paper or report, references are listed in alphabetical order. Thus a sentence in a report might look something like this:

> Research on women and leisure in the 1970s and 1980s included work in Britain (Deem, 1986), in Canada (Bella, 1989), in the United States (Bialeschki and Henderson, 1986) and in Australia (Anderson, 1975).

Note that authors' initials are not used in these references (unless there are two authors with the same surname). At the end of the report a list of references is provided, arranged in alphabetical order, as follows.

References

Anderson, R. (1975) *Leisure: An Inappropriate Concept for Women?* Canberra: AGPS.

Bella, L. (1989) 'Women and leisure: beyond androcentrism', in E.L. Jackson and T.L. Burton (eds) *Understanding Leisure and Recreation*, State College, PA: Venture, pp. 151–80.

Bialeschki, M.D. and Henderson, K. (1986) 'Leisure in the common world of women', *Leisure Studies*, Vol.5, No.3, pp. 299–308.

Deem, R. (1986) *All Work and No Play? The Sociology of Women's Leisure*, Milton Keynes: Open University Press.

Style variation

The style of presentation can be varied; for instance, the above statement could be made in the following alternative ways:

> Interest in research on women and leisure was widespread in the 1970s and 1980s in the English speaking world, as work from authors in Britain, Canada, the United States and Australia indicates (Bella, 1989; Bialeschki and Henderson, 1986; Deem, 1986; Anderson, 1975).

Or, drawing more explicit attention to the authors:

> Recent research on women and leisure in the 1970s and 1980s included Deem's (1986) work in Britain, Bella's (1980) work in Canada the work of Bialeschki and Henderson (1986) in the United States and of Anderson (1975) in Australia.

Specifics and quotations

When referring to specific points from an item of literature, rather than making a general reference to the whole article as above, page references should be given to the specific aspect of interest. For example:

> At least one commentator has suggested that greater understanding of leisure could be obtained by drawing on the Weberian concept of 'lifestyle' (Moorhouse, 1989: 31).

When *quoting* directly from a source, page references should also be given:

> Iso-Ahola makes the point that 'To survive as an academic field, scholars must supply evidence that their methods of investigation are valid and reliable rather than "soft"' (1980: 49).

A longer quotation would be indented in the page and handled like this:

Iso-Ahola argues the case for scientific research in the leisure area and states:

To survive as an academic field, scholars must supply evidence to the effect that their methods of investigation are valid and reliable rather than 'soft'. This becomes increasingly important in obtaining grants from sources inside and outside academic institutions (Iso-Ahola, 1980: 49).

Advantages and disadvantages

The author/date system is an 'academic' style. The referencing is very 'upfront', even obtrusive, in the text. It is not an appropriate style for some practically orientated reports, particularly where the readership is not academic. Large numbers of references using this style tend to 'clutter up' the text and make it difficult to read. The author/date system also has the disadvantage that it cannot accommodate footnotes (at the foot of the page) or endnotes (at the end of the chapter). However, one view is that footnotes and endnotes are undesirable anyway – that is, if something is worth saying it is worth saying in the text. If notes and asides are nevertheless considered necessary it is possible to establish a footnote system for this purpose in addition to using the author/date system for references to the literature only. This of course becomes somewhat complex. If notes are considered necessary then it is probably best to use the footnote style for everything, as discussed below.

The advantages of the author/date system are that it saves the effort of keeping track of footnote numbers; it indicates the date of publication to the reader; the details of any one item of literature have to be written out only once; and it results in a tidy, alphabetical list of references at the end of the document.

Footnote or endnote system

Basic features

The *footnote* style involves the use of numbered references in the text and a list of corresponding numbered references at the foot of the page, at the end of each chapter or at the end of the report or book. The term footnote originates from the time when the notes were invariably printed at the foot of each page – and this can be seen in older books. However, printing footnotes at the bottom of the page came to be viewed as too complex to organise and too expensive to set up for printing, so it was generally abandoned in favour of providing the list of notes at the end of each chapter or at the end of the book. Consequently *endnotes* are now more common. Ironically, the advent of word-processing has meant that the placing of footnotes at the bottom of the page can now be done automatically by computer. Most word-processing packages offer this feature, automatically making space for the appropriate number of footnotes on each page and keeping track of their numbering and so on. Publishers have, however, generally adhered to the practice of placing the notes all together at the end of the chapter or book.

The actual number of the reference in the text can be given in brackets (1) or as a superscript: [1]. Using the footnote system, the paragraph given above would look like this:

> Research on women and leisure in the 1970s and 1980s included Deem's[1] work in Britain, Bella's[2] work in Canada, Bialeschki and Henderson's[3] work in the United States and Anderson's[4] work in Australia.

The list of notes at the end of the report would then be in the numerical order in which they appear in the text:

Notes
1. Deem, R. (1986) *All Work and No Play? The Sociology of Women's Leisure*, Milton Keynes: Open University Press.
2. Bella, L. (1989) 'Women and leisure: beyond androcentrism', in E.L. Jackson and T.L. Burton (eds) *Understanding Leisure and Recreation*, State College, PA: Venture, pp. 151–80.
3. Bialeschki, M.D. and Henderson, K. (1986) 'Leisure in the common world of women', *Leisure Studies*, Vol.5, No.3, pp. 299–308.
4. Anderson, R. (1975) *Leisure: An Inappropriate Concept for Women?* Canberra: AGPS.

It can be seen that this format is less obtrusive in the text than the author/date system. In fact it can be made even less obtrusive by using only one footnote, as follows:

> Research on women and leisure in the 1970s and 1980s included work by researchers in Britain, Canada, the United States and Australia.[1]

At the end of the report the reference list could look something like this:

Notes
1.	In Britain:	Deem, R. (1986) *All Work and No Play? The Sociology of Women's Leisure*, Milton Keynes: Open University Press.
	In Canada:	Bella, L. (1989) 'Women and leisure: beyond androcentrism', in E.L. Jackson and T.L. Burton (eds) *Understanding Leisure and Recreation*, State College, PA: Venture, pp. 151–80.
	In the USA:	Bialeschki, M.D. and Henderson, K. (1986) 'Leisure in the common world of women', *Leisure Studies*, Vol.5, No.3, pp. 299–308.
	In Australia:	Anderson, R. (1975) *Leisure: An Inappropriate Concept for Women?* Canberra: AGPS.

Multiple references

It should never be necessary to write a reference out in full more than once in a document. Additional references to a work already cited can be made using *op. cit.* or references back to previous footnotes. For example, the above paragraph of text might be followed by:

Deem pioneered the study of women and leisure in Britain.[2]

The footnote would then say:

  2. Deem, *op. cit.*   *or*   2. See footnote 1.

Specifics, quotations

Page references for specific references or quotations are given in the footnote rather than the text. So the Iso-Ahola quotation given above would look like this:

> Iso-Ahola makes the point that 'To survive as an academic field, scholars must supply evidence to the effect that their methods of investigation are valid and reliable rather than "soft"'.[4]

The footnote would then say:

  4. Iso-Ahola, S.E. (1980) 'Tools of social psychological inquiry', Chapter 3 of *The Social Psychology of Leisure and Recreation*, Dubuque: Wm. C. Brown, p. 49.

Further quotations from the same work might have footnotes as follows:

  5. Iso-Ahola, *op. cit.* p. 167.

Advantages and disadvantages

One of the advantages of the footnote system is that it can accommodate notes other than references to the literature, as discussed above. A disadvantage of the system is that it does not result in a tidy, alphabetical list of references. This diminishes the convenience of the report as a source of literature references for the reader. Some writers therefore resort to producing a bibliography in addition to the list of references. This results in extra work, since it means that references have to be written out a second time (but *see* 'The best of both worlds' below). Keeping track of footnotes or endnotes and their numbering is much less of a disadvantage than it used to be, since this can now be taken care of by the computer.

The features, advantages and disadvantages of the two systems, author/date and footnote/endnote, are summarised in Figure 5.9.

The best of both worlds

One way of combining the advantages of both systems is for the list of notes in a footnote/endnote system to consist of author/date references and then to provide an alphabetical list of references at the end of the report. So the list of footnotes for the above paragraph would then look like this:

Notes
1. Deem, 1986.
2. Bella, 1989.

Figure 5.9   Reference systems: features, advantages, disadvantages

	Harvard (author/date)	Footnote/endnote
Reference in text	Author (date)	Number, e.g.: [1]
Reference format	Author (date) <u>Title</u> publishing details	1. Author <u>Title</u>, publishing details, date
Reference list format	Alphabetical list at end of report	Numbered list at: • foot of pages • end of chapters, or • end of report
Advantages	• alphabetical bibliography • easy to use	• unobtrusive in text • can add notes/ comments
Disadvantages	• obtrusive in text • can't add notes	• can be difficult to use without computer • no alphabetical list

3. Bialeschki and Henderson, 1986.
4. Anderson, 1975.

An alphabetical bibliography would then follow which would be the same as for the author/date system. This approach is particularly useful when making several references to the same document.

Second-hand references

Occasionally reference is made to an item which the writer has not read directly, but which is referred to in another document which the writer has read. This can be called a *second-hand* reference. It is misleading, somewhat unethical, and dangerous, to give a full reference to the original if you have not read it directly yourself. The reference should be given to the second-hand source, not to the original. For example:

Kerlinger characterises research as 'systematic, controlled, empirical, and critical investigation of hypothetical propositions about the presumed relations among natural phenomena' (quoted in Iso-Ahola, 1980, p. 48).

In this instance I have not read Kerlinger in the original; I am relying on Iso-Ahola's quotation from Kerlinger. The Kerlinger item is not listed in the references; only the Iso-Ahola reference is listed. It is ethical to treat the second-hand reference this way and it is also safe, since any inaccuracy in a quotation then rests with the second-hand source.

Excessive referencing

A certain amount of judgement must be used when a large number of references are being made to a single source. It becomes very tiresome when repeated reference is made to the same source on every other line of a report! One way to avoid this is to be very 'up-front' about the fact that a large section of your literature review is based on a single source. For example, if you are summarising MacCannell's work on tourism, create a separate section of your report and announce it as follows:

The work of MacCannell
This section of the review summarises MacCannell's (1976) seminal work, *The Tourist: A New Theory of the Leisure Class.* . . .

Subsequently, detailed references need only be given when using specific quotations.

Latin abbreviations

A number of Latin abbreviations are used in referencing. If a work has more than two authors, the first author's name and *et al.* may be used in text references, but all authors should be listed in the bibliography. The abbreviation *et al.* stands for the Latin *et alia*, meaning 'and the others', and is generally underlined or in italics. The abbreviation *op. cit.* stands for the Latin *opere citato*, meaning 'in the work cited'. In the footnote system, if reference is made to the same page in a work cited in the previous footnote, the abbreviation *ibid.* is sometimes used, short for *ibidem*, meaning 'in the same place', but care must be taken that *ibid.* is used only when referring to the same page. The use of '*ibid.*, p. 7', when the previous footnote referred to p. 52 of the work, is incorrect.

QUESTIONS AND EXERCISES

1 Compile an *inclusive* bibliography on a topic of your choice, using the sources outlined in this chapter.

2 Choose a research topic and:
   (a) investigate the literature using a library computerised catalogue and any other electronic database available to you;
   (b) explore the literature via literary sources, such as reference lists and indexes in general textbooks, journal contents and lists of references in articles;
   (c) compare the nature and extent of the bibliography arising from the two sources.

FURTHER READING

For examples of bibliographies, *see*: Veal (1990, 1993a); Baretje (1964–); Goeldner and Dicke (1980); Burkhardt *et al.* (1995).

For information on tourism sources, *see*: Goeldner (1994).

Style manuals include American Psychological Association (1983); Australian Government Publishing Service (1994).

The Leisure Studies Association has produced an *Index Book* listing all its conference papers from 1975 to 1992, with author and subject indexes (McFee, 1992).

CHAPTER 6

Secondary data: sources and analysis

INTRODUCTION

This chapter considers the use of existing sources of data, as opposed to the collection of new data which is the subject of most of the rest of the book. The chapter examines mainly published statistical sources, such as the census and national surveys, but other sources, such as archives and management data are also included.

In undertaking research it is clearly wise to use existing information where possible, rather than embarking on expensive and time-consuming new information-collection exercises. One aspect of this has already been touched on in Chapter 5 in relation to the literature. In searching the literature the researcher may come across references to statistical or other data which may not have been fully analysed or exploited by the original collectors of the data, because of their particular interests, or limitations on time and money. Or data may be available which are open to alternative analyses and interpretations. In other cases information may exist which was not originally collected for research purposes – for example, the administrative records of a leisure or tourism organisation – but which can provide the basis for research.

Primary data are new data specifically collected in the current research project – the researcher is the *primary user*. *Secondary* data are data which already exist and which were collected for some other (primary) purpose but which can be used a second time in the current project – the researcher is the *secondary user*. Further analysis of such data is referred to as *secondary analysis*.

As with the literature, secondary data can play a variety of roles in a research project, from being the whole basis of the research to being a vital or incidental point of comparison.

Six main sources of secondary data are examined here, as listed in Figure 6.1. Where appropriate, reference is made to examples in Britain and Australia. In the final part of the chapter case studies of the use of secondary data for planning and management purposes are presented.

Figure 6.1   Types of secondary data

- National leisure participation surveys
- Tourism surveys
- Economic surveys
- The census of population
- Management data
- Documentary sources

NATIONAL LEISURE PARTICIPATION SURVEYS

The national survey phenomenon

In most developed countries surveys of leisure participation are conducted by government departments or agencies on a regular basis. In the USA such surveys have been conducted since the early 1960s, particularly on outdoor recreation. In Britain the *General Household Survey* (GHS), commissioned by government agencies and conducted by the Office of Population Censuses and Surveys (OPCS), has provided leisure participation information every two or three years since 1973. In Australia the Commonwealth government commissioned the first national *Recreation Participation Survey* (NRPS) in 1985/86 and subsequently commissioned the *Population Survey Monitor* to collect information on leisure participation. While such surveys have been carried out in a number of countries over the last two decades, each country has adopted different design principles, so that the findings are not comparable, as a number of attempts at international comparisons indicate (Kamphorst and Roberts, 1989; Hantrais and Kamphorst, 1987; Cushman *et al.*, 1996).

National surveys, and their regional equivalents, are the main source of information available to researchers on overall participation levels in a range of leisure activities. A number of issues arise in the use of these important data bases, including questions of validity and reliability, sample size, the participation reference period used, the age range of the population covered, the range of activities included, and information on the social characteristics of respondents. These topics are discussed in turn below.

Validity and reliability

National surveys suffer from the limitation of all interview surveys in that they are dependent on respondents' own reports of their patterns of leisure participation. How sure can we be, therefore, that the resultant data are accurate? We cannot be absolutely sure, as discussed in Chapter 9. However, a number of features of surveys such as the GHS lend credence to their reliability and value as sources of data.

First, national government survey organisations such as the OPCS have an enviable reputation for excellence and professionalism in their work. Second, the surveys are often based on large sample sizes. Third, in the case of the GHS, the fact that there has been little dramatic variation in the findings of the various surveys over the years is reassuring (Veal, 1993d; Gratton and Tice, 1994; Gratton, 1996). Erratic and unexplainable fluctuations in reported levels of participation would have led to suspicions that the surveys were unreliable, but this has not happened.

Some commentators have questioned the validity of participation surveys, conducting experiments which show that there is a tendency for respondents to exaggerate levels of participation substantially, at least in relation to some activities (Chase and Godbey, 1983; Chase and Harada, 1984). However, as Boothby (1987) suggests, some of the defects of surveys can be overcome by attention to certain aspects of design.

Sample size

In general the larger the sample size the more reliable and precise are the survey findings. The GHS is based on a large sample of around 20 000 interviews, divided into four quarterly samples of 5000 each. The Australian NRPS was based on quarterly samples of around 2000, while the new Population Survey Monitor uses samples of around 5000. These surveys are therefore large and subject to only minimal 'statistical error' – a term explained in Chapter 12.

Main question: reference time period

The main question people are asked in the GHS is what leisure activities they have engaged in during their leisure time *in the previous four weeks* (*see* Table 6.1). Four weeks is the 'reference time period'. In contrast, American surveys have tended to ask people what they have done in the previous *year*. The American approach, of adopting one year as the reference time period, has the advantage of covering participation in all seasons of the year in one survey and including a larger proportion of the infrequent participants. However, it has the disadvantage of introducing possible errors in people's recall of their activities over such a long time period. The GHS avoids this by limiting the time period over which people are asked to recall to one month. Seasonal variations are covered by interviewing at different times of the year. The Australian national survey is even more restrictive, covering just one week (*see* Table 6.2).

As a result of this methodological approach, it is important to note that the surveys do not indicate the total number of people who take part in an activity, but rather the number that take part in a *specified time period* – such as a month or week. The choice of time period affects different activities differently. For example most people who visit zoos do so very rarely, perhaps once in two or three years: so the reported number of people visiting in a month or a week,

Table 6.1 Leisure participation in Britain, 1977–1986

	Per cent participating in 4 weeks prior to interview: ann. ave., persons aged 16+			
	1977	1980	1983	1986
Amateur drama, music	3	3	3	4
Athletics (incl. jogging)	1	1	2	3
Badminton	2	2	2	2
Bowls	1	1	1	1
Bowls, ten-pin	1	1	1	2
Camping or caravanning	1	1	1	1
Cinema or film clubs	10	10	7	8
Cricket	1	1	1	1
Cycling	1	1	2	2
Dancing	15	14	11	11
Darts	9	7	7	6
DIY	35	37	36	39
Exhibitions or shows	2	2	2	3
Fairs, arcades, fetes, carnivals	4	4	2	4
Fishing	2	2	2	2
Football	3	3	3	3
Gardening	42	43	44	43
Going out for a drink	64	54	54	55
Going out for a meal		40	40	47
Golf	2	2	2	3
Gymnastics, indoor athletics	*	1	1	1
Visit historic buildings, sites, towns	8	9	8	9
Horse-riding	1	1	1	1
Keep fit, yoga	1	2	3	3
Listen to records, tapes	62	64	63	67
Visit museums, art galleries	4	3	3	4
Outings by car, motorbike, boat	2	2	1	4
Read books	54	57	56	59
Sewing, knitting	29	28	27	27
Snooker, billiards, pool	6	7	8	9
Squash	2	2	3	2
Swimming (indoor pool)	5	6	7	9
Swimming (sea, outdoor pool)	2	2	3	2
Table tennis	2	2	1	1
Tennis	1	2	1	1
Theatre, ballet, opera	5	5	4	5
Visits to countryside	5	4	3	3
Visits to parks	4	4	4	4
Visits to seaside	7	7	7	7
Walking (2 miles or more)	17	19	19	19
Zoos	1	2	1	1
Sample size	23 171	22 594	19 050	19 209

Source: General Household Surveys/OPCS.   * Less than 0.5%.

Table 6.2　Leisure participation, Australia, Summer 1991

Per cent participating in week prior to interview			
Home-based		**Sport**	
Watch TV	93.6	Athletics	0.5
Entertain at home	35.8	Gymnastics	0.4
Electronic & computer games	11.2	Basketball	2.0
Exercise, keep fit	35.7	Netball – indoors	0.6
Swim in own or friends' pool	23.3	Netball – outdoors	0.8
Play musical instrument	8.8	Tennis	5.8
Arts, crafts	21.4	Squash	1.9
Reading	70.4	Badminton	0.2
Listen to music	65.1	Cricket – indoor	1.5
Gardening for pleasure	41.3	Cricket – outdoor	3.9
Indoor games	17.7	Baseball, softball	0.6
Outdoor play with children	28.9	Rugby League	0.2
Talk on telephone (15 mins +)	48.8	Rugby Union	0.1
Relax, do nothing	58.0	Australian Rules Football	0.3
Social/Cultural		Soccer – outdoor	1.0
Visit friends, relatives	62.8	Soccer – indoor	0.3
Dining, eating out	31.7	Touch football	0.9
Dancing, discotheque	5.9	Boxing, wrestling	*
Visit pub	13.8	Martial arts	0.9
Visit (licensed) club	9.7	Motor sport	0.4
Movies	8.0	Archery/shooting	0.5
Pop concerts	1.6	Orienteering	*
Theatre	1.1	Hockey/lacrosse – indoor	0.3
Music recital, opera	0.5	Hockey/lacrosse – outdoor	0.3
Other live performances	0.8	Cycling	5.0
Special interest courses	1.6	Golf	4.1
Church activities	13.6	Swimming	15.5
Library activities	7.3	Surfing, lifesaving	2.5
Museums, galleries	1.6	Horse-riding	0.6
Exhibitions	0.9	Rink sports	0.3
Play musical instrument	*	Lawn bowls	1.5
Arts, crafts	3.9	Ten-pin bowling	1.5
Hobbies	11.2	**Recreation**	
Picnic, barbecue away from home	13.7	Walk dog	14.2
Visit parks	10.3	Walk for pleasure	26.6
Horse races, trots, dog races	1.7	Aerobics	5.4
Sport spectator	6.6	Jogging, running	3.9
Drive for pleasure	19.0	Bushwalking, hiking	2.3
Bird watching	2.6	Skateboarding	0.3
Play electronic games	4.0	Shooting, hunting	0.3
(Window) Shopping for pleasure	29.6	Fishing	3.4
Source: Centre for Leisure and Tourism Studies. Sample size (persons aged 14+): 2103. UTS, unpublished data from national Recreation Participation Survey *Less than 0.05		Non-power water activities	1.3
		Water activities – powered	0.9

while it may be accurate, includes only a small proportion of the total number of people in the community who visit zoos. By contrast, people who play football are quite likely to do so at least once a week, so those reported as playing football in any one month or week are likely to represent most football players. The effects of the choice of time period were shown in the British and Australian surveys when, in 1991, questions were asked about participation in a shorter and longer time period; four weeks and a year in the case of the GHS and a week and a month in the case of the Australian survey. In both cases, the use of the longer reference time period resulted in much higher reported levels of participation (*see* Gratton, 1996; Darcy, 1994; and Table 10.1).

This illustrates an important point about survey data in general: the meaning of information and the uses to which it can be put depend vitally on the way the data are collected.

Age range

In addition to its restriction to participation in a four-week period, the GHS is also restricted in terms of age range: it covers only those aged 16 and over. Most surveys of this sort are limited in this way: some include respondents as young as 12 years old, while some cover only those aged 18 and over. The Australian survey covers people aged 14 and over. The reasons for not interviewing young children are three-fold. First, it may be difficult to obtain accurate information from very young children; second, it may be considered ethically unacceptable to subject children to the sort of questioning which adults can freely choose to face or not. Third, there is a question as to when children are considered to engage in their own independent leisure activities as opposed to being under the control of parents.

The lower age limit has effects on the results, in that for some activities – for example swimming or cycling – young teenagers may be a significant proportion of total participants. For other activities – for example gardening or going to the opera – the age limit may be inconsequential because young people are not among the most frequent participants. When using data from surveys such as the GHS it is therefore important to bear in mind that under-16-year-olds are excluded.

Activities

The GHS covers a wide range of home-based, indoor, outdoor, sporting and cultural activities, as indicated in Table 6.1. Respondents in the survey are asked whether they have been away on holiday in the previous week, and then what activities they have engaged in during their leisure time in the past month, and, for each activity, how many times.

The results are reported as percentages, either averaged over the year, as in Table 6.1, or in four quarters or seasons (OPCS, annual; Veal, 1984). As can be seen, for many activities, the percentage participation level is small. However, even one per cent of the adult population of Britain is almost half a million people, so small percentages can represent large numbers of people. Although the sample size of the GHS is large, the small percentages produce correspondingly small sub-samples of participants – often only 20 or 30 respondents – so the scope for detailed analysis of participants in individual activities is limited. A further limitation of the sample size is that the survey cannot be subdivided to give detailed results for regions of the country. The Australian survey is even more restricted by sample size.

Social characteristics

In addition to the basic information on participation national surveys generally include a wide range of background information on the people interviewed, including such variables as gender, occupation, age, education level reached, size of family or household unit and country of birth. This information can be used to examine levels of participation by different social groups from either an equity or a marketing point of view, and can also be used to predict demand, as future changes in the underlying social structure of the community affect patterns of demand (*see* Veal, 1994, p. 130).

The importance of participation surveys

Surveys such as the GHS and the Australian NRPS, despite their limitations, are the main source of information, not only on overall levels of participation but also on differences in participation between different groups in the community, such as the young and the old, men and women and different occupational groups. Any leisure researcher or professional should therefore be fully familiar with such key data sources.

TOURISM SURVEYS

In the case of *domestic* tourism there is also reliance on interview surveys for basic statistical information. However, in the case of *international* tourism certain data are available from government international arrivals and departures statistics, which are collected by immigration authorities at ports of entry. The advantage of this latter source of information is that it lends itself to a certain degree of international comparison, a task which is undertaken by the OECD and the World Tourism Organisation (OECD, annual; World Tourism Organisation, annual). However, the information on each traveller is limited, so recourse must also be had to surveys for much of the data on international tourists.

In Britain the main source of information on domestic tourism is the *British Home Tourism Survey*, commissioned each year since 1971 by the English Tourist Board. This is a home-based survey with a substantial monthly sample size, which records origins and destinations of trips with at least one overnight stay in the previous two months. A similar survey, the *Domestic Tourism*

Monitor, is conducted in Australia under the auspices of the government-funded Bureau of Tourism Research.

Information on overseas visitors to Britain and British trips overseas is collected by the *International Visitor Survey*, conducted each year by OPCS. It records such information as destinations, length of trip, levels of expenditure and places and attractions visited. The equivalent Australian survey goes by the same name.

As with leisure surveys, the data on tourist trips are influenced by the definition of 'tourist' and the reference time periods used. Most definitions of tourism require a person to stay away from their normal place of residence for at least one night and travel a certain minimum distance to qualify as a tourist. This means that people who take a trip from London to Southend or Brighton, but do not stay overnight, are not classified as tourists, but as day-trippers. Even people travelling across international borders – such as those taking day-trips across the English Channel – are not tourists by this definition. Comprehensive data on border crossings are no longer collected in Europe because of the sheer volume of such crossings and the increasing liberalisation of travel regulations. Thus, while they are collected by governments and their agencies for official purposes, the 'hard' data on tourism flows are, in reality, every bit as 'soft' as the data on leisure participation (Edwards, 1991).

ECONOMIC SURVEYS

In most developed countries surveys of household expenditure are conducted on a regular basis. In Britain this survey is an annual one and is called the *Family Expenditure Survey* (FES), while the Australian equivalent, the *Household Expenditure Survey*, is conducted every five years. The FES collects information from a cross-section of families throughout Great Britain on their weekly expenditure on scores of items, many of which relate to leisure, as listed in Figure 6. 2. The other form of available economic data relates to employment in the leisure and tourism industries. Data are available from the Department of Employment, at national and regional level, on employment in a number of industry sectors, as listed in Figure 6.2.

These data provide the basis for the regular leisure forecasting and market trend analysis reports produced by such organisations as *Leisure Consultants* (Martin and Mason, annual) and the *Henley Centre for Forecasting* (Henley Centre for Forecasting, quarterly).

THE POPULATION CENSUS

And it came to pass in those days, that there went out a decree from Caesar Augustus, that all the world should be taxed. . . . And all went to be taxed, every one into his own city (*Luke*, 2:1–3).

Figure 6.2   Economic data

(a) Family Expenditure Survey data

Alcoholic drink	Eating out
Arts and crafts	Sport
Musical instruments	Gambling
Audio, tapes, CDs	Television and video
Books, newspapers, magazines	Gardening
Pets	Toys and games
Cinema	Holidays
Photography	Home computers
DIY	

(b) Employment data

Public houses	Hotels
Sport and recreation	Cinemas
Betting and gambling	Theatres
Clubs	Broadcasting
Restaurants	

This quotation from the *Bible* indicates that the taking of a census of the whole population, for taxation and other purposes, is a long-standing practice of governments. Another well-known historical example is the *Domesday Book*, compiled by William the Conqueror for the whole of England in the eleventh century.

The *population census* is an important source of information and any aspiring recreation or tourism manager should be fully aware of its content and its potential. A complete census of the population is taken in Britain by the Office of Population Censuses and Surveys (OPCS) every 10 years; the latest was 1991, and before that 1981, 1971 and so on. In Australia, because the population is growing relatively rapidly, the Australian Bureau of Statistics undertakes a census every five years. As in most countries, it is a statutory requirement for householders (and hoteliers) to fill out a census form on 'census night', indicating the number of people, including visitors, in the building, and their age, gender, occupation and so on. Some people escape the net, for instance people sleeping rough or illegal immigrants, but generally the information is believed to be reliable and comprehensive.

Data from the census are available at a number of levels, from national down to the level of collector districts (CDs) (enumeration districts – EDs – in UK), as shown in Figure 6.3. CDs are small areas, with populations of around 250 to 500, which a single census collection officer deals with on census night. By adding together data from a few CDs, a leisure facility manager can obtain data on the demographic characteristics of the population of the catchment area of the facility. An enormous amount of information is available on each of these areas, as listed in Figure 6.4.

Figure 6.3 Census data: levels of availability

Britain	Australia
• National	• National
• Regions	• State
• Counties	• Postal codes
• Local government areas	• Local government areas
• Parliamentary constituencies	• State and federal Parliament electorates
• Enumeration districts (EDs)	• Census collection districts (CDs)

Figure 6.4 Census data available

Resident population
- Number of males and females
- Number or proportion in 5-year age groups (and single years for under-20s)
- Numbers of people:
  - with different religions
  - born in UK and other countries
  - speaking different languages
  - with parents born in UK and other countries
- Numbers of families or households:
  - of different sizes
  - with different numbers of dependent children
  - which are single parent families
  - with various numbers of vehicles
- Numbers of people:
  - who left school at various ages
  - with different educational or technical qualifications
  - in different occupational groups
  - unemployed
  - living in different types of dwelling

It can be seen that none of the census information is concerned directly with leisure or tourism. So why should the census be of interest to the leisure or tourism researcher? First, many managers in the leisure and tourism industries have general responsibility for a particular geographical area, whether that be a whole country, a region, a local government area or the catchment area of a particular facility or service. One of the cardinal rules for the manager/marketer is to 'know your market or customer'. This applies as much in public sector agencies as in commercial organisations. The census provides valuable information about the numbers and characteristics of customers or potential customers in a geographical area. The census can be used to produce a 'profile' of an area, so that the manager has an overall view of the nature of the community being served. This might apply to the catchment area of a leisure facility or the areas from which a tourism destination draws its visitors. Nearly all the items of information listed in Figure 6.4 can be relevant to such a community profile or market profile.

The census can place a particular leisure or tourism operation into demographic perspective. For example, if a facility or enterprise is intended to serve a particular geographical area and is aimed at teenagers, the census will indicate how many teenagers live in that area. If 5000 teenagers live in an area and the facility has 500 teenage customers then it is reaching ten per cent of the potential market. This may be good or bad, depending on the level of competition and how specialised the product or service is.

More sophisticated uses of the census involve analysing a large range of data by computer in order to classify areas into 'types'. Residential areas can be classified, for example, into retirement areas, working class family areas, affluent areas and so on. In Britain, a system called 'ACORN' (A Classification Of Residential Neighbourhoods) has been developed to do this classification and it has been found that residents of different area 'types' have markedly different leisure participation patterns (Shaw, 1984; Williams *et al*., 1988; Veal, 1993d). This is related to the ideas of *lifestyle* and *psychographics*, as referred to in Chapter 1.

MANAGEMENT DATA

Most leisure and tourism organisations generate routine data which can be of use for research purposes and many have *management information systems* specifically designed to produce data upon which assessments of the performance of the organisation can be based. Examples of such data, which may be available on an hourly, daily, weekly, monthly, seasonal or annual basis, are listed in Figure 6.5. It is usually advisable to explore fully the nature, extent and availability of such data, and their potential utilisation, before embarking on fresh data collection. For example, in Case study 3.1 in Chapter 3, the manager of a facility is concerned about declining levels of visits. Before initiating expensive procedures, such as surveys, to investigate the causes it would be advisable to study the *available visitor data* to see whether the decline was across all services and whether it was taking place at all times or only at certain times of the day, week, season or year.

DOCUMENTARY SOURCES

Documentary sources lie somewhere between literature and management data as an information source for research. Typical examples are listed in Figure 6.6. Many of such sources are important for historical research, either for a primarily historical research project, or as background for a project with a

Figure 6.5   Management data

- Visitor numbers (in various categories)
- Visitor expenditure or income (in various categories)
- Bookings and facility utilisation
- Customer enquiries
- Membership numbers and details
- Customer complaints
- Results of visitor and customer surveys
- Expenditure of the organisation (under various headings)
- Staff turnover, absenteeism, etc.

Figure 6.6   Documentary sources

- Minutes of committee, council or board meetings
- Correspondence of an organisation or an individual
- Archives (may include both of the above and other papers)
- Popular literature, such as novels, magazines
- Newspapers, particularly coverage of specific topics and/or particular aspects, such as editorials, advertising or correspondence columns
- Brochures and advertising material
- Diaries

contemporary focus. In some cases the documents are a focus of research in their own right; for example, some research on women and sport has examined the coverage of women's sport in the media (for example, Rowe and Brown, 1994). As the links between cultural and media studies and leisure and tourism studies increase, so analysis of media content, including television, is likely to increase (Critcher, 1992; Tomlinson, 1990). Approaches to analysing such data are addressed in Chapter 8.

USING SECONDARY DATA

Some useful analysis can be done using secondary sources of data. In fact there are certain forms of analysis which can only be done with such data. Four case studies are given here by way of illustration.

CASE STUDY 6.1

Estimating likely demand for a leisure facility

The problem

A developer or local council is considering whether to build a cinema on a particular site in a town centre, as part of a multi-purpose leisure complex (a cinema is used as an example, but the methodology could be applied equally to other types of facility). The town has a population of 100 000 and already has two 400-seat cinemas. The developer wants to know what demand exists in the area for such a facility. A range of approaches could be considered to investigate this question.

Possibilities

One approach to the problem would be to examine existing cinemas in the area to see whether they are over-used or under-used, that is whether demand is already being adequately met by existing facilities. This however may not give the full answer, since it might be found that a well-managed, well-located cinema is well used while another, perhaps poorly managed and poorly located, is poorly used. It might also be difficult to obtain commercially sensitive data from potential competitors.

Another approach might be to conduct an interview survey of local residents to ask them whether they would like to go to the cinema but do not do so at present because of lack of suitable facilities. Even if the time and money were available to conduct such a survey, the results could not be relied on as the main piece of information on which to base the decision because, while people's honesty and accuracy in recalling activities might be relied on in relation to activities which they have actually taken part in, asking them to predict their behaviour in hypothetical future situations is very risky.

A third approach would be to examine communities of similar population size and type to see what levels of cinema provision they have and how well they are used. Again this may be a time-consuming process and somewhat 'hit-and-miss' because it is not easy to find comparable communities and because some of the data required, being commercially 'sensitive', may not be readily available.

A fourth approach would be to use secondary data, namely the appropriate national survey (NS) and the census, to provide an approximate estimate of likely demand for cinema seats in the area. The aim is to provide an estimate of the level of demand which a community of the size of the study area is likely to generate and compare that with the level of demand already likely to be catered for by existing cinemas, to see whether or not there is a surplus of demand over supply.

The approach

The general approach used here is represented diagrammatically in Figure 6.7.

A Age-specific participation rates

One of the features of cinema attendance is that it varies considerably by age. Cinema is attended more by young people than by older people. If, for example, the study town contains a higher than average proportion of young people, it can be

Figure 6.7 Estimating likely demand for a leisure facility – an approach

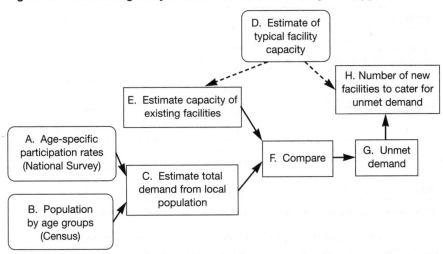

expected to produce a higher than average demand for cinema, and vice versa. The NS gives information on the percentage of people of different ages who go to the cinema, as shown in Table 6.3. It can be seen that teenagers are almost six times as likely to attend the cinema as the over-60s. The particular NS deals only with people aged 16 and over. Obviously children under that age do go to the cinema; but it may be that there is sufficient demand for an additional cinema even without taking account of the under-16s; so the under-16s can be ignored for the moment, only returning to them if necessary.

B Population by age-groups

Suppose the census gives the population of the town as 100 000, and the population aged 16 and over as 80 000. In Table 6.4 the age structure of the national population aged 16 and over is compared with that of the study town. Clearly the town has a

Table 6.3   Cinema attendance by age

Age group	% of age group who go to the cinema in an average week (from National Survey)
14–19 years	14.9
20–24	11.5
25–29	7.4
30–39	5.2
40–49	4.8
50–59	3.5
60+	2.5
Average	6.6

Source: Hypothetical data.

Table 6.4 Study town and national age structure compared

Age groups	National %	Study town %
14–19 years	12.5	19.5
20–24	11.9	19.0
25–29	10.6	14.2
30–39	20.1	21.1
40–49	14.2	9.0
50–59	11.8	7.7
60+	18.9	9.5
Total	100.0	100.0

Source: Hypothetical data. In practice such data would be obtained from the population census.

much younger age profile than the national average with only just over half the proportion of over-55s and correspondingly larger proportions in the young age groups. So it is clearly advisable to give consideration to the question of age structure.

C Estimate total demand from local population

Table 6.5 indicates how demand for cinema attendance would be estimated: attendances are estimated for each age group and summed to give a total of 6543 attendances per week.

D Estimate of typical facility capacity

For this exercise it is assumed that a typical 400-seat cinema auditorium requires 1500 ticket sales a week to be viable (this is entirely hypothetical: in a real situation this information would be checked out with experts).

E Estimate capacity of existing facilities

Two cinemas already exist in the town. If they have a seating capacity of 400 each, then they would accommodate some 3000 visits a week.

Table 6.5 Estimating demand for cinema attendance

	% of age group participating per week (X)	Town population (Y)	Estimated demand (visits per week)
Data source	National Survey	Census	X*Y/100
14–19 years	14.9	15 600	2324
20–24	11.5	15 200	1748
25–29	7.4	11 360	841
30–39	5.2	16 880	878
40–49	4.8	7 200	346
50–59	3.5	6 160	216
60+	2.5	7 600	190
Total		80 000	6543 = 8.2%

F Compare

The total estimated demand is 6500 visits per week, and the existing cinemas have a capacity of 3000 per week.

G Unmet demand

Unmet demand can therefore be estimated as about 3500 visits per week.

H Number of new facilities to cater for unmet demand

It would take two typical 400-seat cinemas to cater for the unmet demand – that is, it is estimated that the town can support four cinemas.

Comment

This exercise does not predict demand precisely. It merely indicates a 'ball park' demand figure. A well-managed and programmed cinema might draw far more demand than is estimated. The NS attendance rates relate to average attendances across the country, so clearly there are places where higher attendance rates occur as well as places where lower rates occur. What the exercise indicates is that, on the basis of data to hand, 6500 cinema attendances a week seems reasonably likely. This seems a very simple and crude calculation, but quite often investors – in the public and private sectors – fail to carry out even this sort of simple calculation to check on 'ball park' demand figures; investments are made on the basis of personal hunch, and then surprise is expressed when demand fails to materialise.

Forecasting note: To provide a simple forecast of future demand for, say, the year 2006 it would be necessary merely to insert population forecasts for the year 2006 into column B of Table 6.5 and rework the calculations.

CASE STUDY 6.2

Tourism trend analysis

Typically tourism statistics are produced on a quarterly basis, as in Table 6.6 (column A). Each quarterly figure of tourist arrivals reflects two factors: seasonal variation and longer-term trends. One way of examining the longer-term trend without the distraction of the seasonal variation is to produce a 'smoothed' series by calculating a 'moving average' (column B). The moving average consists of the average of the previous four quarters' figures. For example:

- the moving average for Aug–Dec 1990 is the average of the four figures for 1990;

- the moving average for Jan–Mar 1991 is the average of the figures from Apr–Jun 1990 to Jan–Mar 1991.

Note: the calculations can be done very easily with a spreadsheet program. The effect is to present a 'smoothed' trend series, as shown graphically in Figure 6.8.

Table 6.6 Tourist arrivals, 1986–1990

Year	Quarter	A. Arrivals millions	B. Moving average
1990	Jan–Mar	1.1	–
	Apr–Jun	2.5	–
	Jul–Sept	4.5	–
	Oct–Dec	3.3	2.9
1991	Jan–Mar	1.3	2.9
	Apr–Jun	2.8	3.0
	Jul–Sept	4.9	3.1
	Oct–Dec	3.9	3.2
1992	Jan–Mar	1.6	3.3
	Apr–Jun	3.0	3.3
	Jul–Sept	5.5	3.5
	Oct–Dec	4.3	3.6
1993	Jan–Mar	1.8	3.7
	Apr–Jun	3.0	3.7
	Jul–Sept	5.2	3.6
	Oct–Dec	3.1	3.3
1994	Jan–Mar	1.7	3.3
	Apr–Jun	2.8	3.2
	Jul–Sept	4.8	3.1
	Oct–Dec	3.0	3.1

Source: Hypothetical; in practice arrivals are obtained from government arrivals/departures statistics.

Figure 6.8 Tourism trends

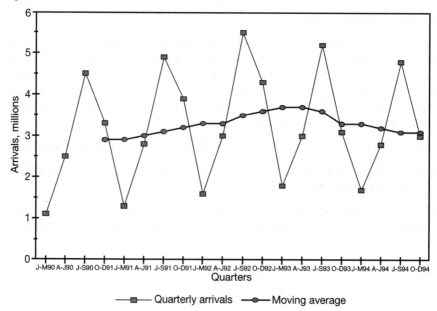

CASE STUDY 6.3

Facility utilisation

Managers often have information available on the use of facilities, but this is also often neglected as a source of data for research. As indicated in Case studies 6.1 and 6.2, the level of utilisation of existing facilities is an important issue for managers and planners: Table 6.7 and Figure 6.9 illustrate how existing data can be used to address this question. Table 6.7 presents data which might be routinely collected on the level of use of particular areas of a leisure facility (for example, various rooms or halls in an indoor leisure centre or various rides in a leisure park). The daily usage levels would have been averaged over a number of weeks. For each of the areas it is necessary to estimate the daily capacity: this is a reasonable assessment of the number of users which would equate to the facility being deemed 'fully used' (*see* Veal, 1994a, pp. 110–12). The actual levels of use are related to the capacity in the form of percentages, and these are presented graphically in Figure 6.9. The graph shows a different pattern of use for Area A, compared with the other two areas. Area A is under-used on Monday, Thursday and Friday, while areas B and C are under-used between Sunday and Wednesday. This suggests the need for different programming and marketing policies for the various areas.

Table 6.7 Facility utilisation data

	Area A		Area B		Area C	
	Number	% used	Number	% used	Number	% used
Mon	120	40.0	60	50.0	310	62.0
Tues	150	50.0	40	33.3	210	42.0
Wed	180	60.0	30	25.0	180	36.0
Thur	120	40.0	80	66.7	375	75.0
Fri	100	33.3	95	79.2	430	86.0
Sat	210	70.0	110	91.7	420	84.0
Sun	250	83.3	40	33.3	310	62.0
Daily capacity	300	100.0	120	100.0	500	100.0

CASE STUDY 6.4

Facility catchment or market area

Leisure and tourism facilities often have available information on users' addresses which can be used to study the catchment or market area – an important aspect of planning and management, as illustrated in Case studies 3.3 and 6.1. Many leisure facilities, for example, have membership or subscriber lists. Hotels and resorts have details of the home addresses of patrons. Figure 6.10 shows how such data can be plotted on a map to produce a visual representation of the catchment or market area of the facility. Such information can be used either to concentrate marketing in the existing area, or to consciously seek to extend the area.

When very large numbers are involved it may be necessary to sample such lists – for example selecting every fifth or tenth member or patron.

Figure 6.9   Facility utilisation

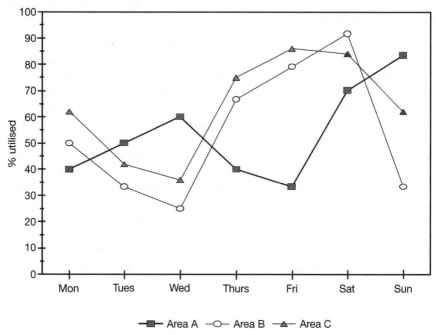

Figure 6.10   Catchment/market area

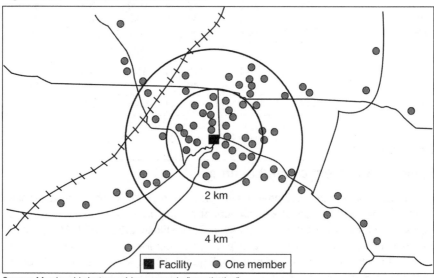

Source: Membership/patron address records (hypothetical).

While this case study is used to illustrate the use of secondary data, catchment areas can also be based on survey data. Indeed they must be if information on client addresses is not available (*see* Chapter 9, particularly discussion of user or site surveys).

QUESTIONS AND EXERCISES

1 Take a leisure activity of your own choice, and a community of your own choice and, using data from the General Household Survey, or equivalent, and data from the census, provide an estimate of the likely demand for the activity in the selected community, using the methodology outlined in Case study 6.1.

2 In relation to exercise 1, what would be the implications of a predicted increase of 15 per cent in the number of people aged 60 and over and a 15 per cent decrease in the number of people aged 25 and under, over the next five years?

3 Refer to the quarterly inbound tourism statistics for the last 10 years and produce a trend line of the sort outlined in Case study 6.2.

4 Undertake an exercise similar to Case study 6.3 for a leisure facility for which you can obtain usage data.

5 Undertake an exercise similar to Case study 6.4 for a leisure facility for which you can obtain user/member address data.

6 Select an activity from the General Household Survey, or equivalent local survey, and provide a profile of the activity, indicating the overall level of participation and how participation is related to age, gender, occupation and education.

FURTHER READING

On the GHS, *see*: Office of Population Censuses and Surveys (annual); Veal (1984, 1993d); Gratton and Tice (1994); Gratton (1996).

On Australian leisure surveys, *see*: Darcy (1994); Veal (1993b, 1993c); Darcy and Veal (1996); Lynch and Veal (1996, Chapter 5).

On employment statistics, *see*: Corley (1982).

On economic data, *see*: Martin and Mason (annual); Henley Centre for Forecasting (quarterly); Lynch and Veal (1996, Chapter 6).

On tourism data sources, *see*: Burkart and Medlik (1981, Part III); Edwards (1991); Goeldner (1994).

On international comparisons, *see*: Kamphorst and Roberts (1989); Hantrais and Kamphorst (1987); Cushman *et al.* (1996).

On documentary sources, *see*: Kellehear (1993).

CHAPTER 7

Observation

THE NATURE AND PURPOSE OF OBSERVATIONAL RESEARCH

This chapter draws attention to the importance of *looking* in research and introduces some of the specific approaches of observational methods. It examines situations in which observation is particularly appropriate and outlines the main steps which should be taken in an observation-based project. Observation is a neglected technique in leisure and tourism research. While it is rarely possible to base a whole project on observation, the technique has a vital role to play, either formally or informally, in most research strategies.

Observation involves *looking*. The results can be recorded and analysed qualitatively or quantitatively. Looking can be done with the naked eye or with the help of sophisticated equipment. For example, time-lapse photography can be used to photograph an area automatically at set periods; aerial photography can be used to gain a panoramic view of a whole recreation or tourism area; and video can also be used. These more sophisticated techniques are considered later in the chapter, but first the more simple approaches are examined.

POSSIBILITIES

A number of types of situation where observation is appropriate or necessary can be identified, as listed in Figure 7.1. These situations are discussed in turn below.

Children's play

There is some research which can only be tackled by means of observation. One example is children's play. Research on children's play is often concerned with discovering play patterns. What types of equipment do children of different ages prefer? Do boys have a different pattern of play from girls? Is there any difference in play patterns between children from different ethnic backgrounds? It is clear that answers to such questions could not be found by *interviewing* children, particularly very young children. The obvious approach is to *observe* children at play and record their behaviour.

Figure 7.1   Situations for observational research

- Children's play

- The use of informal leisure/tourism areas

- Spatial use of sites

- Deviant behaviour

- Consumer testing

- Complementary research

- Everyday life

- Social behaviour

Levels of use of informal recreation or tourism areas

Observation can be used to estimate the level of use of informal recreation areas such as beaches, urban parks or tourist sites, where there is no admission charge. Since there is no charge for entry to this type of area, and therefore no ticket sales data, managers and planners can only obtain estimates of their levels of use by observation.

An indication of the level of use of sites may be required for a variety of reasons. For instance, a public agency might decide that it would be useful, for political or public relations reasons, to be able to state the total number of visitors which a facility serves in a week or a year – in order to justify the level of taxpayers' money being spent on maintaining it. In management terms it is often useful to be able to relate the costs of maintaining a site to the number of visits which it attracts, as an input to decisions on how much money should be spent on different sites. A single site manager might be interested to compare levels of use over time to assess the impact of various management measures. In order to obtain an estimate of use levels it is necessary to *observe* and *count* the number of users.

Where the bulk of users arrive at a facility by private car it may be possible to install automatic vehicle counters to count the number of vehicles entering and leaving the site, and thus give an approximation of use levels. In this case the help of a mechanical device is enlisted to do the counting. However, vehicle counts provide information on the number of *vehicles* using a site but not the number of *people*. To obtain estimates of the numbers of people it is necessary to supplement these data by direct observation for some of the time – to ascertain the average number of persons in vehicles and, at some sites, to estimate the numbers arriving by foot or bicycle, who would not be recorded by the mechanical counting device.

Spatial use of sites

Observation is useful not only for gathering data on the number of users of a site but also for studying the way people make use of a site. This is particularly important in relation to the design and layout of leisure spaces, and their capacity. For instance, if people tend to crowd close to entrances and parking areas (which they often do) then where those entrances and parking areas are positioned will affect the pattern of use of the site. This can be used as a management tool to influence the pattern of use of a site.

Similarly if, as has been found, people tend to locate themselves along 'edges' – such as fences, banks, areas of trees and shrubs, etc. – then this tendency can be used to influence the pattern of use of a site, by determining the nature and location of such 'edges' (Ruddell and Hammitt, 1987). While this applies particularly to outdoor natural areas, it can also have some relevance in built-up areas, such as shopping malls, and in buildings such as museums.

Public buildings and public open spaces are often designed with either little or no consideration as to how people will actually use them, or on the basis of untested assumptions about how they will be used. In reality it is often found that people do not actually behave as anticipated: that some spaces are under-used while some are over-crowded, or that spaces are not designed or equipped for the activities which they are accommodating. The pattern of movement of people around exhibitions can affect the information absorbed, depending on the relative prominence and attraction of exhibits (Pearce, 1988: pp. 100–1). Observation is the means by which these aspects of space utilisation can be discovered.

Deviant behaviour

Deviant behaviour is a situation where observation is likely to be more fruitful than interviews. People are unlikely to tell an interviewer about their litter dropping habits, their lack of adherence to the rules in a park, or their beer-can throwing habits at a football match. Finding out about such things requires observation – usually covert observation! This of course raises ethical issues, such as people's rights to privacy, which are considered in Chapter 11.

Consumer testing

Consumer testing is another potentially fruitful but under-exploited use of observation. While interviews are one way of obtaining information on the quality of the experience offered by a leisure or tourism facility or product, an additional means is to play the role of *incognito* user, customer or observer. Such an observer would be required to make use of facilities or services, armed with a checklist of features to observe – such as cleanliness, information availability and clarity, staff performance – and would make a report after using the facilities or services. Again, ethical and industrial relations issues may arise in such a study because of the element of deception involved in playing the part of a customer.

Complementary research

Observation can be a necessary complement to interview surveys to correct for variation in sampling rates. For instance in a typical urban park or beauty spot two interviewers, working at a steady rate, may be able to interview virtually all users in the less busy periods in the early morning but only manage to interview a small proportion of the users during the busy lunch hour and afternoon. The final sample would therefore, in this case, over-represent early-morning users and under-represent mid-day and afternoon users. If these two groups were to have different characteristics, this may have a biasing effect on, for example, the balance of views expressed by the users. Counts of the hourly levels of use can provide data to give an appropriate *weight* to the mid-day and afternoon users. The process of *weighting* is described in more detail in Chapter 12.

Everyday life

The idea of simply observing *everyday life* as an approach to studying a society is associated with Britain's Mass Observation anthropological study of the British way of life in the 1930s and 1940s and with the work of Irving Goffman (1959). An anthology of Mass Observation sketches, published in 1984 (Calder and Sheridan, 1984) includes descriptions of everyday events in pubs, on the Blackpool promenade and in the wartime blitz in London. Goffman's work was more theoretical than this study and concerned the ways individuals use space and interact in public and private places. An anthology of work in the Goffman style (Birenbaum and Sagarin, 1973) includes observational studies of such leisure activities as pinball, bars, card games and restaurants.

Social behaviour

Observation has been used in sociological research to develop ideas and theories about social behaviour. The research of Fiske (1983) and Grant (1984) on the use of beaches, Cuneen and Lynch (1988) on the riots at the Australian Motor Cycle Grand Prix and Marsh and his colleagues (1978) on soccer fans are examples of this approach. These researchers use an interactive, inductive process to build explanations of social behaviour from what they observe. Very often a key feature of such studies is the way the researchers seek to contrast what they have observed with what has apparently been observed by others, particularly those with influence or authority, such as officials, police and the media. Observational research can challenge existing stereotypical interpretations of events.

Participant observation

The technique of participant observation is not dealt with here since it is covered in Chapter 8 on qualitative methods.

MAIN ELEMENTS OF OBSERVATIONAL RESEARCH

Observation is essentially a simple research method so there is not a great deal of 'technique' to consider. What is mainly required from the researcher is precision, painstaking attention to detail and patience. The main tasks in planning and conducting an observational project are as set out in Figure 7.2.

Figure 7.2   Steps in an observation project

```
 1  Choose site(s)

 2  Choose observation point(s)

 3  Choose study time period

 4  Decide on continuous observation or sampling

 5  Decide on number and length of sampling periods

 6  Decide what to observe

 7  Divide into zones

 8  Design a recording sheet

 9  Conduct study

10  Analyse data
```

As with the elements of the research process outlined in Chapter 3, it is difficult to produce a list of steps which will cover all eventualities. In particular, if the approach is not quantitative but qualitative in nature, then a number of the steps discussed here, particularly those concerning counting, may be redundant.

Step 1: Choice of site(s)

In the case of consultancy research the sites to be studied may be fixed; but where there is some element of choice some time should be devoted to inspecting and choosing sites which will offer the appropriate leisure/tourism behaviour but also provide suitable conditions for observation.

Step 2: Choice of observation point(s)

Choice of observation points within a site is clearly important and needs to be done with care. Some sites can be observed in their entirety from one spot. In other cases a circuit of viewing spots must be devised.

Step 3: Choice of time period

The choice of time period is important because of variations in use of a facility, by time of the year, day of the week, time of day or weather conditions, or according to social factors such as public holidays. Observation to cover all time periods may be very demanding in terms of resources, so some form of sampling will usually be necessary.

Step 4: Continuous observation or sampling?

The question of whether to undertake continuous observation or to sample different periods is related to the resources available and the nature of the site. The issue is particularly important if one of the aims of the research is to obtain an accurate estimate of the number of visitors to the site, when the terminology used to refer to the two approaches would be *continuous counts* or *spot counts*. It could, for example, be very expensive to place observers at the numerous gates of a large urban park for as much as 100 hours in a week to estimate the number of users. A sampling approach will usually have to be adopted. Once the decision is taken to sample it is of course necessary to decide how often to do this. This is discussed further under step 5.

If counting is being undertaken there is also a decision to be made as to whether to count the number of people *entering* the site during specified time periods or the number of people *present* at particular points in time. Counting the number of people present at particular points in time is generally easier since it can be done by one person regardless of the number of entrances to the site, and can provide information on the spatial use of the site at the same time. Thus one person, at specified times, makes a circuit of the site and records the numbers of people present in designated zones.

When qualitative rather than quantitative observation is being undertaken it is more likely that continuous observation will be adopted since the aim will generally be to observe the dynamics of events and behaviour at the site. However, the question of when to undertake such observation in order to cover all aspects of the use of the site still needs careful consideration.

Step 5: Count frequency

Where counts of users are involved, how often should they be undertaken? This will depend to a large extent on the rate of change in the level of use of the site. For example, the four counts in Figure 7.3 are clearly insufficient since, if the broken line is the pattern of use observed in a research project, but

Figure 7.3 Counts of park use – 1

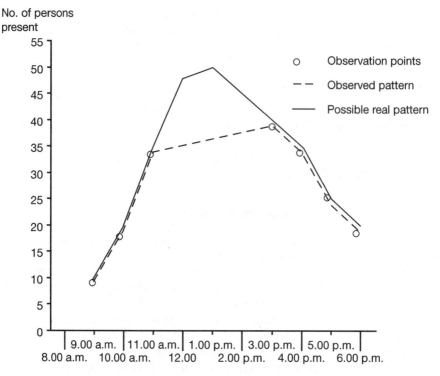

No. of persons present

the unbroken line is the true pattern, the research would have inaccurately represented the true situation. There is little advice that can be given to overcome this problem, except to sample frequently at the beginning of a project until the basic patterns of peaks and troughs in usage have been established; subsequently it may be possible to sample less often.

Step 6: What to observe

One approach to observing the spatial behaviour of visitors within a facility is to record people's positions directly, as indicated in Figure 7.4. In addition to observing numbers of people and their positions, it is possible to observe and record different types of activity. It is also possible, to a limited extent, to record visitor characteristics. For instance men and women could be separately identified. It is also possible to distinguish between children and adults and to distinguish senior citizens, although, if more than one counter is involved, care will need to be taken over the dividing line between such categories as child, teenager, young adult, adult and elderly person. It is also possible, again with care, to observe the size of parties using a site, especially if they are observed arriving or leaving at a car park.

The additional items of information collected would of course complicate the recording sheet and symbols would be necessary to record the different

Figure 7.4 Mapping information: use of a park

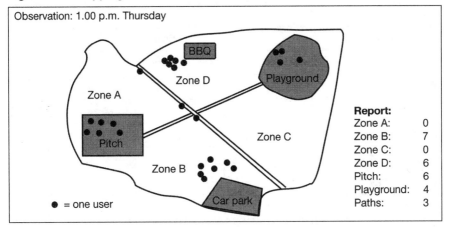

Observation: 1.00 p.m. Thursday

BBQ
Zone D
Playground
Zone A
Pitch
Zone C
Zone B
● = one user
Car park

Report:
Zone A:	0
Zone B:	7
Zone C:	0
Zone D:	6
Pitch:	6
Playground:	4
Paths:	3

types of person on a map. Care needs to be taken not to make the data collection so complicated that it becomes too difficult for the observers to observe and collect and leads to inaccuracies. This is one of those situations where it is necessary to consider carefully *why* the data are being collected and not to get carried away with data collection for its own sake.

In addition to observing people statically, or as they arrive at an entrance, it is also possible to observe visitors' movement through a site. Of course care must be taken not to give offence by letting visitors become aware that they are being 'followed', but routes taken by visitors can be revealing for management.

Car registration numbers can be a useful source of information. First, they can provide information on where people have travelled from. Second, number plates can be used to trace the movement of vehicles within an area – for instance within a national park with a number of stopping points.

Step 7: Division of site into zones

In large sites it is advisable to divide the site into areas or zones and record the number of people and their activities within those zones. The zones should be determined primarily by management concerns – for example, the children's playground, the sports areas, the rose garden. But they should also be designed for ease of counting; ideally zones should be such that they can be observed from one spot and should be clearly demarcated by natural or other features.

Step 8: Design of recording sheet

Figure 7.5 is an example of a counting sheet designed for an area with six zones and the possibility of a variety of activities. The data collected using such a form are ideal for storage, manipulation and presentation in graphic form

Figure 7.5   Example of a count recording sheet

Site:				Date:			
Name of observer:				Start time:			
				Zone:			
Activity	A	B	C	D	E	F	G
Walking							
Sitting							
Playing sport							
Children playing							
Eating							
Total							

using a spreadsheet computer program such as Lotus123 or Excel. An example of a graphical presentation of count data is shown in Figure 7.6; this relates to a whole site and not to a site divided into zones, but similar graphics could be produced for each zone.

Figure 7.6   Park usage

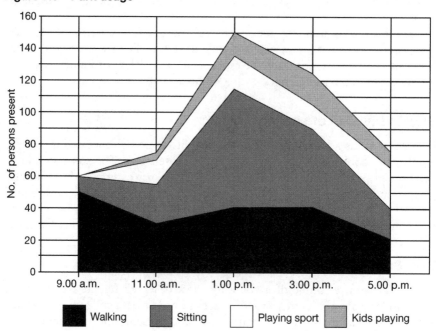

Step 9: Conduct the observation

If the project has been well planned then the conduct of an observational project should be straightforward. The main danger in a major project can be boredom, leading to inaccuracies in observing and recording data. It is therefore advisable to vary the work of those involved so that, where appropriate, data collectors alternate between behavioural observation and counting and, where possible, are switched between sites.

Step 10: Analysis of data

How should sample counts be interpreted to obtain an overall estimate of use? Consider the set of counts shown in Table 7.1, which relate to the numbers of people present in a park, which opens at 8 a.m. and closes at 8 p.m. This pattern is illustrated graphically in Figure 7.7.

Table 7.1 Observed use of a park

Time	No. of people present	Time	No. of people present
8 a.m.	0	3 p.m.	55
9 a.m.	10	4 p.m.	55
10 a.m.	25	5 p.m.	35
11 a.m.	32	6 p.m.	25
12 noon	40	7 p.m.	14
1 p.m.	47	8 p.m.	0
2 p.m.	50	Total	388
		Average/hour	32.3

Source: hypothetical.

It is estimated that there is an average of 32.3 people in the park every hour, over a 12-hour period, giving a total of 388 *visitor-hours*. The number of visitor-hours is a valid measure of use in its own right and could be used to compare different sites or to compare the performance of the same site over time. But, for example, 12 visitor-hours could result from one person visiting the park and staying all day, or two people staying six hours each, 12 people staying one hour each, or 24 people staying half an hour each. So if an estimate is required of the number of different *persons* visiting the park over the course of the day, additional information, on the *length of stay*, is necessary. If the average user, in the example, stayed exactly half an hour, then the number of persons would be estimated at twice the number of visitor-hours, or 776 (388 ÷ ½); if the average user stayed, say, two hours, the number of users would be 194 (388 ÷ 2). Thus the number of visitors is equal to the number of visitor-hours divided by the average length of stay. The length of stay must be obtained either by detailed observation of a sample of groups or by an interview survey.

Figure 7.7   Counts of park use – 2

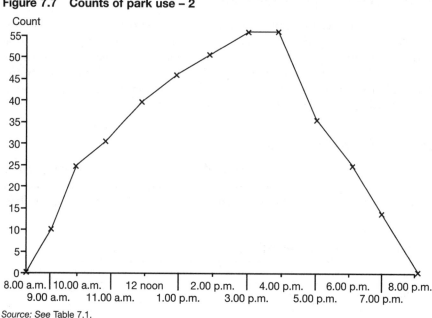

Source: See Table 7.1.

Details of user characteristics obtained from observation can be used as a check on the accuracy of sampling in interview surveys and may be used to 'weight' the results of such surveys so that the final result is a better reflection of the characteristics of the users of the facility. This is similar to the 'time of day' correction discussed above, but relates to the personal characteristics of users, rather than their time of use of the facility. For instance, if it was found by observation that half the users of a site were women but in an interview survey only a third of those interviewed were women, the women in the sample could be given a greater weighting at the analysis stage so that their views and attitudes would receive due emphasis. The details of weighting are described more fully in Chapter 12.

PHOTOGRAPHY AND VIDEO

Aerial photography

The use of aerial photography is well developed in geography and geology, where a whole sub-discipline of *remote sensing* has developed using a variety of techniques. It can also be an effective technique in leisure and tourism studies. Where large areas are concerned – such as coastlines and estuaries, where access is difficult and recreational use of the site is very scattered, aerial photography may be the only way of obtaining estimates of levels and patterns of use. In harbours and estuaries it is probably the best means of obtaining estimates of numbers of craft using the area since, as they are generally moving about, it can be difficult to count manually on a crowded waterway. Needless to say a good quality camera is needed for such work. Generally slides are the best medium because they can easily be projected on a large screen for the subsequent laborious task of counting.

Still photography

The value of ordinary, land-based, photography as an adjunct to direct observation should not be overlooked. The level of crowding of a site, its nature and atmosphere can be conveyed to the reader of a report with the aid of photographs. Particular problems, for instance of erosion, or design faults, can be conveyed better visually than verbally – a picture speaks a thousand words.

Video

Video can be used to record patterns of use of a site, but is likely to be used for illustrative rather than analytical purposes. Video can provide a useful illustration of 'before' and 'after' situations, to illustrate the nature of problems on a site and the effect of measures to ameliorate the problems – for example congestion, erosion or littering.

Time-lapse photography

Time-lapse photography lies somewhere between still photography and video. A time-lapse camera can be set up to take pictures of a scene automatically, say, every 10 seconds or every minute. The resultant sequence of pictures can then be projected as a film or video to show the speeded-up pattern of use of the area viewed. This is the technique used in wildlife documentaries which show a plant apparently growing before your eyes, but it can also be used to show the changing pattern of use of a leisure or tourism site.

JUST LOOKING

Finally we should also not forget how important it is to use our eyes, even if the research project does not involve systematic observational data collection. Familiarity with a leisure activity or a leisure or tourism site helps to design a good research project and aids in interpreting data. Many studies have been based on informal, but careful, observation. All useful information is not in the form of numbers. Careful observation of what is happening in a particular leisure or tourism situation, at a particular facility or type of facility or among a particular group can be a more appropriate research approach than the use of questionnaires or even informal interviews. The good researcher is all eyes.

QUESTIONS AND EXERCISES

1 Select an informal leisure or tourism site, position yourself in an unobtrusive location, but where you can seen what is going on. Over a period of two hours, record what happens. Write a report on: how the site is used; who it is used by; how many people use it; what conflicts there are, if any, between different groups of users; and how the design of the site aids or hinders the activity which people engage in on the site.

2 Establish a counting system to record the number of people present in a leisure or tourism site at hourly intervals during the course of a day. Estimate the number of visitor-hours at the site for the day.

3 In relation to exercise 2, conduct interviews with three or four visitors each hour, and ask them how long they have stayed, or expect to stay, at the site. Establish the average length of stay and, using this information and the data from exercise 2, estimate the number of persons visiting the site in the course of the day.

4 Use photographs to record examples of neglect or damage to leisure or tourism sites known to you.

FURTHER READING

On general or methodological issues, *see*: Burch (1981); Ely (1981); Tyre and Siderelis (1978); TRRU (1983); Kellehear (1993); Adler and Adler (1994); Peine (1984).

Examples of studies using observation are: general: Birenbaum and Sagarin (1973); children's play: Child (1983); Block and Laursen (1996); sporting crowds and riots: Cuneen *et al.* (1989); sporting crowds (football): Marsh *et al.* (1978); beach use: Fiske (1983); Grant (1984); countryside recreation: Glyptis (1981a, 1981b); Heberlein and Dunwiddie (1979); Patmore (1983, p. 146); Van der Zande (1985); parks: Gold (1972); museums: Bitgood, *et al.* (1988); Pearce (1988).

CHAPTER 8

Qualitative methods

INTRODUCTION: QUALITIES AND USES

This chapter reviews methods of research which involve the collection and analysis of *qualitative* information rather than numerical data. The chapter discusses the advantages and features of qualitative methods, their role in market research and the range of methods available, including in-depth interviews, group interviews and focus groups, participant observation and ethnographic approaches. The chapter concludes with a discussion of the analysis of *texts*, which, although it can be undertaken quantitatively as well as qualitatively, has generally been associated with the qualitative tradition.

The term 'qualitative' is used to describe research methods and techniques which use, and give rise to, qualitative rather than quantitative information. In general the qualitative approach tends to collect a great deal of 'rich' information about relatively few people rather than more limited information about a large number of people. It is however possible to envisage qualitative research which actually deals with large numbers of people. For example, a research project on sports spectators, involving observation and participation in spectator activity, could involve information relating to tens of thousands of people.

Qualitative methods can be used for pragmatic reasons, in situations where formal, quantified research is not necessary or is not possible. But there are also theoretical grounds for using qualitative methods. Much quantitative research necessarily imposes the *researcher's* view on a situation; the researcher decides which are the important issues and which questions are to be asked and determines the whole framework within which the discourse of the research will be conducted. Much qualitative research is based on the belief that the people personally involved in a particular (leisure or tourism) situation are best placed to analyse and describe their experiences or feelings in their own words – that they should be allowed to speak without the intermediary of the researcher and without being constrained by the framework imposed by the researcher – a sort of *cinema vérité* or *vox populi* style of research.

Merits of qualitative methods

Kelly (1980), in making a plea for more qualitative leisure research, argued that the approach had been neglected in the field of leisure studies during the 1960s and 1970s, particularly in the United States. He suggested that qualitative research has the following advantages over quantitative research.

1 The method corresponds with the nature of the phenomenon being studied – that is, leisure is a qualitative experience.
2 The method 'brings people back in' to leisure research. By contrast, quantitative methods tend to be very impersonal – *real* people with names and unique personalities do not feature.
3 The results of qualitative research are more understandable to people who are not statistically trained.
4 The method is better able to encompass personal change over time. By contrast much quantitative research tends to look only at current behaviour as related to current social, economic and environmental circumstances, ignoring the fact that most people's behaviour is heavily influenced by their life history and experience.
5 Reflecting the first point, Kelly argues that leisure itself involves a great deal of face-to-face interaction between people – involving symbols, gestures etc. – and qualitative research is well suited to investigating this.
6 Kelly argues that qualitative rather than quantitative techniques are better at providing an understanding of people's needs and aspirations, although some researchers in the psychological field in particular might disagree with him.

In this book it has been argued that different methods are not inherently good or bad, but just more or less appropriate for the task in hand. Thus Kelly's comments relate to particular types of research with particular purposes. A similar list of claims could be made about the merits of various forms of quantitative research, as shown in Chapter 9 in relation to questionnaire surveys.

Uses in market research

Peterson (1994), speaking from a market researcher's perspective, lists the potential uses of qualitative research as:

(a) to develop hypotheses concerning relevant behaviour and attitudes;
(b) to identify the full range of issues, views and attitudes which should be pursued in larger-scale research;
(c) to suggest methods for quantitative enquiry – for example, in terms of deciding who should be included in interview surveys;
(d) to identify language used to address relevant issues (thus avoiding the use of jargon in questionnaires);
(e) to understand how a buying decision is made – questionnaire surveys are not very good at exploring *processes*;
(f) to develop new product, service or marketing strategy ideas – the free play of attitudes and opinions can be a rich source of ideas for the marketer;
(g) to provide an initial screening of new product, service or strategy ideas;
(h) to learn how communications are received – what is understood and how – particularly related to advertising.

THE QUALITATIVE RESEARCH PROCESS

Qualitative methods generally require a more flexible approach to overall research design and conduct. Most quantitative research tends to be *sequential* in nature; the steps set out in Chapter 3 tend to be distinct and follow in a pre-planned sequence. This is inevitable because of the nature of the core data-collection exercise which is generally involved. Much qualitative research involves a more fluid relationship between the various elements of the research – an approach which might be called *recursive*. In this approach hypothesis formation evolves as the research progresses; data analysis and collection take place concurrently; and writing is also often an evolutionary, ongoing, process, rather than a separate process which happens at the end of the project. The two approaches are represented diagrammatically in Figure 8.1. Although these two approaches are presented here in the context of a contrast between quantitative and qualitative methods, in fact quantitative and qualitative methods can both involve sequential and recursive approaches. Thus, it is possible to have an essentially quantitative study which nevertheless involves a variety of data sources and a number of small-scale studies, which build in an iterative way. On the other hand, it is also possible for an essentially qualitative study to be conducted on a large scale, with a single data source – for example, a nationwide study of council leaders, involving fairly standardised in-depth interviews.

Figure 8.1 Sequential and recursive approaches to research

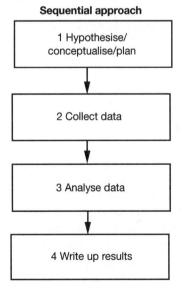

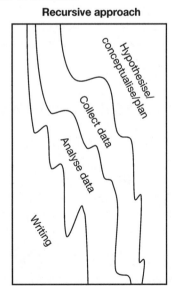

THE RANGE OF METHODS

Qualitative techniques commonly used in leisure and tourism research and which are discussed in more detail in this chapter are listed in Figure 8.2.

Figure 8.2   Qualitative methods: summary

In-depth interviews
- Usually conducted with a relatively small number of subjects
- Interview guided by a checklist of topics rather than a formal questionnaire
- Interviews often tape-recorded and verbatim transcript prepared
- Can take half an hour and may extend over several hours; repeat interviews possible

Group interviews/focus groups
- Similar to in-depth interviews but conducted with a group
- Interaction between subjects takes place as well as interaction between interviewer and subject

Participant observation
- Researcher gathers information by being an actual participant with the subjects being studied
- Researcher may be known by the subjects as a researcher or may be *incognito*

Ethnography
- Utilises a number of the above techniques; not a single technique; borrowed from anthropology

IN-DEPTH INTERVIEWS

Nature

An in-depth interview is characterised by its length, depth and structure. In-depth interviews tend to be much longer than questionnaire-based interviews, typically taking at least half an hour and sometimes several hours. The method may involve interviewing people more than once. As the name implies, the in-depth interview seeks to probe more deeply than is possible with a questionnaire-based interview. Rather than just asking a question, recording a simple answer, and moving on, the in-depth interviewer encourages respondents to talk, asks supplementary questions and asks respondents to explain their answers. The in-depth interview is therefore less structured than a questionnaire-based interview; every interview in a study, although dealing with the same issues, will be different.

Purposes and situations

In-depth interviews tend to be used in three situations.

1 The subjects of the research may be relatively few in number so a question-naire-based quantitative style of research would be inappropriate.
2 The information likely to be obtained from each subject is expected to vary considerably, and in complex ways. An example would be interviews with the management staff of a recreation or tourism department of a local council, or interviews with the coaches of different national sports teams. Each of these interviews would be different and would be a 'story' in its own right. In reporting the research it would be the unique nature and structure of each of these 'stories' which would be of interest; data on 'what percentage of respondents said what' would not be relevant.
3 A topic is to be explored as a preliminary stage in planning a larger study, possibly a quantitative study, such as a questionnaire-based survey.

Checklist

Rather than a formal questionnaire the 'instrument' used in in-depth interviews is often a *checklist* of topics to be raised. For example, a formal questionnaire might ask a question: 'Which of the following countries have you ever visited on holiday?' The informal interview checklist would probably simply include the words 'countries visited'. The interviewer would shape the question according to the circumstances of a particular interview. If the interviewer is interested, for example, in the influence of childhood holiday experiences on adult visit patterns, in some interviews it may be necessary to ask a specific question such as: 'What overseas holiday trips did you take as a child?' In other interviews the interviewee might volunteer detailed information on childhood trips in response to the interviewer's initial question. It is then not necessary to ask the separate question about childhood trips. Thus in-depth interviews vary from interview to interview; they take on a life of their own. The skill on the part of the interviewer is to ensure that all relevant topics are covered – even though they may be covered in different orders and in different ways in different interviews.

The design of the checklist should nevertheless be as methodical as the design of a formal questionnaire; in particular, the items to be included on the checklist should be based on the conceptual framework for the study and the resultant list of data needs, as discussed in Chapter 3. An example of a checklist is included as Appendix 8.1. The example given is in the form of a fairly terse list of topics. An alternative is to include fully worded questions, as would appear in a questionnaire; this may be necessary when interviewers other than the researcher are being used. The problem with fully worded questions is that actually turning to the clipboard and reading out lengthy questions can interrupt the flow and informality of the interview.

The interviewing process

Conducting a good in-depth interview could be said to require the skills of a good investigative journalist. As Dean and his colleagues put it:

> Many people feel that a newspaper reporter is a far cry from a social scientist. Yet many of the data of social science today are gathered by interviewing and observation techniques that resemble those of a skilled newspaper man at work on the study of, say, a union strike or a political convention. It makes little sense for us to belittle these less rigorous methods as 'unscientific'. We will do better to study them and the techniques they involve so that we can make better use of them in producing scientific information. (Dean, Eichhorn and Dean, quoted in McCall and Simmons, 1969, p. 1)

An important skill in interviewing is to avoid becoming so taken up in the conversational style of the interview that the interviewee is 'led' by the interviewer. The interviewer should avoid agreeing – or disagreeing – with the interviewee or suggesting answers. This is more difficult than it sounds because in normal conversation we tend to make friendly noises and contribute to the discussion. In an in-depth interview we are torn between the need to maintain a friendly conversational atmosphere and the need *not* to influence the interviewee's responses.

Some of the carefully planned sequencing of questions which is built into formal questionnaires must be achieved by the interviewer being very sensitive and quick thinking. For example, having discovered that the respondent does not go to the theatre, the interviewer should not lead the respondent by asking: 'Is this because it is too expensive?' Rather the interviewee should be asked a more open question, such as: 'Why is that?' If the interviewee does not mention cost, but cost is of particular interest in the study, then the respondent might be asked a question such as: 'What about seat prices?' But this would be only *after* the interviewee has given his or her own unprompted reasons for not attending the theatre.

Whyte (1982) lists a sort of hierarchy in interviewer responses which vary in their degree of *intervention* in the interview. Whyte also sees this as the interviewer exercising varying degrees of *control* over the interview. Whyte's list, which begins with the least intrusive style of intervention, is as shown in Figure 8.3. It should be noted that, except for the sixth of these responses, the interviewer is essentially drawing on what the subject has already said and is inviting her or him to expand on it.

An important skill in interviewing of this sort is not to be afraid of silence. Some questions puzzle respondents and they need time to think. The interviewer does not have to fill the space with noise under the guise of 'helping' the interviewee. The interviewee should be allowed time to ponder. The initiative can be left with the respondent to ask for an explanation if a question is unclear. While it is pleasant to engender a conversational atmosphere in these situations, the in-depth interview is in fact different from a conversation. The interviewer is meant to listen and encourage the respondent to talk – not to engage in debate!

Figure 8.3 Interviewing interventions – Whyte

1 'Uh-huh'	A non-verbal response which merely indicates that the interviewer is still listening and interested.
2 'That's interesting'	Encourages the subject to keep talking or expand on the current topic.
3 Reflection	Repeating the last statement as a question – e.g. 'So you don't like sport?'
4 Probe	Inviting explanations of statements – e.g. 'Why don't you like sport?'
5 Back tracking	Remembering something the subject said earlier and inviting further information – e.g. 'Let's go back to what you were saying about your school days.'
6 New topic	Initiating a new topic – e.g. 'Can we talk about other leisure activities – what about entertainment?'

Recording

Tape-recording of in-depth interviews is common, although in some cases it might be felt that such a procedure could inhibit respondents. If tape-recording is not possible then notes must be taken during the interview or immediately afterwards. There can be great value in producing complete *verbatim* (word-for-word) transcripts of interviews. This is a laborious process – one hour of interview taking as much as six hours to transcribe. Such transcripts can however be used to analyse the results of interviews in a more methodical and complete manner than is possible with notes.

Analysis

There are various ways of analysing interview transcripts or notes. The essence of any analysis procedure must be to return to the terms of reference, and the conceptual framework, and research questions or hypotheses of the research, and begin to sort and evaluate the information gathered in relation to the questions posed and the concepts identified. In qualitative research however those original ideas may be very fluid; data gathering and hypothesis formulation, and even the identification of concepts, is a two-way process. Ideas are refined and revised in the light of the information gathered, as in the above discussion of the 'recursive' approach.

In addition to the problem of ordering and summarising the data conceptually, the researcher is faced with practical problems of how to approach the pile of interview notes or transcripts.

The initial steps in analysis involve fairly methodical procedures to classify and organise the information collected. On a very practical note, it is advisable to ensure that the transcripts have wide margins so that they can be annotated with key words for analytical purposes. It can also be useful to number the paragraphs, or use the line numbering facility which is available in word-processor packages. This is necessary not only to identify topics across a number of interviews but also because very often the same topic is covered several times in the same interview so some sort of *flagging* is necessary for analysis. Also, a particular part of the dialogue may not be related to the substantive topic specifically raised by the interviewer but may relate, for example, to underlying attitudes expressed by interviewees, which might arise at any time in an interview.

Analysis can be carried out directly from the annotated transcripts or the information can be transferred to a card index system, in which data could be recorded, for example, as follows:

Negative views of school sport: Interview 2, p. 12, para. 34
                                       Interview 3, p. 5, paras. 6–7
                                       Interview 5, p. 4, paras. 20–22, p. 10, para. 40

Attitudes to package holidays: Interview 1, pp. 2–3
                                         Interview 3, p. 3, paras. 3–4

It is possible to use data analysis techniques which are similar to those used in quantitative analysis. For example, in Figure 8.4, a form of analysis similar to

Figure 8.4 'Cross-tabulation' of interview responses

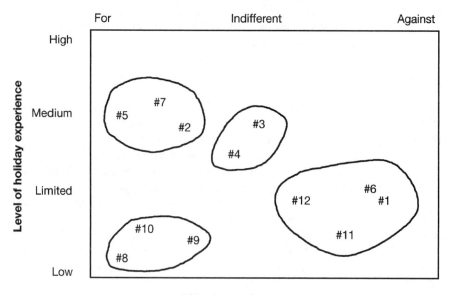

Numbers refer to interviewees.

a cross-tabulation is shown, with 12 hypothetical interviewees 'plotted' on a two-dimensional space with 'attitudes towards holiday packages' along one dimension and 'level of holiday experience' along the other. The placing of the respondents depends on a qualitative assessment based on the interview transcripts. It can be seen that, in the example, the respondents fall into four groups. Such a grouping would provide the basis for further analysis of the transcripts (*see* Huberman and Miles, 1994, p. 437).

Computer packages are now available to analyse interview transcripts (Fielding and Lee, 1991), taking advantage of the fact that interview transcripts typed on a word-processor are available in electronic form. Standard word-processing packages can aid analysis in a simple way, for example by using the *search* facility to locate particular words or phrases or the *list* facility usually provided as part of the *table of contents* procedure. Specialist computer packages, such as *NUD•IST* (Richards and Richards, 1994), enable the researcher to classify and *flag* the text, as discussed above. This speeds up the subsequent process of transcript analysis. In order for the text of the transcript to be flagged for computer analysis, a hierarchical flagging *system* has to be established. Logically this should be based on the conceptual framework established for the project. Figure 8.5 shows such a system which might arise from the interview checklist in Appendix 8.1. Using the package, appropriate sections of the interview transcripts (lines, sentences or paragraphs) would be marked A1, A2, B1, etc. The computer aids subsequent analysis by identifying and printing out, or writing to a file, all sentences or paragraphs which contain references to, for example, participation in sport (D2) and school influence (A2).

Detailed analysis may be less important when the purpose of the in-depth or informal interviews is to provide input into the design of a formal questionnaire. In that case the interviewer might make a series of notes arising from the interview which might be of relevance to the questionnaire design process, and

Figure 8.5   Example of framework for analysing interview transcripts

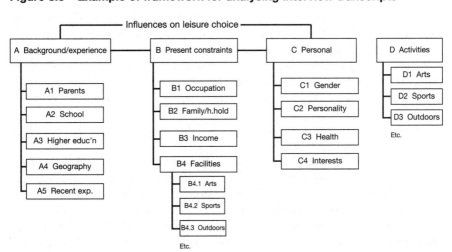

may provide input from memory as long as the questionnaire design work is undertaken fairly soon after the interviews.

GROUP INTERVIEWS AND FOCUS GROUPS

Nature

The idea of interviewing groups of people together rather than individually is becoming increasingly popular in market research. In this technique the interviewer becomes the *facilitator* of a discussion rather than an interviewer as such. The aim of the process is much the same as in an in-depth interview, but in this case the 'subjects' interact with each other as well as with the researcher.

Purposes

The technique can be used:

- when a particular group is important in a study but is so small in number that members of the group would not be adequately represented in a general community survey – for example, members of minority ethnic groups or people with disabilities;
- when the interaction/discussion process itself is of interest – for example, in testing reactions to a proposed new product, or when investigating how people form political opinions;
- as an alternative to the in-depth interview, when it may not be practical to arrange for individual in-depth interviews but people are willing to be interviewed as a group – for example, some youth groups or members of some ethnic communities.

Methods

A group will usually comprise between five and 12 participants. They may be chosen from a 'panel' of people who make themselves available to market researchers for this sort of exercise, or they may be chosen because they are members of a particular group of interest to the research – for instance local residents in a particular area, members of a sports club, or a group of people on a holiday package. The members of the group may or may not be known to one another.

The usual procedure is to tape-record the discussion and for the researcher to produce a summary from the recording.

Many of the same considerations apply here as in the in-depth interview situation: the process is informal but the interviewer (or convenor or discussion leader) still has a role in guiding the discussion and ensuring that all the aspects of the topic are covered. In addition, in the group interview, the interviewer has the task of ensuring that everyone in the group has their say and that the discussion is not dominated by one or two vociferous members of the group.

Analysis

As with the in-depth interview, one approach to analysis is to produce a complete transcript of the interviews and proceed as for in-depth interviews. Of course, in addition to the transcript identifying interviewer and interviewee, it must now distinguish between different members of the focus group. This may be difficult or even impossible from a tape recording. Detailed analysis would also be difficult because of the number of 'actors'. It is therefore more common for summary notes to be produced directly from the tape. In this case the *analysis* is effectively proceeding at the same time as the notes are being taken, since the note-taker must be drawing out key elements of the discussion in the light of the objective of the study. It would therefore be good practice to listen to the tape more than once to ensure that the notes accurately reflect the content of the discussion. If resources permit it is advisable for another person to listen to the tape and assess the accuracy of the notes taken from it.

PARTICIPANT OBSERVATION

Nature

In participant observation the researcher becomes a participant in the social process being studied. The classic study of this type is Whyte's *Street Corner Society* (1955), in which the researcher spent several years living with an inner city US Italian community. Smith's (1985) study of pubs in England is a direct leisure example as is Wynne's (1986) study of community involvement with recreation facilities.

Purposes

In leisure and tourism elements of 'participant observation' are common in many types of research. For instance, a researcher involved in studying the use of a park or resort can easily spend periods as a user of the facility. This is however a very minimalist view of participant observation. Traditionally the process has involved much more interaction of the researcher with the people being researched. In many cases some sort of participant observation is the only way of researching particular phenomena – for instance it would be difficult to study what really goes on in a drug sub-culture or in some youth sub-cultures using a questionnaire and clipboard. Becoming part of the group is the obvious way of studying the group.

Methods

Participant observation raises a number of practical and tactical problems. For example, in some cases actually gaining admittance to the social setting of interest may be a problem – for instance where close-knit groups are involved. Having gained admittance to the setting, the question arises as to whether to pose as a 'typical' member of the group, whether to adopt a plausible 'disguise' (for example, a 'journalist' or 'writer') or whether to admit to being a researcher.

Selection of informants is an issue to be addressed by the participant observer in the same way that sampling must be considered by the survey researcher. The members of the study group who are most friendly and talkative may be the easiest to communicate with, but may give a biased picture of the views and behaviour of the group.

In addition there are practical problems to be faced over how to record information. When the researcher's identity has not been revealed, the taking of notes or the use of a tape-recorder may be impossible. Even when the researcher has identified her or himself as such, or has assumed a plausible 'identity', the use of such devices may interfere with the sort of natural relationship which the researcher is trying to establish. The question of the researcher's relationship with informants also raises ethical questions, which are discussed in Chapter 11.

Recording of information can present problems, especially if the researcher is *incognito*, or simply wishes to avoid introducing the distancing and inhibitions which the presence of a notebook may entail. The taking of regular and detailed notes is, however, the basic data-recording method. This may be supplemented by photographs and even video and tape-recordings in some instances.

Analysis

Since the researcher is also the front-line data gatherer and recorder, the process of analysis is an ongoing process. The researcher must constantly be relating what she or he sees to the objectives of the study, and drawing interim conclusions. The very act of deciding what to view, what to say and what to record involves choices, which will be influenced by the researcher's evolving understanding of the phenomenon being studied. This iterative process results in what Glaser and Strauss (1967) termed *grounded theory*. The process is a complex and personal one, as described in Strauss's *Qualitative Analysis for Social Scientists* (1987).

ETHNOGRAPHY

The ethnographic style of research is not one technique but an approach drawing on a variety of techniques. Generally, as applied to leisure and tourism research, it seeks to see the world through the eyes of those being researched, allowing them to speak for themselves, often through extensive direct quotations in the research report. Often also, the aim is to debunk conventional, establishment, 'common-sense' views of 'social problems', 'deviants', sexual and ethnic stereotypes and so on. In leisure studies the approach has become particularly associated with 'cultural studies', for example of youth sub-cultures and ethnic groups.

140

It is better to read the results of the research than to read about the methodology *per se*. Examples are Griffin *et al.* (1982) on women and leisure, Hollands (1985) on unemployed youth and Hall and Jefferson (1976) on youth sub-cultures.

ANALYSING TEXTS

The analysis of texts, such as plays and novels, is the very basis of some disciplines in the humanities, such as English, media studies and cultural studies. As researchers from these disciplines have turned their attention to leisure and tourism issues, and as the relationships between leisure, tourism and 'cultural products' have become recognised, the approach is playing an increasingly important role in leisure and tourism research. The term *text* is now used to embrace not just printed material, but also pictures, recorded music, film and television. Indeed, virtually any cultural product can, in the jargon, be *read* as *text*. The trend is reflected in the increasing use of the term *gaze* to describe the activity of both leisure and tourism researchers and the subjects of their research. John Urry, in his book *The Tourist Gaze* (1990), states the following.

> Tourism research should involve the examination of texts, not only written texts but also maps, landscapes, paintings, films, townscapes, TV programmes, brochures, and so on. ... Thus, social research significantly consists of interpreting texts, through various mainly qualitative techniques, to identify the discursive structures which give rise to and sustain, albeit temporarily, a given tourist site. (Urry, 1994, pp. 238–9)

It is not proposed to outline analysis techniques in detail here, since approaches are very varied, including the qualitative, literary 'reading' of texts, the *interpretation* of texts sometimes referred to as *hermeneutics* and the highly quantified form of analysis known as *content analysis*. The approach here is, rather, to introduce the readers to some examples of work in this area.

Novels and other literature

Sönmez *et al.* (1993) examine the concept of leisure as portrayed in the novels of Kenyan author Ngugi wa Thiong'o. The analysis provides a perspective on a non-western view of leisure and its place in a culture faced with the upheaval of the colonial and post-colonial experience. In two papers, Hultsman and Harper (1992, and Harper and Hultsman, 1992) analyse a collection of 1930s essays on life in the 'Old South' of the USA to reveal new insights into leisure and class at that time. One chapter in Paul Barry's (1994, pp. 414–44) biography of Kerry Packer provides a fascinating insight into one, very rich, man's approach to 'serious leisure' (Stebbins, 1992) – in this case polo. This illustrates the value of biographies as a source of material on leisure.

Media coverage

Media coverage of selected topics can be studied quantitatively by measuring the column centimetres devoted to the topic in newspapers or the time devoted to the topic on television. Examples are the studies by Brown (1995) and Rowe and Brown (1994) of press coverage of women's sport in Australian newspapers and Toohey's (1990) analysis of the television coverage of the Seoul Olympic Games. The study by Cuneen *et al.* (1989) involves an analysis of the verbal and pictorial press coverage of a sporting event.

Film

MacCannell (1993) provides an extensive analysis of the tourist film *Cannibal Tours*, upon which he builds a detailed theoretical interpretation of the role of tourism in the modern world. Rojek (1993) provides an analysis of Disney films and their role in contemporary culture, in his paper 'Disney culture'.

Material culture

In his paper on 'The interpretation of documents and material culture', Hodder (1994) devotes relatively little space to documents, but concentrates on the idea of studying 'material culture' or artefacts. Among the latter he includes dress fashions, national flags and the archaeological study of garbage. The scope for the direct study of leisure-related cultural products is enormous. Among examples in the research literature are the study of the theme parks of the Disney Corporation (Rojek, 1993; Klugman *et al.*, 1995), postcards (Cohen, 1993), American musicals (Dyer, 1993) and heavy metal rock music (Straw, 1993).

QUESTIONS AND EXERCISES

1 Select an example of a quantitative and a qualitative research report from a recent edition of one of the leisure or tourism journals and consider whether the qualitative research project could have been approached using quantitative methods and whether the quantitative project could have been approached using qualitative methods.

2 On the basis of exercise 3 in Chapter 3, or one of the case studies in Chapter 3, suggest a group of people who might be studied using in-depth interviews, and devise an interview checklist for such an interview.

3 Use the checklist in Appendix 8.1 to interview a willing friend or colleague. Assess your performance as an interviewer.

4 If you are studying with others, organise yourselves into groups of five or six and organise a focus group interview, with one person as facilitator, choosing a topic of mutual interest, such as 'the role of education and qualifications in the leisure/tourism industries' or 'holiday choice processes' or 'fitness versus sport'. Take turns in acting as convenor and assess each other's skills as convenor.

5 Using the issues of a newspaper for one week, provide a qualitative and quantitative analysis of the coverage of a topic of interest, such as: the environment, ethnic minorities, women and sport or overseas locations.

6 Arrange to view a copy of *Cannibal Tours* and discuss the film in the light of MacCannell's (1993) essay on the film. Or, view any Disney cartoon film and discuss it in relation to Rojek's (1993) paper.

FURTHER READING

On qualitative methods generally, *see*: Lofland and Lofland (1984); Burgess (1982); Denzin (1989); Denzin and Lincoln (1994); Silverman (1993); Barton and Lazarsfield (1969).

On qualitative methods in relation to leisure, *see*: Henderson (1990, 1991); Godbey and Scott (1990); Kelly (1980); Kamphorst, Tibori and Giljam (1984). For examples in leisure studies, *see*: Cuneen *et al.* (1988); Griffin *et al.* (1982); Hollands (1985); Marsh *et al.* (1978); Walker (1988); Wynne (1986).

In relation to tourism, *see*: Cohen (1988); Peterson (1994).

On informal and in-depth interviews, *see*: Moeller *et al.* (1980a); Rapoport and Rapoport (1975).

On participant observation, *see*: Campbell (1970); Glancy (1986).

On focus groups, *see*: Calder (1977); Krueger (1988); Reynolds and Johnson (1978); Stewart and Shamdasani (1990); Morgan (1993).

On grounded theory, *see*: Glaser and Strauss (1967); Strauss (1987); Strauss and Corbin (1994).

On the link between media studies and leisure studies, *see*: Critcher (1992).

APPENDIX 8.1
EXAMPLE OF A CHECKLIST FOR IN-DEPTH INTERVIEWING

This is part of a checklist devised in connection with a study of people's use of leisure time and attitudes towards leisure.

Current activities: explore each one – compare	How often? Why? Where?　　home /away from home Who with? Meaning/importance Type of involvement
Activities would *like* to do	Why not?
Meaning of 'leisure' to you	
Constraints:	Home Work (time/energy/colleagues) Family roles Being a woman/man Being a parent Money/costs Car/transport
Past activities Why changes?	School College/university Family
Facilities	Locally　　Favourite City　　Use/non-use　　Why? Region　　Access
Clubs/associations	
Personality	
Skills	
Dislikes	Aspirations

CHAPTER 9

Questionnaire surveys

INTRODUCTION: ROLES AND LIMITATIONS

This chapter presents an overview of the range of types of questionnaire survey. Questionnaire surveys involve the gathering of information from individuals using a formally designed schedule of questions called a *questionnaire* or *interview schedule*. The technique is arguably the most commonly used in leisure and tourism research.

Questionnaire surveys usually involve only a proportion, or *sample*, of the population in which the researcher is interested. For example the national surveys discussed in Chapter 6 are based on samples of only a few thousand to represent tens of millions of people. How such samples are chosen, how the size of the sample is decided and the implications of relying on a sample to represent a population, are issues that are discussed in Chapter 12.

Questionnaire surveys rely on information from respondents. What respondents say depends on their own powers of recall, on their honesty and, fundamentally, on the format of the questions included in the questionnaire. There has been very little research on the validity or accuracy of questionnaire data in leisure and tourism studies. However, some research has suggested that respondents exaggerate levels of participation, at least in some activities (*see* Chase and Godbey, 1983; Chase and Harada, 1984; Bachman and O'Malley, 1981). It has been suggested that interviewees are affected by the desire to be helpful and friendly towards the interviewer, so that, for example, if the interview is about sport or the arts, respondents will tend to exaggerate their interest in and involvement with sport or the arts, just to be helpful and positive. Clarke and Critcher (1985) warn against attempts to assess complex concepts such as job satisfaction using over-simplified, leading questions in questionnaires. The conclusion of their discussion does not follow clearly from their argument since it shifts from the study of attitudes to the measurement of activities, but it is nevertheless worthy of repeating.

> There is always a gap between what people say and what they actually do and no study of work or leisure can afford to take what people say at face value, especially when the answers are contained in the questions (Clarke and Critcher, 1985, p. 27).

This warns against poor questionnaire design but also suggests that the researcher and the user of research results should always bear in mind the nature and source of the data and not fall into the trap of believing that, because information is presented in numerical form and is based on large numbers, it represents immutable 'truth'.

Questionnaire surveys usually involve substantial numbers of 'subjects' (the people being surveyed), ranging from perhaps 50 or 60 to many thousands. This, together with the complexity of some forms of quantitative analysis, means that computers are invariably used to analyse the results. The practical implications of this are considered in Chapter 10, which deals with questionnaire design.

Following a discussion of the merits of questionnaire methods and of completion by interviewer or respondent, this chapter discusses, in turn, the household questionnaire survey, the street survey, the telephone survey, the postal or mail survey, user or site surveys, and captive group surveys.

MERITS OF QUESTIONNAIRE SURVEYS

Compared with the qualitative techniques discussed in Chapter 8, questionnaire surveys usually involve quantification – the presentation of results in numerical terms. This has implications for the way the data are collected, analysed and interpreted. In Chapter 8 a list of merits of qualitative methods, as put forward by Kelly, was presented. The merits of questionnaire surveys can be similarly examined. Some of the qualities of questionnaire surveys which make them useful in leisure and tourism research are set out below.

1 Contemporary leisure and tourism are often mass phenomena, requiring major involvement from governmental, non-profit and commercial organisations, which rely on quantified information for significant aspects of their decision-making. Questionnaire surveys are an ideal means of providing some of this information.
2 While absolute 'objectivity' is impossible, questionnaire methods provide a 'transparent' set of research procedures. Just how information was collected and how it was analysed or interpreted is clear for all to see. Indeed, data from questionnaire surveys can often be re-analysed by others if they wish to extend the research or provide an alternative interpretation.
3 Quantification can provide relatively complex information in a succinct, easily understood form.
4 Methods such as longitudinal surveys and annually repeated surveys provide the opportunity to study change over time, using comparable methodology.
5 Leisure and tourism encompass a wide range of activities, with a range of characteristics, such as frequency, duration and type of participation, expenditure, location, level of enjoyment. Questionnaires are a good means of ensuring that a complete picture of a person's patterns of participation is obtained.
6 While qualitative methods are ideal for exploring attitudes, meanings and perceptions on an individual basis, questionnaire methods provide the means to gather and record simple information on the incidence of attitudes, meanings and perceptions among the population as a whole.

Comparison of this list and the one referring to qualitative methods at the beginning of Chapter 8 reinforces the view that each method has its merits and appropriate uses – the 'horses for courses' idea. Questionnaire surveys have a role to play when the research questions indicate the need for fairly structured data and generally when data are required from samples which are explicitly representative of a defined wider population. Examples of the role of questionnaire surveys as compared with other methods are shown in Figure 9.1.

INTERVIEWER COMPLETION OR RESPONDENT COMPLETION?

Questionnaire surveys can be either interviewer-completed or respondent-completed. When completed by the interviewer, the questionnaire provides the *script* for an interview; an interviewer reads the questions out to the respondent and records the respondent's answers on the questionnaire. When the questionnaire is completed by the respondent, respondents read and fill out the questionnaire themselves. Each approach has its particular advantages and disadvantages, as summarised in Figure 9.2.

Interviewer completion is more expensive in terms of interviewers' time (which usually has to be paid for) but the use of an interviewer usually ensures a more accurate and complete response. Respondent completion can be cheaper and quicker but often results in low response rates, which can introduce bias in the results because the people who choose not to respond or are unable to respond, perhaps because of language or literacy difficulties, may differ from those who do respond. When designing a questionnaire for respondent completion, greater care must be taken with layout and presentation since it must be read and completed by 'untrained' people. In terms of design, respondent-completion questionnaires should ideally consist primarily of 'closed' questions – that is questions which can be answered by ticking boxes. 'Open-ended' questions – where respondents have to write out their answers – should be avoided, since they invariably achieve only a low response. For example, in an interview, respondents will often give expansive answers to questions such as: 'Do you have any comments to make on the overall management of this facility?' But they will not as readily write down such answers in a respondent-completion questionnaire.

There may, however, be cases when respondent completion is to be preferred, or is the only practicable approach – for example when the people to be surveyed are widely scattered geographically, which would make face-to-face interviews impossibly expensive and a postal survey an obvious choice, or when it is felt that, on sensitive matters, respondents might prefer the anonymity of the respondent-completed questionnaire. Some of the issues connected with respondent-completion questionnaires are discussed more fully in the section on postal surveys.

Figure 9.1   The use of questionnaire surveys versus other methods – examples

Organisation	Topic	Questionnaire survey	Qualitative methods	Other methods
Political party	Voting intentions of electors	• Party's current level of support *vis-à-vis* other parties – telephone survey	• Concerns and attitudes of different types of voter – focus groups	• Past voting patterns; previous election voting returns • Overall characteristics of electors in different seats; census data
Leisure facility management	How to increase number of visitors	• Information on what types of people use which services and when – user survey • Information on socio-demographic characteristics of users vs non-users and perceptions of facility – community survey	• The experience of visiting the facility; quality, atmosphere, service – observation and/or focus groups	• Information on relative popularity of different activities/services – ticket sales and utilisation data
Tourism Commission	Data for Tourism Strategic Plan	• Accommodation used, sites visited, expenditure patterns and socio-demographic characteristics of visitors from different places	• Quality of visitor experience – in-depth interviews or focus groups with visitors • Resident attitudes towards tourists and tourist development – focus groups	• Arrival and departure data (if national study)
Individual researcher	The role of the holiday in leisure (Case study 3.2)	• Socio-demographic characteristics and numbers of those who do and do not take holidays – measures of income, health and attitudes	• Meanings and importance of holidays and local leisure in individuals' lifestyle – in-depth interviews	–

Figure 9.2   Interviewer versus respondent completion

	Interviewer completion	Respondent completion
Advantages	More accuracy Higher response rates Fuller and more complete answers Design can be less 'user-friendly'	Cheaper Quicker Relatively anonymous
Disadvantages	Higher cost Less anonymity	Patchy response Incomplete response Risk of frivolous responses More care needed in design

TYPES OF QUESTIONNAIRE SURVEY

Questionnaire surveys in the leisure and tourism field can be divided into six types:

- *Household survey*: people are selected on the basis of where they live and are interviewed in their home.
- *Street survey*: people are selected by stopping them in street, in shopping malls, etc.
- *Telephone survey*: interviews are conducted by telephone.
- *Mail survey*: questionnaires are sent and returned by mail.
- *Site or user survey*: users of a leisure or tourism facility or site are surveyed on-site.
- *Captive group survey*: members of groups such as classes of school children, members of a club or employees of an organisation are surveyed.

Each of these is discussed in more detail below and some of their basic characteristics are summarised in Figure 9.3.

Figure 9.3   Types of questionnaire survey – characteristics

Type	Self or interviewer completion	Cost	Sample	Possible length of questionnaire	Response rate
Household	Either	Expensive	Whole population	Long	High
Street	Interviewer	Medium	Most of population	Short	Medium
Telephone	Interviewer	Medium	People with telephone	Short	High
Mail	Respondent	Cheap	General or special	Varies	Low
On-site	Either	Medium	Users only	Medium	High
Captive	Respondent	Cheap	Group only	Medium	High

THE HOUSEHOLD QUESTIONNAIRE SURVEY

Nature

Much of the quantified data in the field of leisure and tourism derive from household questionnaire surveys. While academics draw on the data extensively, the majority of such surveys are commissioned by government and commercial leisure and tourism organisations for policy or marketing purposes. The advantage of such household surveys is that they are generally representative of the community, as the samples drawn tend to include all age groups, above a certain minimum, and all occupational groups. They also generally represent a complete geographical area, whether that be a country, a region, a local government area or a neighbourhood. Household surveys are therefore designed to provide information on the reported leisure or tourism behaviour of the community as a whole.

While some household leisure or tourism surveys are specialised, many are broad ranging in their coverage. That is, they tend to ask, among other things, about participation in a wide range of leisure activities, holiday-taking patterns or buying habits. This facilitates exploration of a wide range of issues which other types of survey cannot so readily tackle.

Conduct

Normally household questionnaire surveys are completed by the interviewer but it is possible for questionnaires to be left at the respondent's home for completion by the respondent and later collection. The fieldworker then has the responsibility of checking that questionnaires have been fully completed and perhaps conducting an interview in those situations where respondents have been unable to fill in the questionnaire, because they have been too busy, have forgotten, have lost the questionnaire, or because of literacy or language problems or infirmity.

Being home based this sort of survey can involve quite lengthy questionnaires and interviews. By contrast, in the street, at a leisure or tourism facility, or over the telephone, it can be difficult to conduct a lengthy interview. Leisure participation surveys in particular, with their huge range of possible activities, often involve a very complex questionnaire which is difficult to administer 'on the run'. With the home-based interview it is usually possible to pursue issues at greater length. An interview of three-quarters of an hour in duration is not out of the question and 20–30 minutes is quite common.

A variation on the standard household questionnaire interview survey is to combine interviewer-completed and respondent-completed elements. This often happens with leisure surveys: the interviewer conducts an interview with one member of the household about the household – how many people live there, whether the dwelling is owned or rented, perhaps information on recreational equipment, or anything to do with the household as a whole. Then an individual questionnaire is left for each member of the household to complete, concerning their own leisure behaviour. The interviewer calls back later to collect these individual questionnaires.

The potential length of interviews, the problems of contacting representative samples and, on occasions, the wide geographical spread of the study area, mean that household surveys are usually the most expensive to conduct, per interview. Costs of the order of £15 or £20 per interview are typical, depending on the amount of analysis included in the price. When samples of several thousands are involved, it can be seen that the costs can be substantial.

Omnibus surveys

While considering household surveys mention should be made of the *omnibus* survey. Omnibus surveys are single surveys conducted by a market research or survey organisation for several clients who each contribute their own particular questions to the questionnaire. In an omnibus survey the main costs of the survey, which lie in sampling and contacting respondents, are shared by a number of clients. In addition, in an omnibus survey the cost of collecting fairly standard demographic and socio-economic information – such as age, gender, family structure, occupation and income – is shared among the clients. With regular omnibus surveys many of the procedures, such as sampling and data processing, have become a matter of routine, and interviewers are in place throughout the country already trained and familiar with the type of questionnaire and the requirements of the market research company; these factors can reduce costs significantly.

The British *General Household Survey* is an omnibus survey of 20 000 people run by the government Office of Population Censuses and Surveys, the clients being government departments and agencies. In the years when leisure questions are included, the clients for those questions are the various national leisure and recreation agencies, such as the Sports Council and the Countryside Commission. In Australia the national *Recreation Participation Survey* and the annual *Domestic Tourism Monitor* use a commercially run omnibus survey, the AGB:McNair *Market Monitor*.

THE STREET SURVEY

Nature

The street survey involves a relatively short questionnaire and is conducted, as the name implies, on the street – usually a shopping street or tourist area – or in squares or shopping centres, where a cross-section of the community, or of visitors to an area, might be expected to be found.

Conduct

Stopping people in such environments for an interview places certain limitations on the interview process. First, an interview conducted in the street cannot generally be as long as one conducted at someone's home – especially when the interviewee is in a hurry. Of course there are some household interviews which are very short because the interviewee is in a hurry or is a reluctant respondent and there are street interviews which are lengthy because the respondent has plenty of time. As a general rule, however, the street interview must be shorter. In both the home and street interview situation, before committing themselves to an interview, potential respondents often ask 'How long will it take?' In the home-based situation a reply of '15–20 minutes' is generally acceptable but in the street situation anything more than 'five minutes' would generally lead to a marked reduction in the proportion of people prepared to co-operate. The range of topics, issues and activities which can be covered in a street interview is therefore restricted and this must be taken into account in designing the questionnaire.

The second limitation of the street survey is the problem of contacting a representative sample of the population. Certain types of people might not frequent shopping areas at all, or only infrequently – for instance people who are housebound for various reasons or people who have other people to do their shopping. Some types of tourist – for example business tourists or those visiting friends or relatives – may not be found in the popular tourist areas. Such individuals might be of particular importance in some leisure and tourism research, so their omission can significantly compromise the results. There is little that can be done to overcome this limitation; it has to be accepted as a limitation of the method. The other side of this coin is that certain groups will be over-represented in shopping streets – notably full-time home/child carers, the retired and the unemployed in suburban shopping areas, or office workers in business areas. It might also be the case that certain areas are frequented more by, for example, young people than old people or by men rather than women, so any sample would be representative of the users of the area, but not of the local population or visitor population as a whole.

Quota sampling

The means used to attempt to overcome the problem of unrepresentative samples is the technique of *quota sampling* in which the interviewer is given a 'quota' of different types of people – by age, gender, occupation, etc. – to interview. The proportions in each category are determined by reference to the census or other appropriate information sources. When the survey is complete, if the sample is still not representative with regard to the key characteristics, further adjustments can be achieved through the process of *weighting*, discussed in Chapter 12.

THE TELEPHONE SURVEY

Nature

The telephone survey is particularly popular with political pollsters because of its speed and the ease with which a widespread sample of the community can be contacted. It is also used extensively in market and academic research for the same reasons.

An obvious limitation of the technique is that it excludes non-telephone subscribers – generally low income groups and some mobile sections of the population. With telephones in the great majority of homes in developed countries this is not now as serious a problem as it was in the past. In fairly simple surveys like political opinion polls, where the researcher has access to previous survey results using telephone and face-to-face interviews, this problem may be overcome by the use of a correction factor. For instance it might be known that non-telephone subscribers always add x per cent to the Labour vote. In certain kinds of market research the absence of the poorer parts of the community from the survey may be unimportant because they do not form a significant part of the market. For much public policy and academic research however, this can be a significant limitation.

Conduct

Length of interview can be a limitation of telephone surveys, but not as serious as in the case of street interviews; telephone interviews of 10 or 15 minutes are acceptable.

The technique has its own unique set of problems in relation to sampling. Generally the numbers to be called are selected at random from the telephone directory. Many market research companies have equipment which will automatically dial random telephone numbers as required. If a representative cross-section of the community is to be included then it is necessary for this type of interviewing to be done in the evening and/or at weekends if those who have paid jobs away from the home or who are in full-time education are to be included.

A further limitation of the telephone interview is that respondents cannot be shown such things as lists. This is particularly relevant to leisure and tourism surveys. In leisure participation surveys respondents are frequently shown lists of activities and asked if they have participated in them. Such lists can include 20 or 30 items, which could be tedious to read out over the telephone. Similarly in tourism studies respondents may be shown a list of places and asked which they have visited. Surveys which involve long checklists – for example of attitude dimensions – are also not easily conducted by telephone.

It can be argued that telephones have an advantage over face-to-face interviews in that respondents may feel that they are more anonymous and may therefore be more forthcoming in their opinions. But it could also be argued that the face-to-face interview has other advantages in terms of eye contact and body language which enable the skilled interviewer to conduct a better interview than is possible over the telephone.

The main advantage of the telephone survey is that it is quick and relatively cheap to conduct. A further advantage is that, because the interviewer is office based, arrangements can be made for the interviewer to key answers directly into a computer, so dispensing with the printed questionnaire. This speeds up the analysis process considerably and cuts down the possibility of error in transcribing results from questionnaire to computer. It explains how the results of overnight political opinion polls can be published in the newspapers the next morning.

THE MAIL SURVEY

Nature

There are certain situations where the mail or postal method is the only practical survey technique to use. The commonest example is where members or customers of some national organisation are to be surveyed. The costs of conducting face-to-face interviews with even a sample of the members or customers would be substantial, so a mail survey is the obvious answer. The mail survey has the advantage that a large sample can be included. In the case of a membership organisation, there may be advantages in surveying the whole membership, even though this may not be necessary in statistical terms. It can however be very helpful in terms of the internal politics of the organisation for all members to be given the opportunity to participate in the survey and to 'have their say'.

The problem of response rates

The most notorious problem of postal surveys is low response rates. In many cases as few as 25 or 30 per cent of those sent a questionnaire bother to reply. There are even notorious instances, for example in community surveys on local government planning strategies, of only three or four per cent response rates. Surveys with only 30 per cent response rates are regularly reported in the research literature, but questions must be raised as to their validity when 70 per cent of the target sample is not represented.

What affects the response rate? Seven different factors can be identified, as listed in Figure 9.4. These factors and ways of dealing with them are discussed in Chapter 11.

THE USER OR SITE SURVEY

Nature

The terms *on-site*, *site*, *user* or *visitor* survey are used to refer to this type of survey. *On-site* and *site survey* tend to be used in the context of outdoor

Figure 9.4   Factors affecting mail survey responses

1   The interest of the respondent in the survey topic

2   The length of the questionnaire

3   Questionnaire design/presentation/complexity

4   The style, content and authorship of the accompanying letter

5   The provision of a postage-paid reply envelope

6   Rewards for responding

7   The number and timing of reminders/follow-ups

recreation studies, *user survey* in the context of indoor recreation facilities, and *visitor survey* when tourists or daytrippers are involved, or types of facility where visits are relatively infrequent, such as museums or zoos. A fourth term, *audience survey*, is used in the arts environment, for example for surveys of theatre audiences. The term user survey is utilised in this chapter to cover all these situations.

The user survey is the most common type of survey used by managers in leisure and tourism. Surveys of tourists and local users are carried out at recreation or leisure facilities and surveys of tourists are carried out at hotels and *en route* on various types of transport, particularly international air trips. General surveys of visitors to a tourist area often take the form of street surveys. Visitors are interviewed in the street, in squares or plazas or in seafront areas – anywhere where tourists are known to congregate. In this case the 'facility' is the tourist town or area, so the 'street survey' and the 'site survey' overlap and consideration must be given to the features of both types of survey. In general the site survey is more controlled than the street survey; interviewers are seen by respondents to be part of the management of the facility and usually it is possible to interview users at a convenient time when they are not 'in a rush', as they may be in the street or shopping mall.

Conduct

User surveys can be conducted by interviewer or by respondent completion. Unless carefully supervised, respondent-completion methods can lead to a poor standard in the completion of questionnaires and a low response level. And as with all low response levels this can be a source of serious bias in that those who reply may be unrepresentative of the users or visitors as a whole.

The usual respondent-completion survey involves handing users a questionnaire on their arrival at the site and collecting them on their departure, or conducting the whole procedure upon departure. Where respondent completion is thought to be desirable or necessary then sufficient staff should be employed to check all users leaving the site, to ask for the completed questionnaires, to provide replacements for questionnaires which have been mislaid, and to assist in completing questionnaires, including completion by interview if necessary.

Conducting user surveys by interview is generally preferable to respondent completion for the reasons discussed earlier in this chapter. The use of interviewers obviously has a cost disadvantage but, depending on the length of the interview, costs per interview are usually comparatively low. Typically a user-survey interview will take about five minutes. Given the need to check through completed questionnaires, the gaps in user traffic and the need for interviewers to take breaks, it is reasonable to expect interviewers in such situations to complete about six interviews in an hour. Such estimates are of course necessary when considering project budgets and timetables.

The survey methods considered so far have been fairly multi-purpose; they could be used for market research for a range of products or services, by public agencies for a variety of policy orientated purposes, or for academic research. User surveys are more specific. While academics conduct user surveys as a convenient way of gathering data on particular leisure or tourism activities, the more usual use of such surveys is for policy, planning or management purposes. User surveys are the type of survey which readers of this book are most likely to be involved with; they are the most convenient for students to 'cut their teeth' on, and they are the most common surveys for individual managers to become involved in. For these reasons the roles of user surveys are considered in some detail below.

The uses of user surveys

What can user surveys be used for? The most obvious use is to provide direct feedback to management on a range of issues, including the following.

Catchment area

What is the *catchment* or *market* area of the facility or service? That is, what geographical area do most of the users come from? This can be important in terms of advertising policy. Management can concentrate on their existing catchment area and focus advertising and marketing accordingly or they can take conscious decisions to use marketing to attempt to extend the catchment area. But in order to do this it is necessary to establish the catchment area. In some cases this information is already available from membership records, but in many cases it can only be discovered by means of a survey.

User profile

What is the socio-economic or demographic profile of the users? It might be thought that a management capable of observation would be able to make this assessment without the need for a survey. This depends on the type of facility, the extent to which management is in continuous contact with users and the variability of the user profile. For example, a restaurant, hotel or resort manager might be very well informed on this but managers of beaches, urban parks, national or state parks or theatres might, for various reasons, be less well informed, or even misinformed.

Profile information can be used in a number of ways. It can be used, in the same way as the data on catchment area, to concentrate or extend the market. Very often the commercial operator will opt to concentrate – to focus on a particular client group and maximise the market share of that group. In the case of a public sector facility the remit is usually to attract as wide a cross-section of the community as possible, so the data would be used to highlight those sections of the community not being catered for and therefore requiring marketing attention.

User opinions

What are the opinions of users? These data are invariably collected in user surveys and are usually of great interest to managers, but the interpretation of such data is not without its difficulties (Veal, 1988). If management are looking for pertinent criticisms current users may be the wrong group to consult. Those who are most critical are likely no longer to be using the facility. Those using the facility may be reluctant to be very critical because it undermines their own situation – if the place is so poor why are they there? Those who are prepared to be critical may not be the sorts of clients for whom the facility is designed. As Lucas has said:

> It seems misleading to give equal weight to evaluations by people who are seeking a different type of area or experience. By analogy, a Chinese restaurant would do well to ignore the opinion about the food by someone who ate there by mistake while seeking an Italian restaurant. (Lucas, 1970, p. 5)

In some situations people have little choice between facilities so criticisms are perhaps more easily interpreted. For example, parents' comments about the suitability of a local park for children's play can be particularly pertinent when it is the only play area available in the neighbourhood.

When opinion data have been collected it is often difficult to know precisely what to do with the results. Very often the largest group of users has no complaint or suggestion to make, either because they cannot be bothered to think of anything in the interview situation or because of the 'respondent selection' process referred to above. Often the most common complaint is raised by as few as 10 per cent of users. If this is the most common complaint, then logically something ought to be done about it by the management. But it could also be said that 90 per cent of the users are not concerned about that issue, so perhaps there is no need to do anything about it! Very often, therefore, management can use survey results to suit their own needs. If they want to do something about X, they can say that X was complained about by more users than anything else: if they do not want to do anything about X they can say that 90 per cent of users are satisfied with X the way it is.

Managers mostly want to enhance and maximise the quality of the experience enjoyed by their visitors: it may not be criticism of specific features that is important but users' overall evaluation of the experience. Thus users can be asked to rate a facility or area using a scale such as: Very good/Good/Fair/Poor/Very poor or Very satisfied/Satisfied/Dissatisfied/Very dissatisfied. The results of such an evaluation can be used to compare users' evaluation of one facility with another – for example, in a system of parks. Or they could be used to examine the same facility at different times to see if satisfaction has increased or declined. This can be important in evaluation research of the sort discussed by Hatry and Dunn (1971) and discussed in Chapter 3.

Non-users

User surveys by definition involve only current users of a facility or current visitors to an area. This is often cited as a limitation of such surveys, the implication being that non-users may be of more interest than users if the aim of management is to increase the number of users or visitors. Caution should however be exercised in moving to consider conducting research on non-users. For a start the number of non-users or non-visitors is usually very large. For example, in a city of a million population, a facility which has 5000 users has 995 000 non-users! In a country with a population of 50 million, a tourist area which attracts a million visitors a year has 49 million non-visitors, and if management is interested in international visitors, they have around five billion non-visitors! The idea that all non-users are potential users, and should therefore be researched, is therefore somewhat naive.

The user survey can nevertheless assist in focusing any research which is to be conducted on non-users. For example, in the case of a local recreation facility, the user survey defines the catchment area and, unless there is some reason for believing that the catchment area can or should be extended, the non-users to be studied are those who live within that area. Similarly the user profile indicates the type of person currently using the facility, and again, unless there is a conscious decision to attempt to change that profile, the non-users to be studied are the ones with that profile living within the defined catchment area. Comparison between the user profile and the profile of the population of the catchment area, as revealed by census data, will indicate the numbers and characteristics of non-users in the area. Thus user surveys can reveal something about non-users!

CAPTIVE GROUP SURVEYS

Nature

The 'captive group' survey is not referred to in other research methods texts. It refers to the situation where the people to be included in the survey comprise the membership of some group where access can be negotiated *en bloc*. Such groups include school children, adult education groups, clubs of various kinds and groups of employees – although all have their various unique characteristics.

Conduct

A roomful of co-operative people can provide a number of respondent-completed questionnaires very quickly. Respondent completion is less problematic in 'captive' situations than in less controlled situations because it is possible to take the group through the questionnaire question by question and therefore ensure good standards of completion.

The most common example of a captive group is school children: the easiest way to contact children under school leaving age is via schools. The method may, however, appear simpler than it is in practice. Research on children for education purposes has become so common that education authorities are cautious about permitting access to children for surveys. Very often permission for any survey work must be obtained from the central education authority; the permission of the class teacher or head teacher is not sufficient.

The most economical use of this technique involves using a respondent-completed questionnaire, but interview methods can also be used. The essential feature is that access to members of the group is facilitated by their membership of that group and the fact that they are gathered together in one place at one time. It is important to be aware of the criteria for membership of the group and to compare that with the needs of the research. In some cases an apparent match can be misleading. For example attendees at a retired people's club meeting does not include all retired people, for example, 'non-joiners' and the housebound. While schools include all young people, care must be taken over their catchment areas, compared with the study area of the research, and with the mix of public and private schools.

QUESTIONS AND EXERCISES

What type of survey would you conduct for a sample of 500 of the following?

1 Tourists who are visiting a seaside resort.

2 Members of 'Greenpeace'.

3 The users of a theatre.

4 The users of a large urban park.

5 Overseas visitors to Great Britain.

6 People who do not play sport.

7 People who play sport.

8 People who rent videos.

9 People aged 14 and over living in the local council area.

10 Young people aged 11–13 living in the local council area.

FURTHER READING

See reading list for Chapter 6 for details of large-scale, national household surveys.

On surveys generally, *see*: Hudson (1988); Hoinville and Jowell (1978); Frank Small and Associates (1988); Marriott (1987); Veal (1988); Tourism and Recreation Research Unit (1983); Williamson *et al.* (1982); Ryan (1995).

On telephone surveys, *see*: Lavrakas (1993); Field (1972).

On mail surveys, *see*: Hoinville and Jowell (1978); Dillman (1978).

On visitor (user) surveys versus conversion (coupon) surveys in tourism, *see*: Perdue and Botkin (1988); Woodside and Ronkainen (1994).

CHAPTER 10

Questionnaire design

INTRODUCTION: RESEARCH PROBLEMS AND INFORMATION REQUIREMENTS

This chapter reviews in detail the factors which must be considered in designing questionnaires for leisure and tourism studies. First, the relationship between research problems and information requirements is examined. This is followed by consideration of the types of information typically included in leisure and tourism questionnaires, the wording of questions, the ordering and layout of questions, coding of questionnaires for computer analysis and the problem of validity. Finally some consideration is given to the special requirements of time-budget studies.

The important principle in designing questionnaires is to take it slowly and carefully and to remember why the research is being done. Very often researchers move too quickly into 'questionnaire design mode' and begin listing all the things 'it would be interesting to ask'. In many organisations a draft questionnaire is circulated for comment and everyone in the organisation joins in. The process begins to resemble Christmas tree decorating: nobody must be left out and everybody must be allowed to contribute their favourite bauble. This is not the best way to proceed!

The decision to conduct a questionnaire survey should itself be the culmination of a careful process of thought and discussion, involving consideration of all possible techniques, as discussed in Chapter 3. The concepts and variables involved, and the relationships to be investigated – possibly in the form of hypotheses, theories, models or evaluative frameworks – should be clear and should guide the questionnaire design process, as illustrated in Figure 10.1. It is not advisable to *begin* with a list of questions to be included in the

Figure 10.1 Questionnaire design process

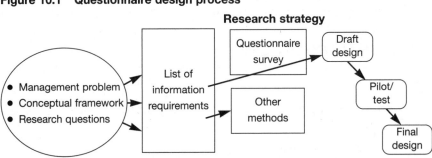

questionnaire. The starting point should be an examination of the management, planning, policy or theoretical questions to be addressed, and this should be followed by the drawing up of a list of information required to address the problems. This is outlined in Chapter 3 as elements 1–5 of the research process. Element 6, deciding the research strategy, involves determining which of the listed information requirements should be met by means of a questionnaire survey. Questions should be included in the questionnaire only if they relate to requirements listed in element 5. This means that every question included must be linked back to the *research questions*.

In designing a questionnaire, the researcher should of course have sought out as much previous research on the topic or related topics as possible. This can have an effect on the overall design of a project, as discussed in Chapter 3. More specifically, if it is decided that the study in hand should have points of comparison with other studies, then data will need to be collected on a similar basis. Questionnaires from previous studies therefore become part of the input into the questionnaire design process.

TYPES OF INFORMATION

Generally the information to be gathered from questionnaire surveys can be divided into three groups:

1 Respondent characteristics: Who?
2 Activities/behaviour: What?
3 Attitudes/motivations: Why?

Figure 10.2 lists some of the more common types of information collected under these three headings. The items covered are of course necessarily general in nature and do not cover all the specialised types of information which can be collected by questionnaire surveys. Some of these items of information require more intrusive questions than others – for example, income. And some can be difficult to ascertain accurately – for example, occupation or details of expenditure while on a tourist trip. They are not therefore all equally suitable for all survey situations.

The items of information discussed here are often referred to as *variables* – that is, they are characteristics or behaviour patterns which *vary* from one individual to another. The term variable is widely used in research generally and in particular in computer analysis of data, as discussed in later chapters.

WORDING OF QUESTIONS

Principles

In wording the questions for a questionnaire the researcher should:

- avoid jargon
- simplify wherever possible

Figure 10.2   Range of information in leisure and tourism questionnaires

Respondent characteristics

- Gender
- Age
- Economic status
- Occupation/social class
  (own or 'head of household')
- Previous employment history
- Income (own or household)
- Education/qualifications
- Marital/family status

- Household type/family size
- Life cycle
- Ethnic group/country of birth
- Residential location
- Mobility - driving licence, access
  to private transport
- Party/group size/type (site/visitor
  surveys)

Activities

(a) Site/visitor surveys

- Activities while on site or in the
  area
- Use of site attractions/facilities
- Frequency of visit
- Time spent on site
- Expenditure per head –
  amounts/purposes
- Travel-related information
- Trip origin (where travelled from)
- Trip purpose
- Home address
- Travel mode
- Travel time
- Accommodation type used

(b) Household surveys

- Leisure activities (including
  holidays) – what, where, how
  often, time spent, when, who
  with?
- Use of particular facilities/sites
- Travel mode to out-of-home leisure
- Expenditure patterns
- Past activities (personal leisure
  histories)
- Planned future activities

Attitude/motivation information – examples

(a) Site/visitor surveys

- Reasons for choice of site/area
- Meaning/importance/values
- Satisfaction/evaluation of
  experience or services
- Comments on facility
- Future intentions/hopes

(b) Household surveys

- Leisure/travel aspirations/needs
- Evaluation of services/facilities
  available
- Psychological meaning of activities/
  satisfactions
- Reactions to development/provision
  proposals
- Values – re environment etc.

- avoid ambiguity
- avoid leading questions
- ask only one question at a time (i.e. avoid multi-purpose questions)

Examples of good and bad practice in question wording are given in Figure 10.3.

Figure 10.3   Question wording: examples of good and bad practice

Principle	Bad example	Improved version
Use simple language	What is your frequency of utilisation of retail travel outlets?	How often do you use travel agents?
Avoid ambiguity	Do you play sport very often?	Have you played any of the following sports within the last four weeks? (present list)
Avoid leading questions	Are you against the extension of the airport?	What is your opinion on the extension of the airport? Are you for it, against it or not concerned?
Ask just one question at a time	Do you use the local arts centre, and if so what do you think of its facilities?	1 Do you use the local arts centre? Yes/No 2 What do you think of the facilities in the local arts centre?

Pre-coded versus open-ended questions

As illustrated in Figure 10.4, an *open-ended* question is one where the interviewer asks a question without any prompting of the range of answers to be expected, and writes down the respondent's reply verbatim. In a respondent-completed questionnaire a line or space is left for respondents to write their answers. A closed or pre-coded question is one where the respondent is offered a range of answers to choose from, either verbally or from a show card or, in the case of a respondent-completed questionnaire, having the range of answers set out in the questionnaire and (usually) being asked to tick boxes.

With an open-ended question there is no prior list of responses. With the closed/pre-coded question there is a list of responses which is shown to the respondent. A third possibility, in an interviewer-administered survey, is a combination of the two. Here the question is asked in an open-ended manner, but no card is shown to the respondent: the questionnaire includes a pre-coded list where the answer is recorded. If respondents answer 'other' it is usual to write in details of what the 'other' is.

The advantage of the open-ended question is that the respondent's answer is not unduly influenced by the interviewer or by the questionnaire wording and

Figure 10.4   Open-ended versus pre-coded questions – example

Open-ended
What is the main constraint on your ability to study?

_____

Pre-coded/closed
Which of the following (or items listed on the card) is the main constraint on your ability to study? (show card – if interviewer completed questionnaire)

(a) My job	☐₁
(b) Timetabling	☐₂
(c) Child care	☐₃
(d) Spouse/partner	☐₄
(e) Money	☐₅
(f) Energy	☐₆
(g) Other _____	☐₇

Card shown to respondent:

> (a) My job
> (b) Timetabling of course
> (c) Child care
> (d) Spouse/partner
> (e) Money
> (f) Energy
> (g) Other _____

the verbatim replies from respondents can provide a rich source of varied material which might have been hidden by categories on a pre-coded list. Figure 10.5 gives an example of the range of responses which can result from a single open-ended question.

Pre-coded groups are often used when asking respondents about quantified information, such as age, income, expenditure, because of convenience and to save any embarrassment respondents may have about divulging precise figures. There is, however, an advantage in using the open-ended approach for such data – obtaining actual figures rather than group codes. Recording the

Figure 10.5   Example of range of replies resulting from an open-ended question

Question: Do you have any complaints about this (beach/picnic) area?
(Site survey in a beachside national park with boating and camping. Number of responses in brackets)

Sand bars (22)
Parking (5)
Wild car driving (1)
Lack of beach area (1)
Too few shops (1)
Too few picnic tables (4)
No timber for barbecue (2)
Need more picnic space (3)
Need boat hire facilities (1)
Need active recreation facilities (1)
Litter/pollution (74)
Urban sprawl (1)
Need wharf fishing access (1)
Lack of info. on walking trails (1)
Not enough facilities (3)
Slow barbecues (2)
Uncontrolled camping (1)
Lack of or poor toilets (9)
Amenities too far from camp site (1)
Too much development (4)
(Speed) boats (44)
Need more trees for shade (1)
'Yobbos drinking beer on beach' (1)
Spear fishermen (1)
Water skiers (2)
Against nudism (3)
Loud music (1)
Dumped cars (1)
Traffic (1)
Poor roads (1)
Sand flies (1)
More barbecues (1)
Shells/oysters (1)
Need outdoor cafes (1)
Need more food places (1)
Water too shallow (1)

Uncontrolled boats (23)
Jet skis (39)
Surveys (1)
Should be kept for locals (1)
Seaweed (3)
Need showers (1)
Administration of national park (1)
Maintenance and policing of park (1)
Trucks on beach (2)
Anglers (1)
Crowds/tourists (26)
Having to pay entry fee (6)
Houses along waterfront (2)
Unpleasant smell (drain) (2)
Sales people (1)
Need electric barbecues (1)
Dogs (21)
No access to coast (1)
Park rangers not operating in interest
    of the public (1)
Behaviour of others (20)
Access – long indirect road (1)
Need more shops (2)
Navigation marks unclear (1)
Need more taps (1)
Need more swings (1)
No first-aid facilities (1)
Need powered caravan sites (1)
Allow dogs (1)
Private beach areas (1)
Lack of restaurant (1)
Need rain shelters (1)
Can't spear fish (1)
No road shoulders for cyclists (1)
Remove rocks from swim areas (1)
Dangerous boat ramp pollutant
    activities (1)

Source: Robertson and Veal, 1987.

actual number permits the flexible option of grouping categories in alternative ways when carrying out the analysis. It also enables *averages* and other measures to be calculated and facilitates a range of statistical analysis which is not possible with groups. The actual figure is therefore often more useful for analytic purposes.

Open-ended questions have two major disadvantages. First, the analysis of verbatim answers to qualitative questions for computer analysis is laborious and may result in a final set of categories which are of no more value than a well-constructed pre-coded list. In the case of the answers in Figure 10.5, for example, for detailed analysis it may be necessary to group the answers into, say, six groups – this would be time-consuming and would involve a certain amount of judgement in grouping individual answers, which can be a source of errors. This process is discussed in more detail under coding below.

The second disadvantage of the open-ended approach is that, in the case of respondent-completed questionnaires, response rates to such questions can be very low: people are often too lazy or too busy to write out free-form answers. When to use open-ended or closed questions is therefore a matter of judgement.

Common questions

In Case studies 10.1, 10.2 and 10.3 at the end of this chapter, examples are given of typical questions used in household, site and captive group surveys, with interviewer-completed and respondent-completed examples. Annotations in the margins indicate the type of question involved. The case studies cannot, of course, cover all situations, but they give a wide range of examples of questions and appropriate formats. Below are some comments on some of the more common questions used, beginning with a number of respondent characteristics.

Age

Any examination of leisure participation and tourism data will show the importance of age in differentiating leisure and tourism behaviour and attitudes; it is therefore one of the data items most commonly included in questionnaires. The main decision to be made is whether to use pre-coded groups or ask for respondents' actual age. The advantages and disadvantages of the two approaches are discussed above, under pre-coded versus open-ended questions. If using pre-coded groups, ensure that there are no overlapping age categories. For example, if the following categories were used it would not be clear into which group a 14-year-old respondent would fall.

A   0–14

B   14–19

Note that, to ensure comparability with census data, age groups should be specified as: 15–19, 20–24, 25–29, etc., *not* 16–20, 21–25, 26–30, etc.

Economic status, occupation, socio-economic group or class

A person's economic and occupational situation clearly impinges on leisure and tourism behaviour. Information on such matters is important for marketing and planning and also in relation to public policy concerns with equity. Economic status is a person's situation *vis-à-vis* the formal economy, as listed in Figure 10.6. In contemporary developed economies, only about half the population is engaged in the paid work-force.

Occupation is generally used to denote a person's type of paid work, so it is generally asked only of those identified from the economic status question as being in paid work. Others are sometimes asked what their last paid job was or what the occupation of the 'main breadwinner' of the household is. Such questions can, however become complex because of full-time students living with parents or independently, single parents living on social security and so

Figure 10.6   Economic status, occupational and socio-economic groupings

Economic status

- In full-time paid work
- In part-time paid work
- Full-time home or child care
- In full-time education
- Retired
- Unemployed or looking for paid employment
- Other

Market research occupation/SEG classification

AB   Managerial, administrative, professional (at senior or intermediate level)
C1   Supervisory or clerical (i.e. white collar) and junior managerial, administrative or professional
C2   Skilled manual
DE   Semi-skilled, unskilled and casual workers and those entirely dependent on state pensions

Census occupation/SEG classification

- Professional
- Employers, managers
- Other self-employed
- Skilled workers and foremen
- Non-manual
- Service, semi-skilled and agricultural
- Armed forces
- Unskilled

on. In a household survey it may be possible to pursue these matters, but in other situations, such as site surveys, it may not be appropriate because it would seem too intrusive. For those in paid work the sorts of question asked are:

- What is your occupation?
- What sort of work do you do?
- Which of the groups on this card best describes your occupation?

Sufficient information should be obtained to enable respondents to be classified into an appropriate occupational category. Market researchers and official bodies, such as OPCS, tend to use slightly different classifications, as shown in Figure 10.6. Such groupings, along with economic status, are often referred to as a person's *socio-economic group* or SEG. This is closely related to the idea of *class* or social class. Space does not permit a discussion of this complex concept here, but sources are given in the list of Further Reading at the end of the chapter.

Because people can be vague in response to an open-ended question on occupation it is wise to include a supplementary question to draw out a full description. For example 'office worker', 'engineer' or 'self-employed' are not adequate answers because they can cover such a wide variety of grades of occupation. A supplementary question could be: 'What sort of work is that?' In a household survey it may be possible to ask additional questions to be absolutely sure of the respondent's occupation. Such questions would check on the industry involved and the number of staff supervised by the respondent (Hoinville and Jowell, 1978, p. 172).

Income

A typical wording of a question on income would be:

- What is your own personal gross income from all sources before taxes? or
- Which of the groups on the card does your own personal gross income from all sources fall into?

Gross income is normally asked for, since it can be too complicated to gather information on income net of taxes and other deductions. Since there is often a major difference between gross and net income, this makes the variable a somewhat imprecise one. A further problem with income as a variable is that personal income is not a particularly useful variable for those who are not income recipients or who are not the main income recipients of the household. This can be overcome if all members of the household are being interviewed or if the respondent is asked about the 'main income earner' in the household. However, many teenage children, for example, do not know their parents' income and it might be seen as improper to ask them. Income is a sensitive issue and, in view of the limitations discussed above, is often excluded in site or visitor surveys.

Marital status

Since legal marital status fails to indicate the domestic situation of increasing numbers of people, the usefulness of this variable is declining. In terms of leisure and tourism behaviour, whether or not a person has responsibility for children is likely to be a more important variable. Usual categories for marital status are:

- married
- single – never married
- widowed/divorced/separated

Respondents who are not formally married but living in a *de facto* relationship can then decide for themselves how they want to be classified, or a separate category can be created.

Household type

Household type is a useful variable for many leisure and tourism studies but, except in the household interview situation, the data may be difficult to collect, because a number of items of information are required. In a household interview it is possible to ask 'Who lives here?' A simplified version would be to ask about the number of children of various ages in the household. Classifying the information into 'household type' must be done subsequently. Typical categories are as set out in Figure 10.7.

Group type

In the case of user/site surveys it is more usual to ask about the size of the party or group and its composition – for example, how many children and adults of various ages are present. Clearly such information is important for planning, marketing, managing and programming facilities. A typical categorisation of groups is as shown in Figure 10.7.

Life cycle

Some researchers have argued that individual variables, such as age and marital status, are not good predictors of leisure and tourism behaviour; rather, we should examine the composite variable *life cycle* (Rapoport and Rapoport, 1975). As with household type, a person's stage in the life cycle is not based on a single question but built up from a number of items of information, including age, economic status and marital/family status. A possible classification is as set out in Figure 10.8. Life*style*, as discussed in Chapter 2, is a further development of this idea, but generally involves collection of a considerable amount of additional data.

Figure 10.7 Classifying groups

Household type – Household survey

Question format
Can you please tell me who lives here?

Person	Relationship to Respondent	Gender M/F	Age	Occupation
1	Respondent			
2				
3				
4				
5				
6				

Group classification
(a) Single parent and one dependent child
(b) Single parent and two or more dependent children
(c) Couple and one dependent child
(d) Couple and two or more dependent children
(e) Couple, no children
(f) Related adults only
(g) Unrelated adults only
(h) Single person
(i) Other.

Visitor groups – Site survey

Question format
(a) How many people are there in this group, including yourself?   _____
(b) How many children aged under 5 are there in the group?   _____
(c) How many children aged between 5 and 15 are there?   _____
(d) How many people aged 60 or over are there?   _____

Group classification
(a) Youngest member aged 0–4
(b) Youngest member aged 5–15
(c) Lone adult
(d) Two adults (under 60)
(e) Older couple (60 and over)
(f) 3–5 adults
(g) 6+ adults.

Figure 10.8   Life-cycle stages

1 Child/young single – dependent (on parents)

2 Young single – independent

3 Young married/partnered – no children

4 Parent – dependent children

5 Parent – children now independent

6 Retired – up to 70

7 Retired – over 70

Ethnic group

Ethnic group is included in leisure and tourism surveys because ethnically based cultures influence leisure and tourism behaviour and also because of policy concerns for equity between social groups. Everyone belongs to an ethnic group – that is, a social group that shares religious, language and other cultural values and practices and experiences – including leisure and tourism. Ethnicity therefore becomes important in leisure and tourism policy, planning and management, particularly as regards minority groups whose needs may not be met by mainstream facilities and services. A common approach to ethnicity in the past was to ask the respondent's country of birth, since most ethnic minority groups were migrant groups. But this of course does not identify members of ethnic minority groups not born overseas. Parents' place of birth identifies the second generation of migrant groups but not third and subsequent generations. Country of birth has therefore become less and less useful as an indicator of ethnic group membership. Observation is an obvious solution but is not reliable for many groups. The solution is to ask people what ethnic group they consider they belong to. While this may cause offence to some, it is the most satisfactory approach overall.

Residential location and trip origin

Where a person lives can be a significant determinant of access to leisure facilities and is a reflection of socio-economic position and related patterns of consumption (Shaw, 1984; Zukin, 1990). Residential location and trip origin are the basis of catchment area analysis for individual facilities. In the case of a household survey the residential location would be known by the interviewer and some sort of code – for street, suburb, local government area, county, as appropriate – can be recorded on the questionnaire. In the case of site or visitor surveys, in order to study the catchment area of the facility, it is necessary to ask people where they live or where they have travelled from. How much detail is required? In some surveys the suburb/town is sufficient. In other cases it is necessary to know the street. The number of the dwelling in the street is rarely necessary. For overseas visitors the country is usually adequate information. In Case study 6.4, an example is given of the use of data on home location to show the catchment area of a facility. In that example the information came from membership records, but the information could equally well arise from a questionnaire survey of users.

Market research firms often record full addresses and/or telephone numbers of survey respondents in order to undertake subsequent quality checks on interviewers, to ensure that the respondents have in fact been interviewed.

Housing information

Information on the type of dwelling in which respondents live is usually collected in household surveys because it can easily be gathered by observation. The information is clearly relevant in leisure research because of the implications of dwelling type for access to private recreational space. Whether or not people own their own home is an important socio-economic variable. Typical categories for these items of information are shown in Figure 10.9.

Figure 10.9   Housing information

Type of dwelling	Tenure
1 Separate house	1 Owned outright
2 Semi-detached house	2 Being purchased
3 Terrace house	3 Rented
4 Flat/maisonette	4 Other
5 Caravan, houseboat	
6 Other	

Transport

Because mobility is such an important factor in leisure behaviour, leisure questionnaires often include questions on ownership of and access to vehicles. People are sometimes asked if they possess a current driver's licence. In site surveys, there is often a question on the mode of transport used to travel to the site. If people claim to have used two or more modes of transport, the various modes can all be recorded or respondents can be asked to indicate the one on which they travelled the furthest.

Leisure activities

The problem in leisure participation surveys of devising questions to gather information on leisure activities is a difficult one. The difficulties centre on two main issues:

- whether to use an open-ended or pre-coded format
- the time period for participation

An open-ended question simply asks respondents to list the activities they have engaged in during their leisure time or free time over a specified period. Without any prompting of the range of activities which are intended to be included respondents might have difficulty in recalling all their activities, and in any case may not understand the full scope of the words 'leisure' or 'free time'. The word 'leisure' has different connotations for different people. Without explanation, some people might assume that having a cup of coffee and chatting with a friend was not leisure, or that knitting or gardening could not be leisure. Using the words 'free time' might help a little, but the question is still open to variation in interpretation.

Although providing people with checklists of activities to choose from may be unwieldy, it at least ensures that all respondents consider the same range of options. The disadvantage of the checklist is that the length of the list may be daunting to some respondents, particularly the less literate. In the case of an interviewer-completed questionnaire the main problem may be the time it takes to read out the list and the problem of patience and tedium which it may entail. The General Household Survey compromises by offering a check-list of about a dozen 'types' of leisure activity, such as home-based activities, outdoor recreation, arts and entertainment, as an *aide-mémoire* for the respondent.

The time period for recalling activities is crucial to the nature of the findings. Table 10.1 shows the results from the General Household Survey of 1987 in which respondents were asked about participation in sporting and physical recreation activities in the previous four weeks, but if they had not participated in the previous four weeks they were asked if they had participated in the last year. The results are plain to see (for similar data for Australia, *see* Darcy, 1994). The time period used to measure participation affects the absolute levels of participation recorded and also the apparent relative popularity of activities. The shorter the time period used the more accurate the results are likely to be, but shorter time periods exclude large proportions of participants in those activities which are engaged in relatively infrequently.

In addition to being asked whether they have participated in an activity respondents can also be asked *how often* they have participated and *how much time* was spent on the activity. This can lead to very lengthy interviews for people who have engaged in a wide range of activities. To avoid this, in some surveys a particular leisure occasion, say the last trip to the countryside, is explored in more detail – where the respondent went, who with, what day of the week and what time of day, what specific activities were engaged in, and so on.

In local surveys or surveys with an interest in specific policy areas, it may be of interest to explore the use of specific, named leisure facilities – for example visits to particular national parks or to sports centres – using a variety of approaches to measuring use.

Table 10.1   Sport and physical recreation participation, Great Britain, 1987 – effects of varying reference time period

% participating, persons aged 16+

	In 4 weeks prior to interview (ann. ave.)	In 12 months prior to interview
Walking (at least 2 miles)	37.9	60.1
Snooker/billiards/pool	15.1	22.9
Swimming: outdoor	3.5	34.6
Swimming: indoor	10.5	
Darts	8.8	15.4
Keep fit/yoga	8.6	14.3
Cycling	8.4	14.8
Athletics – track & field	0.5	2.0
Other running/jogging	5.2	10.5
Football	4.8	8.9
Weightlifting/training	4.5	8.2
Golf	3.9	9.2
Badminton	3.4	8.2
Squash	2.6	6.7
Table tennis	2.4	6.3
Fishing	1.9	5.8
Tennis	1.8	6.6
Ten-pin bowling/skittles	1.8	5.7
Lawn/carpet bowls	1.7	3.7
Cricket	1.2	4.2
Water sport (excl. sailing)	1.1	4.7
Horse-riding	0.9	2.6
Self-defence (excl. boxing)	0.8	1.7
Ice-skating	0.8	3.7
Basketball	0.6	1.7
Sailing	0.6	2.5
Motor sports	0.4	1.1
Rugby	0.4	1.1
Netball	0.4	1.4
Gymnastics	0.3	0.6
Boxing/wrestling	0.2	0.4
Hockey	0.2	0.3
Field sports	0.2	0.2
Climbing	0.1	0.2
Curling	–	0.2
Other	0.7	1.5
At least 1 activity	60.7	77.6
Sample	19 500	19 500

Source: General Household Survey, adapted from Gratton, 1996, p.118, OPCS (1987).

In the case of site or user surveys there is usually little problem in asking about activities. Many leisure sites offer opportunity for more than one activity – for example, swimming, picnicking and sunbathing at the beach – so it is usual to ask people what activities they plan to engage in or have engaged in during their visit. Use of specific facilities, such as refreshment facilities, may also be explored.

Tourism activity

In household questionnaire surveys concerned with tourism, the 'activity' question concerns trips taken away from the home area over a specified time period. As with local leisure activities, a major consideration is the recall time period. For major holidays a one-year recall period is not out of the question, but for short breaks, asking about trips during that length of time may lead to inaccuracies in recall, so a shorter time period of, say, three months may be adopted.

A second time period issue concerns the definition of tourist 'trip'. The definition used in a survey may follow an accepted definition of tourism, for example a trip involving a stay away from home of one night or more. However, in some local tourism studies *day-trips* may also be of interest.

In addition to asking about trips taken, household tourism questionnaires also generally include questions on where the respondent has been on the trip, length of stay, travel mode and type of accommodation used. Tourism surveys are usually much more concerned with economic matters than local leisure surveys, so questions on the cost of the trip and of expenditure in various categories are often included.

For site surveys in a tourism context, including *en route* surveys, the activity questions asked of tourists and locals will generally be identical.

Measuring leisure and tourism activity

Clearly leisure and tourism activity encompasses a wide range of variables. The variety of possible measures of leisure and tourism activity is indicated in Figure 10.10. In any study consideration should be given to which types of measure are necessary.

Media use

Questionnaires often include questions on media use because such information can be used when considering advertising policy. To obtain accurate information in this area would require a considerable number of questions on frequency of reading, viewing or listening and, in the case of electronic media, the type of programmes favoured. When the research is concerned with small-scale local facilities or services, television advertising is generally out of the question because of cost, so information on television watching need not be gathered. Similar considerations may apply to magazine and

Figure 10.10 Measuring leisure and tourism demand

Measure	Definition	Leisure example	Tourism example
A The participation rate	The proportion of a defined population which engages in an activity in a given period of time	6 per cent of the adult population of community X go swimming at least once a week	5 per cent of the adult population of country X make an overseas trip each year
B Number of participants	Number of people in a defined community who engage in an activity in a given period of time (A × pop'n. or C ÷ frequency of visit)	20 000 people in community X swim at least once a week	700 000 residents of country X visit country Y in a year
C Volume of activity (visits)	The number of visits made to a defined geographical area by, or the number of games played by, members of a defined community in a specified time period (B × visits/games per time period)*	There are 1.2 million visits to swimming pools in community X (one million by local residents) in a year	850 000 trips are made to country Y by residents of country X in a year**
D Time	The amount of leisure time available to the individual in a defined community, over a specified period – or time spent on specific activity (C × time per visit)	The average retired person has 5 hours leisure time per day/or spends an average of 3 hours watching television per day	The average tourist visiting region Z spends 5.5 nights in the region
E Expenditure	The amount of money spent per individual or by a defined community on leisure or particular leisure goods or services over a specified time period (C × spend per visit)	Consumer expenditure on leisure in Britain is over £50 billion a year	Tourists visiting region Z spend £25 million in the region per annum

* In tourism a further distinction is made between 'trips' (e.g. a complete holiday) and visits (i.e. places visited during the holiday).
** In tourism the measure 'bed-nights' is often used.

national newspaper reading. For many surveys therefore, two questions are involved (show cards would usually be used):

- What (local) newspapers do you read regularly – that is at least weekly?
- What (local) radio stations do you listen to regularly – that is at least twice a week?

Attitudes and opinions

Attitudes and opinions are more complex aspects of questionnaire design. A range of techniques exists to explore people's opinions and attitudes, as listed in Figure 10.11. The first two formats, direct, open-ended questions and checklists, are straightforward, but the other formats presented merit some comment.

3 *Ranking.* Asking respondents to rank items in order of importance is a relatively straightforward process, provided the list is not too long: more than five or six items could test respondents' patience. Again, the responses can be quantified – for example, in the form of average ranks.

4 *Likert scales.* Scaling techniques are sometimes known as 'Likert scales' after the psychologist who developed their use and analysis. In this technique respondents are asked to indicate their agreement or disagreement with a proposition or the importance they attach to a factor, using a standard set of responses. One of the advantages of this approach is that the responses can be quantified, as discussed below under coding.

5 *Attitude statements.* Attitude statements are a means of exploring respondents' attitudes towards a wide range of issues, including questions of a philosophical or political nature. Respondents are shown a series of statements and asked to indicate, using a scale, the extent to which they agree or disagree with them.

  Responses to both Likert scale questions and attitude statements can be scored, as indicated by the numerals beside the answer boxes in Figure 10.11. For example, 'Agree strongly' could be given a score of 1, 'Agree' a score of 2, and so on to 'Disagree strongly' with a score of 5. Scores can then be averaged across a number of respondents. So, for example, a group of people who mostly either agreed or agreed strongly with a statement would produce an average score between 1 and 2, whereas a group who disagreed or disagreed strongly would produce a higher score, between 4 and 5. Such scores enable the strength of agreement with different statements to be compared, and the opinions of different groups of people to be compared.

6 *Semantic differential.* The semantic differential method involves offering respondents *pairs* of contrasting descriptors and asking them to indicate how the facility, place or service being studied relates to the descriptors. This technique is suitable for a respondent-completion questionnaire, since the respondent is required to place a tick on each line. It would be difficult to replicate this exactly in an interview situation with no visual prompts, such as in a telephone survey; the effect would be to reduce the possible

Figure 10.11   Opinion or attitude question formats

1 Open-ended or direct
What attracted you to apply for this course?

_____

2 Checklist
Of the items on the card, which was the most important to you in applying for this course?

> (a)   Good reputation
> (b)   Easy access
> (c)   Curriculum
> (d)   Level of fees
> (e)   Easy parking

3 Ranking
Please rank the items on the card in terms of their importance to you in choosing a course. Please rank them 1 for the most important to 5 for the least important.

	Rank
(a) Good reputation	____
(b) Easy access	____
(c) Curriculum	____
(d) Level of fees	____
(e) Easy parking	____

4 Likert scales
Looking at the items on the card, please say how important each was to you in deciding to choose this course. Was it: Very important, Quite important, Not very important or Not at all important?

	Very important	Quite important	Not very important	Not at all important
Good reputation	$\Box_1$	$\Box_2$	$\Box_3$	$\Box_4$
Easy access	$\Box_1$	$\Box_2$	$\Box_3$	$\Box_4$
Curriculum	$\Box_1$	$\Box_2$	$\Box_3$	$\Box_4$
Level of fees	$\Box_1$	$\Box_2$	$\Box_3$	$\Box_4$
Easy parking	$\Box_1$	$\Box_2$	$\Box_3$	$\Box_4$

5 Attitude statements
Please read the statements below and indicate your level of agreement or disagreement with them by ticking the appropriate box.

	Agree strongly	Agree	No opinion	Disagree	Disagree strongly
The learning experience is more important than the qualification in education	$\Box_1$	$\Box_2$	$\Box_3$	$\Box_4$	$\Box_5$
Graduate course fees are too high	$\Box_1$	$\Box_2$	$\Box_3$	$\Box_4$	$\Box_5$

6 Semantic differential
Please look at the list below and tick the line to indicate where you think this course falls in relation to each factor listed.

Difficult	|_____|_____|_____|_____|	Easy
Irrelevant	|_____|_____|_____|_____|	Relevant
Professional	|_____|_____|_____|_____|	Unprofessional
Dull	|_____|_____|_____|_____|	Interesting

answers to three: close to one end or the other and 'in the middle'. The choice of pairs of words used in a semantic differential list should arise from the research context and theory.

A further development of this approach is the *repertory grid* technique, in which the pairs of words – called *personal constructs* – are developed by the respondent (Kelly, 1955). This technique is not explored further here, but references to examples of its use in leisure and tourism are given in the Further Reading section.

ORDERING OF QUESTIONS AND LAYOUT OF QUESTIONNAIRES

Introductory remarks

Should a questionnaire include introductory remarks, for example explaining the purpose of the survey and asking for the respondent's assistance? In a mail survey such material is generally included in the covering letter. In other forms of respondent-completion questionnaire such a note is also advisable, unless the fieldworkers handing out the questionnaires have sufficient time to provide the necessary introduction and explanation. In interviewer-administered questionnaires the remarks can be printed on the top of each questionnaire or can be included in the interviewers' written instructions.

In fact interviewers are unlikely to approach potential interviewees actually reading from a script. When seeking the co-operation of a potential interviewee it is usually necessary to maintain eye contact, so interviewers must know in advance what they want to say. In household surveys potential interviewees may require a considerable amount of information and proof of identity from the interviewer before agreeing to be interviewed. But in site interviews respondents are generally more interested in knowing how long the interview will take and what sort of questions they will be asked, so only minimal opening remarks are necessary. For example, for a site survey the introduction could be as brief as: 'Excuse me, we are conducting a survey of visitors to the area; would you mind answering a few questions?'

It is usually necessary for an interviewer to indicate what organisation they represent, and this can be reinforced by an identity badge. Market research or consultancy companies often instruct interviewers to indicate only that they represent the company and not the client. This can ensure that unbiased opinions are obtained, although in some cases it can raise ethical considerations if it is felt that respondents have a right to know what organisation will be using the information gathered.

One function of opening remarks can be to ensure the respondent of confidentiality. In site surveys, where names and addresses are not generally collected, confidentiality is easy to maintain. In household and some postal surveys respondents can be identified. One way of ensuring that confidentiality is maintained is to arrange for names and addresses to be kept separate from the questionnaires and for questionnaires to include only an identifying number. This issue is discussed further in Chapter 11, in relation to research ethics.

Ordering

It is important that an interview based on a questionnaire flow in a logical and comfortable manner. A number of principles should be borne in mind.

1 Start with easy questions.
2 Start with 'relevant' questions – for example, if the respondent has been told that the survey is about holidays, begin with some questions about holidays.
3 Personal questions, dealing with such things as age or income, are generally best left to near the end: while they do not generally cause problems, and respondents need not answer those personal questions if they object, they are less likely to cause offence if asked later in the interview when a rapport has been established between interviewer and respondent. Similar principles apply in relation to respondent-completion questionnaires.

Layout

A questionnaire must be laid out and printed in such a way that the person who must read it – whether interviewer or interviewee – can follow all the instructions easily and answer all the questions that they are meant to answer.

Layout becomes particularly important when a questionnaire contains filters – that is when answers to certain questions determine which subsequent questions must be answered. An example, with alternative ways of dealing with layout, is shown in Figure 10.12.

Figure 10.12   Filtering: examples

Layout 1

1 (a) Have you studied at this university before?

      Yes $\square_1$
      No $\square_2$

  (b) If YES: How long ago did you study here? ___ years

Layout 2

1 Have you studied at this university before?

      Yes $\square_1$ Go to question 2
      No $\square_2$ Go to question 3

2 How long ago did you study here? ___ years

In respondent-completion questionnaires extra care must be taken with layout because it can be very difficult to rectify faults 'in the field'. Clarity of layout, and the overall impression given by the questionnaire can be all-important in obtaining a good response.

Mail surveys, where the researcher does not have direct contact with the respondent, are the most demanding. A professionally laid out, typeset and printed questionnaire will pay dividends in terms of level, accuracy and completeness of response. In so far as the length of a questionnaire can affect the response rate in a postal survey, a typeset format can reduce the number of pages considerably.

Even where interviewers are used there are advantages in keeping the questionnaire as compact as possible for ease of handling. A two-column format, as used in Case study 10.2, is worth exploring. Columns can be easily achieved with modern word-processing packages.

The questionnaire shown in Case study 10.3 is designed for respondent completion and the layout therefore uses boxes for the respondent to tick. This is ideal for respondent completion. Boxes can, however, be laborious to type and lay out. Where questionnaire completion is done by an interviewer, rather than ticking boxes, the interviewer can circle codes, as shown in Case studies 10.1 and 10.2. The 'office use' column is not always necessary in such interviewer-administered questionnaires, but is included in Case studies 10.1 and 10.3 for exposition purposes. This type of layout can be used for respondent completion in some situations – for example in certain 'captive group' situations or where respondents are known to be highly literate and are unlikely to be deterred by the apparent technicalities of the layout.

CODING

Most questionnaire survey data are now analysed by computer. This means that the information in the questionnaire must be coded – that is converted into numerical codes and organised in a systematic, 'machine-readable' manner. Different procedures apply to pre-coded and open-ended questions and these are discussed below.

Pre-coded questions

The principle for coding of pre-coded questions is illustrated in many of the examples in the case study questionnaires. For example, for question 1 in Case study 10.1, the codes are as shown beside the boxes. Only one answer is possible, so only one *code* is recorded as the answer to this question.

Where the answer is already numerical, there is no need to code the answer because the numerical answer can be handled by the computer. For example, in question 1 of Case study 10.1 the number of times the respondent has been on a trip is a number, which does not require coding.

Scaled answers, as in Likert scales and attitude statements, readily lend themselves to coding, as shown by the numerals in the examples given in Figure 10.11. In the case of the semantic differential each of the sections of the response line can be numbered, say, 1–4, so that answers can be given a numerical code, depending on where the respondent marks the line.

Open-ended questions

In completely open-ended questions quite an elaborate procedure must be followed to devise a coding system. As already suggested, the answers to open-ended questions can be copied from the questionnaires and presented in a report 'raw', as in Figure 10.5. If this is all that is required from the open-ended questions then there is no point in spending the considerable labour necessary to code the information for computer analysis: the computer will merely reproduce what can be more easily achieved manually.

Computer analysis comes into its own if it is intended to analyse the results in more detail – for example, comparing the opinions of two or more groups. If such comparisons are to be made it will usually be difficult to do so with, say, 50 or 60 different response groups to compare, especially if many of the responses are only given by one or two respondents. The aim then is to devise a coding system which groups the responses into a manageable number of categories.

If a large sample is involved, it is advisable to select a representative sub-sample of the responses, say 50 or 100, and write out the responses, noting, as in Figure 10.5, the number of occurrences of each answer. Then give individual codes for the most frequent responses and group the others into meaningful categories; this is a matter of judgement. The aim is not to leave too many responses in the 'other' category. An example of this process is given in Figure 10.13.

Recording coded information

Computer analysis is conducted using the coded information from a questionnaire. This is best illustrated by an example: a completed questionnaire from Case study 10.3 is set out in Figure 10.14.

The questionnaire is laid out for respondent-completion, so it is made fairly simple by providing boxes to be ticked and the codes for the answers are discreetly printed beside the boxes. An 'office use' column is provided into which the coded information is transferred ready for keying into the computer. This layout might be different for an interviewer-completed questionnaire, as discussed in the section on layout.

In the 'office use' column, *spaces* are provided into which the codes from the answers can be written. The 'variable names' in the office column – *qno*, *crse*, *lib*, etc. – are explained in Chapter 13.

- Questionnaire number, in the 'office use' column, is an identifier so that a link can be made between data in the computer and actual questionnaires; the example questionnaire is number 001

Figure 10.13   Coding open-ended questions – examples

Answers from 25 respondents to the question: 'What did you like most about this course?'	

Learned new skills ////	Opportunity to read in new area /
Networking ///	Broadened my outlook //
Convenience ///	Got me a new job! /
Helpful to my work /	Interesting ///
Friendly staff //	Clearly presented //
Good qualification to have /	Good opportunities for discussion ////
Helpful study guide //	Up-to-date material //
Relevent information ///	Easy assignments ///
Interesting tutorials /	Group project ///
Accessible lecturer //	Learning about leadership //
Guest lectures //	Computer exercises //

Suggested coding system

Comments on course content	1
Comments on course structure	2
Comments on course delivery	3
Comments on lecturer	4
Comments on skills/knowledge gained	5
Other	6

- Question 1 has only one space, because only one answer/code can be given
- Question 2 requires four spaces because respondents can tick up to four boxes
- Question 3 requires five spaces because five ranks must be recorded
- Question 4 asks for an actual number and this will be transferred into the computer without coding
- Question 5 consists of three Likert scale items, so three spaces are provided
- Question 6 is an open-ended question. It is envisaged that some respondents might give more than one answer, so spaces have been reserved for three answers (although in the example, only one has been given). The answers have a coding system (devised as discussed above) as follows:

Comments on course content	1
Comments on structure	2
Comments on delivery/organisation	3
Comments on lecturer	4
Comments on skills acquired	5
Other	6

The data from this particular completed questionnaire in Figure 10.14 therefore become a single row of numbers, as shown in the first row of Figure

Figure 10.14 Completed questionnaire

STUDENT SURVEY 1996

1 What type of course are you enrolled in?

		Office Use
		# _1_
		qno

Undergraduate ☐₁

Graduate diploma ☑₂   _2_ crse

Masters ☐₃

Other _____ ☐₄

2 Which of the following university services have you used in the last six months?

Library ☑₁   _1_ lib

Canteen ☑₁   _1_ cant

Union computer services ☐₁   _0_ comp

Student counselling service ☐₁   _0_ scs

3 Please rank the items below in terms of their importance to you in choosing a course. Rank them from 1 for the most important down to 5 for the least important.

Rank

(a) Good reputation   _1_   _1_ rep

(b) Easy access   _4_   _4_ access

(c) Curriculum   _2_   _2_ curr

(d) Level of fees   _3_   _3_ fees

(e) Easy parking   _5_   _5_ park

4 How much have you spent on books for the course in the last year?   £ _100_   _100_ cost

5 Please indicate the importance of the following to you in studying.

	Very important	Important	Not at all important	
Good textbook	☑₃	☐₂	☐₁	_3_ text
Knowledgeable lecturer	☑₃	☐₂	☐₁	_3_ lect
Easy assignments	☐₃	☐₂	☑₁	_1_ assgn

6. Do you have any suggestions for improving the course?

_1_ sug1

_____ *Less theory* _____   __ sug2

__ sug3

_____

Figure 10.15 Data from five completed questionnaires

		Question number															
		1	2				3					4	5			6	
Data	1	2	1	1	0	0	1	4	2	3	5	100	3	3	1	1		
	2	2	1	1	1	0	1	4	2	3	5	50	2	3	1	2	1	
	3	3	1	0	0	0	2	5	1	3	4	250	2	2	2	3	4	
	4	4	0	0	0	0	2	3	1	4	5	25	3	2	2	1	2	4
	5	3	1	0	0	1	1	4	3	2	5	55	3	3	1			

Based on questionnaire in Figure 10.14. The first row represents the answers given in Figure 10.14.
Subsequent rows relate to a further five completed questionnaires not shown here.

10.15, which shows how data from five completed questionnaires would look. How such a set of data may be analysed by computer is discussed in Chapter 13.

VALIDITY

Questionnaires are designed to gather information from individuals about their characteristics, behaviour and attitudes. Whether or not they actually achieve this depends on a number of considerations. The interview situation is not always conducive to careful, thoughtful responses. Respondents may tend to exaggerate or understate in their answers to some questions. They may also have problems in recalling some information accurately. Respondents may tend to give answers which they believe will please the interviewer. Thus the *validity* of questionnaire-based data – the extent to which they accurately reflect what they are meant to reflect – is a constant source of concern. To some extent the researcher must simply live with these limitations of the survey method and hope that inaccuracies are not significant and that some of them cancel each other out. There are however some measures which can be taken to check on the presence of this type of problem.

One approach is to include 'dummy' categories in some questions. For example, in a survey of recreation managers in Britain in the early 1980s respondents were asked to indicate, from a list, what books and reports they had heard of and had read. Included in the list was one plausible, but non-existent title. A significant proportion of respondents indicated that they had heard of the report and a small proportion claimed to have read it! Such a response does not necessarily mean that respondents were lying; they may simply have been confused about the titles of particular publications. But it does provide cautionary information to the researcher on the degree of error in responses to such questions, since it suggests that responses to the genuine titles may also include a certain amount of inaccuracy. For example, if two per cent of respondents claim to have heard of the non-existent report, this could suggest that all answers are subject to an error of plus or minus 2 per cent.

A similar approach is to include two or more questions in different parts of the questionnaire, which essentially ask the same thing. For example an early question could ask respondents to rank a list of activities or holiday areas in order of preference. Later in the questionnaire, in the context of asking some detailed questions, respondents could be asked to indicate their favourite activity or holiday area. In the analysis, the responses could be tested for consistency.

One possibility is that the interview experience itself may cause respondents to change their opinion, because it causes them to think through in detail something which they might previously have only considered superficially. Similar questions at the beginning and end of the interview may detect this. In an Australian survey of gambling behaviour and attitudes towards a proposed casino development Grichting and Caltabiano (1986) asked, at the beginning of the interview: 'What do you think about the casino coming to Townsville? Are you for it or against it?' At the end of the interview they asked: 'Taking everything you have said into consideration, what do you think now about the casino coming to Townsville? Are you for it or against it?' It was found that about 'one in six respondents changed their attitude toward the casino during the course of the interview'.

TIME-BUDGET STUDIES

Time-budget studies are designed to collect information on people's use of time. Such information is usually collected as part of a household survey, but in addition to answering a questionnaire, respondents are asked to complete a diary, typically covering a period of between two and four days. Respondents are asked to record their activities during their waking hours, including starting and stopping times, together with information on where the activity was done, with whom, and possibly whether the respondent considered it to be paid work, domestic work or leisure.

Coding and analysis of such data presents a considerable challenge, since every possible type of activity must be given a code and information processed for, say, 60 or 70 quarter-hour periods each day. Space does not permit a detailed treatment of this specialised topic here, but it can be followed up in the literature indicated in the Further Reading section.

CASE STUDY 10.1

Household survey questionnaire – interviewer completed

Respondent No.	**SHORT STAY HOLIDAY SURVEY** _____ # **Introductory remarks:** Hallo. We are from St. Anthony's College and we are conducting a survey on people's short-stay holidays. Would you mind answering a few questions? It will take just a few minutes and the results will be kept confidential.
Pre-coded, factual	1 In the last six months, have you been on a short holiday trip of one, two or three nights away from home? Yes 1 (go to Q. 2) No 2 (go to Q. 5) ____
Open ended, factual, numerical	2 How many times did you go on such trips in the six months? Number of times: ___ go to Q. 3 ____
Open ended, factual	3 On your last trip, where did you go? _____ ____

Multiple response categories

4 What were the main activities you engaged in on your visit?

(a) Sightseeing	□₁	(e) Arts activities/events	□₁	__ __
(b) Eating and drinking	□₁	(f) Visit friends/relatives	□₁	__ __
(c) Sporting activities	□₁	(g) Just doing nothing	□₁	__ __
(d) Walking	□₁	(h) Other	□₁	__ __

Attitude statement

5 To what extent do you agree with the following statements?

	Agree strongly	Agree	Neither	Disagree	Disagree strongly	
A short break is as valuable as long holiday	1	2	3	4	5	____
Holidays make life worth living	1	2	3	4	5	____

Pre-coded with show-card, factual

6 Can you tell me which of the following age groups you fall into?

Under 15	A
15–19	B
20–29	C
30–59	D
60+	E

   ____

Pre-coded with show-card, factual

7 Which of the following best describes your current situation?

In full-time paid work	A
In part-time paid work	B
In full-time education	C
Full-time home/child care	D
Retired	E
Looking for work	F
Other	G

   ____

Pre-coded, factual, observed

THANK YOU FOR YOUR HELP

Observe gender:	Male	1	
	Female	2	____

CASE STUDY 10.2

Site survey questionnaire – interviewer completed

The survey is being carried out for the local council to find out what users of the park think of the park, and what changes they would like to see. A total of 100 users of the park are interviewed at the only entrance, in batches of 10, on different days of the week, at different times of the day, and in different weather conditions

---

Ramsey Street Park Survey

Introductory remarks:
Excuse me. We are carrying out a survey for the council to find out what people think about the park. Could you spare a few minutes to answer a few questions?

Simple pre-coded, factual	1 How often do you visit this park? Every day — 1 Several times a week — 2 Once a week — 3 Every 2 or 3 weeks — 4 Once a month — 5 Less often — 6 First visit — 7	6 What do you like most about the park? _____	*Open-ended, opinion*

6 What do you like most about the park?
_____ — *Open-ended, opinion*

7 What do you like least about the park?
_____ — *Open-ended, opinion*

8 Looking at the card, where would you place this park, in relation to others you know?

(a)	Way below average	1
(b)	Below average	2
(c)	Average	3
(d)	Above average	4
(e)	Well above average	5

Checklist with show-card

2 Where have you travelled from today? — *Simple pre-coded, factual*
Home — 1
Work — 2
School/college/univ. — 3
Other — 4

3 What suburb is that in? — *Open-ended, factual*
_____

9 Can you tell me which of these age groups you fall into?

Under 15	A
15–19	B
20–29	C
30–59	D
60+	E

Pre-coded factual with show-card

4 How long did it take you to get here? — *Simple pre-coded, factual*
5 minutes or less — 1
6–15 minutes — 2
16–30 minutes — 3
31 minutes or more — 4

10 How many people are there in your group here today, including yourself? — *Pre-coded, factual*

5 How did you travel here? — *Simple pre-coded, factual*
Walk — 1
Car — 2
Motorbike — 3
Bicycle — 4
Bus/tram — 5
Other — 6

Alone — 1
Two — 2
3–4 — 3
5 or more — 4

THANK YOU FOR YOUR HELP

| Observe: | Male | 1 |
| | Female | 2 |

Observe, factual

CASE STUDY 10.3

Captive group survey – respondent completed

	STUDENT SURVEY 1996	Office Use

STUDENT SURVEY 1996   Office Use
                                                                      # _____
                                                                        qno

1 What type of course are you enrolled in?

Standard pre-coded

Undergraduate   ☐₁

Graduate diploma   ☐₂   __ crse

Masters   ☐₃

Other _____   ☐₄

Pre-coded, multiple response – dichotomous

2 Which of the following university services have you used in the last six months?

Library   ☐₁   __ lib

Canteen   ☐₁   __ cant

Union computer services   ☐₁   __ comp

Student counselling service   ☐₁   __ scs

Ranking

3 Please rank the items below in terms of their importance to you in choosing a course. Rank them from 1 for the most important down to 5 for the least important.

                                   Rank
(a) Good reputation   —   __ rep
(b) Easy access   —   __ access
(c) Curriculum   —   __ curr
(d) Level of fees   —   __ fees
(e) Easy parking   —   __ park

Numerical, uncoded

4 How much have you spent on books for the course in the last year?   £_____

                                                                  ____
                                                                  cost

Likert scales

5 Please indicate the importance of the following to you in studying.

	Very important	Important	Not at all important	
Good textbook	☐₃	☐₂	☐₁	__ text
Knowledgeable lecturer	☐₃	☐₂	☐₁	__ lect
Easy assignments	☐₃	☐₂	☐₁	__ assgn

Open-ended, multiple response – categories

6 Do you have any suggestions for improving the course?

_____   __ sug1
                                                                 __ sug2
_____   __ sug3

QUESTIONS AND EXERCISES

1 Design a questionnaire in relation to one of the studies discussed in Case studies 3.2, 3.3 or 6.1, limiting the questionnaire to 10 questions only.

2 Design a question on people's attitudes towards legalisation of drugs, using three alternative question formats.

3 If you are a member of a leisure/tourism class, invite members of the class to complete the questionnaire in Case study 10.3 and devise a coding system for the answers to the open-ended question based on the answers obtained.

4 Locate a published research report or thesis which includes a questionnaire survey and contains a copy of the questionnaire used (usually in an appendix) and provide a critique of the questionnaire design.

FURTHER READING

On questionnaire design generally, *see*: Hoinville and Jowell (1978); Kidder (1981); Oppenheim (1992).

On life cycle, *see*: Rapoport and Rapoport (1975).

On class, *see*: Giddens (1993, pp. 211–50).

On class and lifestyle, *see*: O'Brien and Ford (1988).

On use of repertory grid technique, *see*: Botterill (1989); Stockdale (1984).

On time-budget diaries, *see*: Burton (1971); BBC (1978); Australian Bureau of Statistics (1994); Szalai (1972).

CHAPTER 11

Research practice

INTRODUCTION: DOING RESEARCH

In Chapter 3 the research process was outlined and discussed in the context of planning research projects and preparing proposals, but the discussion stopped short of implementation – actually doing research. The intervening chapters are concerned with discussions of various methods and techniques with which the researcher needs to be familiar in order to prepare a research plan and proposal. This and subsequent chapters focus more specifically on the doing of research. This chapter addresses four features of research implementation: the planning and organisation of fieldwork; the conduct of pilot surveys; measures to boost response rates – particularly in postal surveys; and the question of research ethics.

PLANNING FIELDWORK ARRANGEMENTS

The scale and complexity of the data collection, or fieldwork, part of a research project can vary enormously. At one extreme the process is largely a matter of personal organisation; at the other extreme a staff of hundreds may need to be recruited, trained and supervised. Some of the items which need consideration are listed in Figure 11.1. Brief notes on these tasks are given below.

1 *Seek permissions.* It is important to remember that permission is often needed to interview in public places, such as streets and beaches, because of local by-laws. Many areas which are thought of as 'public' are in fact the responsibility of some public or private organisation – for example, shopping centres and parks. Permission must be sought from these organisations to conduct fieldwork. It is also good practice to inform the local police if interviewing is being conducted in public places, in case of complaints from the public.

2 *Obtain lists.* Obtaining lists, such as voters or membership lists for sampling, may seem routine, but often apparently straightforward tasks can involve delays, or the material may not be in quite the form anticipated and it may take time to sort out. Often research projects are conducted on very tight schedules and delays of a few days can be crucial. Therefore the earlier these routine tasks are tackled the better.

Figure 11.1 Fieldwork planning tasks

1 Seek permissions – to visit sites, obtain records, etc.
2 Obtain lists for sampling – e.g. voters lists
3 Arrange printing – of questionnaires etc.
4 Check insurance issues
5 Prepare written instructions for interviewers
6 Prepare identity badges/letters for interviewers
7 Recruit interviewers and supervisors
8 Train interviewers and supervisors
9 Obtain quotations for any fieldwork to be conducted by other organisations
10 Appoint and train data coders/processors

3 *Arrange printing.* Again, printing sounds straightforward, but an in-house printing office may have busy periods when it may not be possible to obtain a quick job turnround. Checking on printing procedures and turn-round times at an early stage is therefore advisable.

4 *Check insurance.* When conducting fieldwork away from a normal place of work, insurance issues may arise, including public liability and workers' compensation for interviewers. In educational institutions staff and students are normally covered as long as they are engaged in legitimate university/college activities, but these matters should be checked with a competent legal authority in the organisation.

5 *Prepare written instructions for interviewers.* Written instructions might cover:

- detailed comments on questionnaires and/or other instruments
- instructions in relation to checking of completed questionnaires etc. for legibility and completeness
- instructions on returning questionnaires etc.
- dress and behaviour codes
- roster details
- 'wet weather' instructions, if relevant
- instructions on what to do in the case of 'difficult' interviewees etc.
- details of time-sheets, payment etc.
- contact telephone numbers.

A note on questionnaire-based interviewing is appropriate here. The general approach to interviewing when using a questionnaire is that the interviewer should be instructed to adhere precisely to the wording on the questionnaire.

If the respondent does not understand the question, the question should simply be repeated exactly as before; if the respondent still does not understand then the interviewer should move on to the next question. If this procedure is to be adhered to then the importance of question wording and the testing of such wording in one or more pilot surveys is clear.

The above procedure is clearly important in relation to attitude questions. Any word of explanation or elaboration from the interviewer could influence, and therefore bias, the response. In relation to factual questions, however, it may be less important: a word of explanation from the interviewer may be acceptable if it results in obtaining accurate information.

6 *Prepare identity badges/letters.* If working in a public or semi-public place, fieldworkers should be clearly identified. A badge with the institutional logo and the fieldworker's name is advisable. A letter from the research supervisor indicating that the fieldworker is engaged in legitimate research activity for the organisation may also be helpful.

7 *Recruit interviewers and supervisors.* Where paid interviewers, supervisors or other fieldworkers are to be used it will be necessary to go through the normal procedures for employing part-time staff. Advice from the organisation's human resources unit, or someone familiar with their procedures, will need to be sought.

8 *Training.* The length of training will vary with the complexity of the fieldwork and the experience of the fieldwork staff. Paid fieldworkers should be paid for the training session(s) (and this payment should be budgeted for). A two- or three-hour session is usually sufficient, but more may be necessary for a complex project. It is advisable for interviewers to practise interviews on each other and report back on difficulties encountered.

9 *Obtain quotations.* In some cases certain aspects of the project are to be undertaken by other organisations – for example, data processing. Obtaining detailed quotations on price as early as possible is clearly advisable.

10 *Appoint and train data processors.* In some cases the coding, editing and processing of data for computer analysis is a significant task in its own right, requiring staff to be recruited. Recruitment and training procedures will need to be followed as for fieldworkers.

CONDUCTING A PILOT SURVEY

Pilot surveys are small-scale 'trial runs' of a larger survey. Pilot surveys relate particularly to questionnaire surveys, but can in fact relate to trying out any type of research procedure. It is always advisable to carry out one or more pilot surveys before embarking on the main data-collection exercise. The purposes of pilot surveys are summarised in Figure 11.2. Clearly the pilot can be used to test out all aspects of the survey, not just question wording. Item 4, 'Familiarity with respondents', refers to the role of the pilot in alerting the

Figure 11.2   Pilot survey purposes

```
1 Test questionnaire wording

2 Test question sequencing

3 Test questionnaire layout

4 Familiarity with respondents

5 Test fieldwork arrangements

6 Train and test fieldworkers

7 Estimate response rate

8 Estimate interview etc. time

9 Test analysis procedures
```

researcher to any characteristics, idiosyncrasies or sensitivities of the respondent group with which he or she may not have been previously familiar. Such matters can affect the design and conduct of the main survey. Items 7 and 8, concerned with the response rate and length of interview, can be most important in providing information to 'fine tune' the survey process. For example, it may be necessary to shorten the questionnaire and/or vary the number of field staff so that the project keeps on schedule and within budget.

In principle at least some of the pilot interviews should be carried out by the researcher in charge, or at least by some experienced interviewers, since the interviewers will be required to report back on the pilot survey experience and contribute to discussions on any revisions to the questionnaire or fieldwork arrangements which might subsequently be made. The de-briefing session following the pilot survey is very important and should take place as soon as possible after the completion of the exercise, so that the details are fresh in the interviewers' minds.

BOOSTING MAIL SURVEY RESPONSE RATES

In Chapter 9 reference was made to the range of factors which affect response rates in mail surveys and techniques which might be used to overcome the common problem of low response rates in such surveys. The various factors and measures listed in Figure 9.4 are discussed in detail below.

1 The interest of the respondent in the survey topic

A survey of a local community about a proposal to route a six-lane highway through the neighbourhood would probably result in a high response rate, but a survey of the same community on general patterns of leisure behaviour would probably result in a low response rate. Variation among the population in the level of interest in the topic can result in a biased, that is unrepresentative, response. For example a survey on sports facility provision might evoke a high response rate among those interested in sport and a low response rate among those not interested – giving a false impression of community enthusiasm for sports facility provision. To some extent this can be corrected by weighting (*see* Chapter 12) if the bias corresponds with certain known characteristics of the population. For example, if there was a high response rate from young people and a low response rate from older people, information from the census on the actual proportions of different age groups in the community could be used to weight the results.

2 Length of the questionnaire

It might be expected that a long questionnaire would discourage potential respondents. It has however been argued that other factors, such as the topic and the presentation of the questionnaire, are more important than the length of the questionnaire – that is, if the topic is interesting to the respondent and is well presented then length is not an issue.

3 Questionnaire design, presentation and complexity

More care must be taken in the design and physical presentation of a respondent-completed questionnaire than of one completed by the interviewer. Typesetting, colour coding of pages, graphics and so on may be necessary. Leisure and tourism surveys often present awesome lists of activities which can make a questionnaire look very complicated and demanding to complete.

4 The accompanying letter

The letter from the sponsor or researcher which accompanies the questionnaire may have an influence on people's willingness to respond. Does it give a good reason for the survey? Is it from someone, or the type of organisation, whom the respondent trusts or respects?

5 Postage-paid reply envelope

It is usual to include a postage-paid envelope for the return of the questionnaire. Some believe that an envelope with a real stamp on it will produce a better response rate than a business reply-paid envelope. Providing reply envelopes with real stamps is more expensive because, apart from the time spent in sticking stamps on envelopes, stamps are provided for both respondents and non-respondents.

6 Rewards

The question of rewards for taking part in a survey can arise in relation to any sort of survey but it is a device used most often in mail surveys. One approach is to send every respondent some small reward, such as a voucher for a firm's or agency's product or service, or even money. A more common approach is to enter all respondents in a draw for a prize. Even a fairly costly prize may be money well spent if it results in a substantial increase in the response rate. When the cost of the alternative household surveys involving face-to-face interviews is considered, a substantial prize which results in a significant increase in responses may be considered good value. It could however be argued that the introduction of rewards causes certain people to respond for the wrong reasons and that it introduces a potential source of bias in responses. It might also be considered that the inclusion of a prize or reward 'lowers the tone' of the survey and places it in the same category as other, commercial, junk mail that comes through people's letter boxes every day.

7 Reminders and follow-ups

Sensible reminder and follow-up procedures are perhaps the most significant tool available to the researcher. Typically, a post-card reminder might be sent one week or ten days after the initial mailing. After two weeks a letter accompanied by a second copy of the questionnaire ('in case the first has been mislaid') should be sent. A final reminder card can be sent a week or so after that. The effects of these reminders and follow-ups can be seen in Figure 11.3, which relates to a survey of residents' recreational use of an estuary. It can be

Figure 11.3 Mail survey response pattern

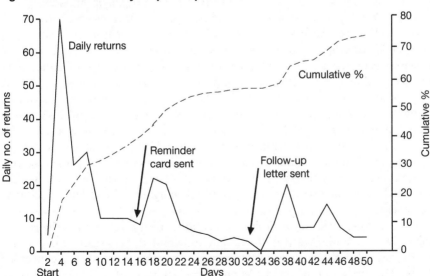

Source: Centre for Leisure and Tourism Studies, UTS, unpublished data.

seen that the level of responses peaked after only three days and looked likely to cease after about 16 days, giving a potential response rate of just 40 per cent. The surges in responses following the sending of the post-card and the second copy of the questionnaire can be seen and the net result was a 75 per cent response rate, which is very good for this type of survey. The need for follow-ups must be considered when budgeting for a postal survey, since postage and printing costs are often the most significant items in such budgets.

Of course the sending out of reminders means that it must be possible to identify returned questionnaires, so that reminders are not sent to those who have replied. This means that questionnaires or envelopes must have an identifying number which can be matched with the mailing list. Some respondents resent this potential breach of confidentiality but it cannot be avoided if only non-respondents are to be followed up. There is often a further advantage to being able to identify responses; they can be used to check the representativeness of the response. For instance, the questionnaire may not include respondents' addresses, but the geographical spread of the response can be examined if the identity of the responses is known, and any necessary weighting can be carried out.

RESEARCH ETHICS

Ethical behaviour is important in research, as in any other field of human activity. Certain ethical considerations, concerned with such matters as plagiarism and honesty in reporting of results, arise in all research, but additional issues arise when the research involves human subjects, in both the biological and social sciences. The principles underlying research ethics are universal: they concern things like honesty and respect for the rights of individuals.

Professional groups, such as market researchers, have established explicit codes of ethics to which members are obliged to adhere. Most universities now have codes of ethics enforced by ethics committees, which must approve all research projects involving humans or animals. Such codes of ethics have intrinsic value in protecting the rights of humans and animals who may become involved in research, but they also serve a professional and organisational function. Researchers may be subject to litigation and can lose professional indemnity if they are not seen to have adhered to the appropriate code of ethics. A related consideration is the question of public relations and the standing, within the community, of organisations responsible for the research. Some practices may be ethical, but still give offence, so the value of the data collected using such practices must be weighed against the ill-will which may be generated.

Ethical issues arise in the design and conduct of research and in the reporting of results. With regard to the design and conduct of research many codes of ethics deal with practices in laboratories, but this discussion is concerned with ethical issues in the 'field'. As far as the reporting of results is concerned, the same ethical principles apply, regardless of the methods involved.

The general principles usually invoked in codes of research ethics are, first, that no harm should befall the research subjects and second, that subjects should take part freely and on the basis of informed consent. These ideas are discussed further below.

Harm

The question of harm arises particularly in medical/biological research, where an individual's health may be put at risk by an experimental procedure. But such risks can also arise in psychological research, where stress and distress can result, and in socio-psychological research where inter-personal relationships can be damaged. In social research, where most leisure and tourism research falls, the question of 'harm' is more likely to arise in the use of data rather than in the collection process, in particular over the issue of confidentiality and privacy.

Privacy is a valued right in western society. Even if no serious harm is *apparently* done, people can still be offended and suffer stress if their affairs are made public or divulged to certain third parties. There is therefore an obligation on the researcher to ensure confidentiality of any data collected. In many questionnaire survey situations, the issue of confidentiality of data does not arise since the data are collected anonymously. But even in an anonymous situation, informants may be reluctant to give certain types of information to 'a complete stranger'. Where such sensitivity is encountered, the usual approach is to stress the voluntary nature of the information-giving process.

In some research projects named individuals are inevitably involved – for example, where the number of subjects is small and they are key figures associated with particular organisations or communities. In this case the issue of confidentiality does arise. Where data are collected directly from the individual, care must be taken to adopt the journalist's practice of checking whether information is being given 'on the record' or 'off the record'. Thus, in interviews where sensitive matters arise, it is wise to ask informants whether they are prepared to be quoted. However, some information is obtained from third parties, and the researcher, like the journalist, must give careful consideration to just how such information is to be used. Unlike newspapers, few research organisations can afford to take the risk of publishing defamatory material, even if it does make a good story!

When data are confidential, measures must be taken to protect that confidentiality through ensuring the security of the raw data, such as interview tapes, transcripts or questionnaires. And care must be taken in the way the results are written up. Data can be stored with code numbers or false names, with a key to the code numbers or names being kept securely in a place apart from the data. Mail surveys are an 'in-between' case. If returns cannot be identified, then there is no way of identifying non-respondents in order to send reminders. Sending reminders to *everyone* is costly, and an irritation to those who have already responded. One solution is to place an identifying number on the return envelope rather than on the questionnaire, with an assurance that the number will not be transferred to the questionnaire.

In reporting results, the use of false names or numbers to identify individuals, organisations, events, places and communities is the obvious solution, although it is often not sufficient. For those 'in the know', the places and the people involved in the research project may be all too easily identifiable. Occasionally this is exacerbated by the author's own list of acknowledgements, which clearly identifies people and places! The situation is akin to the practice of some novelists using friends or acquaintances in their books: some are flattered and others are very offended!

Confidentiality issues often arise with regard to the relationship between the researcher and the sponsoring organisation. In particular, if the sponsoring organisation 'owns' the data, the researcher may wish to protect the confidentiality of informants by *not* passing on to the sponsoring organisation any information which could identify informants by name.

Free choice

It seems obvious that subjects should not be coerced to become involved in research projects, but there are some 'grey' areas. Some of these are institutional and some are intrinsic to the design and nature of the research.

In universities, students are often used as subjects in research. In some places students are *required* to be available for a certain amount of experimental or survey work conducted by academic staff, and in some cases they receive credit for this involvement. Although, no doubt, students can opt out of such activities, there is moral pressure on them to conform and possibly fear of sanctions if they do not. Clearly it is unethical for the university to allow such undue moral pressure to be brought to bear.

Other 'captive group' cases involve classes of school children or members of organisations, whose participation is agreed to by the person in charge. Again, while opting out may be possible, in practice it may be difficult and the subject is, to all intents and purposes, coerced. Research in prisons and mental and other hospitals raises similar questions about genuine freedom of choice on the part of the subject.

The principle of freedom of choice is constantly infringed by governments: it is an offence, for example, not to complete the population census forms or to refuse co-operation with a number of other official surveys. In these cases, the social need for accurate data is considered to outweigh the citizen's right to refuse to give information.

In some types of research – such as observational research where large numbers of subjects are involved – choice on the part of the subject is virtually impossible. Studies of traffic flows, pedestrian movements or crowd behaviour are examples of such research. In many observational research situations, if the subjects knew that they were being observed they might well modify their behaviour, and so invalidate the research. This would apply particularly in situations where anti-social, and even illegal, behaviour may be involved.

These considerations might apply in research ranging from people's interpersonal behaviour in a gym through to research on the milieux of prostitution, gambling or drinking.

The problem of freedom to participate arises particularly in research using participant observation (Bulmer, 1982). The whole basis of such research may rely on the researcher being accepted and trusted by the group being investigated: such trust may not be forthcoming if it is known that the participant is a researcher. If the researcher does 'come clean', there is the risk – even the likelihood – of the subjects modifying their behaviour, thus invalidating the research. To what extent is it ethical for researchers to disguise their identity to the people they are interacting with and studying – in effect to lie about their identity? When researchers are involved with groups engaging in illegal and/or anti-social activities, for example drug-taking or some youth gangs, where do their loyalties lie?

In a celebrated case in recreation research, Moeller and his colleagues (1980a) used *incognito* interviewers, posing as campers, to investigate campers' attitudes to pricing and discovered different results from those collected by formal, identified interviewers. The ethics of this practice raised considerable controversy in the *Journal of Leisure Research* (Christensen, 1980; Moeller *et al.*, 1980b; LaPage, 1981).

If it is accepted that research of this type is permissible, despite the lack of freedom of consent, then the issue of confidentiality in reporting, as discussed above, comes even more to the fore.

Informed consent

In experimental research, where there is a risk, however remote, of physical harm to the subject (for example, where allergies might be involved, or a risk of muscle strains or even of heart attack), it is clearly necessary for the subject to be fully aware of the risks involved in order to be able to give their 'informed consent' to participate. The level of risk of harm is a matter of judgement, and often only the researcher is fully aware of the extent of risk involved in any given research procedure. This raises the question of the extent to which the subject can be fully 'informed'. Subjects can never be as fully informed as the researcher. A judgement has to be made about what is reasonable. In the traditional science laboratory setting, verbal and written explanations of the nature of the research are given to the potential subjects and they are asked to sign a document indicating their agreement to being involved in the research. A researcher could of course 'go through the motions' of following this procedure, but abuse it by providing misleading information about the level of risk – hence the need for clear guidelines and monitoring of these matters.

Such physical or mental risks do not generally arise in leisure and tourism research, but they are only one aspect of being 'informed'. There may be a moral dimension also. For example, some people may object to being involved in research which is being conducted for certain public, political or commercial organisations. So being informed also involves being informed about the purpose of the research and the nature of the sponsor or beneficiary.

In some cases the status of the researcher is ambivalent, for example when students conduct a project on behalf of a client organisation, or when part-time students conduct research for a university assignment using their fellow employees as subjects or conduct research on competitors. It is clearly un-ethical for students to identify themselves only as students and not to identify to their informants the organisation which will be the beneficiary of the research.

But again there are some grey areas. In some cases the research would be invalidated if subjects knew fully what its purpose was: for example, quasi-experimental research on people's attitudes based on reactions to pictures, or to interviewers of differing race or gender. In some attitudinal research, for example on potentially sensitive topics such as race or sex, it may be thought that responses will be affected if respondents are told too much about the research and therefore placed 'on their guard'. Clearly such deception raises ethical issues and judgements have to be made about whether the value of the research justifies the use of mild deception.

In some cases the provision of detailed information to informants, and obtaining their written consent is neither practicable nor necessary. Thus the typical leisure or tourism survey:

- is anonymous
- involves only a short interview (for example, three or four minutes)
- involves fairly innocuous, non-personal questions
- takes place at a facility/site with the agreement of the management or authorities

In this type of situation most respondents are not interested in detailed explanations of the research. Most people are familiar with surveys and their main concern is that the interview should not take up too much of their time! Potential respondents can become impatient with attempts to provide detailed explanations of the research and would prefer to 'get on with it'. Often questions about the purpose of the survey, if they arise at all, do so later during the interview process, when the respondent's interest has been stimulated.

A suggested set of guidelines for such surveys is as follows:

1 Interviewers should be identified with a badge including their name and the name of the organisation involved (the host organisation or university).
2 Interviewers should be fully briefed about the project so that they can answer questions if asked.
3 If a respondent-completion questionnaire is used, a brief description of the purpose of the project should be provided on the questionnaire (but not too long so that it takes a long time to read), with phone numbers for those requiring more information.
4 Interviewers approaching potential respondents should introduce them-selves and seek co-operation using the following words, or similar: 'We are

conducting a survey of users of ——; would you mind answering a few questions?'

5 Telephone numbers of supervisors should be available and can be given to respondents if required.

6 A short printed handout should be available with more information for those respondents who are interested.

General research ethics

The discussion so far has been concerned with the relationship between the researchers and subjects or informants and, to some extent, with client organisations. We should not leave this topic without considering a number of other issues, some of which might be considered 'obvious' to the moral person, but which are nevertheless included for completeness.

1 *Competence.* A researcher should not embark on research involving the use of skills in which they have not been adequately trained; to do so may risk causing harm to subjects, may be an abuse of subjects' goodwill, may risk damaging the reputation of the research organisation, and may involve waste of time and other resources.

2 *Literature review.* Any research should be preceded by a thorough review of the literature to ensure, as far as possible, that the proposed research has not already been done elsewhere.

3 *Plagiarism.* The use of others' data or ideas without due acknowledgement and, where appropriate, permission, is unethical.

4 *Falsification of results.* The falsification of research results or the misleading reporting of results is clearly unethical.

FURTHER READING

On research conduct generally, *see* readings in Chapters 3 and 9. On mail surveys, *see* Hoinville and Jowell (1978); Dillman (1978).

On research ethics, *see*: Beauchamp *et al.* (1982); Bulmer (1982); Christensen (1980); Kimmel (1988); LaPage (1981); Moeller *et al.* (1980a, 1980b); Punch (1994); Sieber (1992).

CHAPTER 12

Sampling

INTRODUCTION

This chapter is an introduction to the principles of sampling rather than a complete guide. It addresses the idea of sampling; samples and populations; representativeness and random sampling; sample sizes and their consequences in terms of 'confidence intervals'; and weighting.

THE IDEA OF SAMPLING

In most survey research and some observational research it is necessary to sample. Mainly because of costs, it is not usually possible to interview all the people who are the focus of the research. For example, if the aim of a research project was to study the leisure patterns or holiday-making behaviour of the adult population of Britain, no one has the resources to conduct interviews with 50 million people! The only time when the whole population is interviewed is every 10 years, when the Office of Population Censuses and Surveys conducts the Census of Population – and the cost of collecting and analysing the data runs into tens of millions of pounds.

At a more modest level, it would be virtually impossible to conduct face-to-face interviews with all the users of an urban park or a busy tourist area since, in busy periods, many hundreds might enter the site and leave in a short space of time. It might be possible to hand self-completion questionnaires to all users but, as discussed in Chapter 9, this approach has disadvantages in terms of quality and level of response. The usual procedure is to interview a sample – a proportion – of the users.

In Chapter 7, on observation, the problems of continuous counting of numbers of users of recreation sites were discussed and it was noted that often available resources demand that sample counts be undertaken – that is the numbers entering the site or present at the site are counted on a sample of occasions.

SAMPLES AND POPULATIONS

One item of terminology should be clarified initially. The total category of subjects which is the focus of attention in a particular research project is known as the *population*. A *sample* is selected from the population. The use of the term population makes sense when dealing with communities of people – for instance the adult population of Britain or the population of London. But the term also applies in other instances; for example the visitors to a resort over the course of a year constitute the *population of resort visitors*; and the users of a sports facility are the *population of users*.

The term *population* can also be applied to non-human phenomena – for example, if a study of the physical characteristics of Australia's beaches found that there were 10 000 beaches in all, from which 100 were to be selected for study, then the 10 000 beaches would be referred to as the *population of beaches* and the 100 selected for study would be the sample. In some texts the word *universe* is used instead of population.

If a sample is to be selected for study then two questions arise.

1 What procedures must be followed to ensure that the sample is representative of the population?
2 How large should the sample be?

These two questions are related, since, other things being equal, the larger the sample the more chance it has of being representative.

REPRESENTATIVENESS

A sample which is not representative of the population is described as *biased*. The whole process of sample selection must be aimed at minimising bias in the sample. Representativeness is achieved, and bias minimised, by the process of *random sampling*. This is not the most helpful term since it implies that the process is not methodical. This is far from the case: random does not mean haphazard! The meaning of random sampling is as follows:

> **In random sampling all members of the population have an equal chance of inclusion in the sample.**

For example, if a sample of 1000 people is to be selected from a population of 10 000 then every member of the population must have a one in 10 chance of being selected. In practice most sampling methods involving human beings can only approximate this rule. The problems of achieving random sampling vary with the type of survey.

Household surveys

The problem of achieving randomness can be examined in the case of a household survey of the adult residents of a country. If the adult population of the country is, say, 40 million and we wish to interview a sample of 1000, then every member of the adult population should have a one in 40 000 chance of being included in the sample. How would this be achieved? Ideally there should be a complete list of all 40 million of the country's adults; their names should be written on slips of paper and placed in a revolving drum, physically or electronically, as in a lottery draw, and 1000 names should be drawn out. Each time a choice is made everyone has a one in 40 million chance of selection. Since selection happens 1000 times, each person has a total of 1000 in 40 million or one in 40 000 chance of selection.

This would be a very laborious process. Surely a close approximation would be to forget the slips of paper and the drum and choose every 40 000th name on the list. But where should the starting point be? It should be some random point between one and 40 000. There are published 'tables of random numbers', which can also be produced from computers, which can be used for this purpose. Strictly speaking the whole sample should be chosen using random numbers, since this would approximate most closely to the 'names in a drum' procedure.

In practice, however, such a list of the population being studied rarely exists. The nearest thing to it would be the electoral registers of all the constituencies in the country. Electoral registers are fairly comprehensive because adults are required by law to register, but they are not perfect. Highly mobile or homeless people are often not included; many who live in multi-occupied premises are omitted. The physical task of selecting the names from such a list would be immense, but there is another disadvantage with this approach. If every 40 000th voter on the registers were selected the sample would be scattered throughout the country. The cost of visiting every one of those selected for a face-to-face interview would be very high.

In practice therefore, organisations conducting national surveys compromise by employing 'multi-stage' sampling and 'clustered' sampling. Multi-stage means that sampling is not done directly but is done by stages. For example if the country had, say, four states or regions a sample of, say, 2000 would be subdivided in the same proportions as the populations of the regions, as shown in Table 12.1. Within each region local government areas would then be divided into country and urban and, say four urban and two rural areas would be selected at random – with the intention of selecting appropriate sub-samples, of perhaps 25, 40 or 50 from each area. These sub-samples could be selected from electoral registers, or streets could be selected and individuals contacted by calling on, say, every fifth house in the street. In any one street interviewers may be instructed to interview, say, 10 or 15 people. By

Table 12.1 Multi-stage sampling

Region	Population		Sample	
	Millions	%	Number	%
A	10	25.0	500	25.0
B	5	12.5	250	12.5
C	20	50.0	1000	50.0
D	5	12.5	250	12.5
Total	40	100.0	2000	100.0

interviewing 'clusters' of people in this way costs are minimised. But care must be taken not to reduce the number of clusters too much or the full range of population and area types would not be included.

Site, user or visitor surveys

Conditions at leisure or tourism sites or facilities vary enormously, depending on the type and size of facility, the season, the day of the week, the time of day or the weather. This discussion can only therefore be in general terms. To ensure randomness, and therefore representativeness, it is necessary for interviewers to adhere to strict rules. Site interviewers operate in two ways. First, the interviewer can be stationary and the users mobile – for instance when the interviewer is located near the entrance and visitors are interviewed as they enter or leave. Alternatively the user may be stationary and the interviewer mobile – for instance when interviewing beach users or users of a picnic site.

In the case of stationary interviewers, the instructions they should follow should be something like:

> When one interview is complete, check through the questionnaire for completeness and legibility. When you are ready with a new questionnaire stop the next person to enter the gate. Stick strictly to this rule and do not select interviewees on any other basis.

The important thing is that interviewers should not avoid certain types of user by picking and choosing whom to interview. Ideally there should be some rule such as interviewing every fifth person to come through the door/gate but, since users will enter at a varying rate and interviews vary in length, this is rarely possible.

In the case of stationary users and a mobile interviewer, the interviewer should be given a certain route to follow on the site and be instructed to interview, say, every fifth group they pass.

Where interviewers are employed, the success of the process will depend on the training given to the interviewers and this could involve observation of them at work to ensure that they are following the rules.

As indicated in Chapter 9, sampling in site or visitor surveys leads inevitably to variation in the proportion of users interviewed at different times of the day. Where users tend to stay for long periods – as in the case of beaches – this may not matter, but where people stay for shorter periods and where the type of user may vary during the course of the day or week, the sample will probably be unrepresentative – that is, biased. This should be corrected by weighting, as indicated at the end of the chapter.

When surveys involve the handing out of questionnaires for completion by the respondent – as for example in a number of tourist *en route* or hotel surveys – unless field staff are available to encourage their completion and return, respondents will be self-selected. Busy hotel or leisure facility receptionists can rarely be relied upon to do a thorough job in handing out and collecting in questionnaires, unless the survey is a priority of the management and therefore closely supervised. Normally a significant proportion of the population will fail to return the questionnaire, but it is unlikely that this self-selection process will be random. For example, people with difficulties in reading or writing English, or people who are in a hurry, may fail to return their questionnaires. Those with 'something to say', whether positive or negative, are more likely to return their questionnaires than people who are apathetic or just content with the service, thus giving a misleading impression of the proportion of users who have strong opinions. Thus it can be seen that this type of 'uncontrolled' survey is at risk of introducing serious bias into the sample and should therefore be avoided if at all possible.

Street surveys and quota sampling

Although the technique of quota sampling can be used in other situations, it is most common in street surveys. The street survey is usually seen as a means of contacting a representative sample of the community but in fact it can also be seen as a sort of 'site survey', the site being the shopping area. As such a street survey which involved a random sample of the users of the street would be representative of the users of the shopping area rather than of the community as a whole. In a suburban shopping centre it would for instance have a high proportion of retired people or full-time home or child carers.

If the aim is in fact to obtain a representative sample of the whole community, then to achieve this interviewers are given 'quotas' of people of different types to contact, the quotas being based on information about the community which is available from the census. For example, if the census indicates that 12 per cent of the population is retired then interviewers would be required to include 12 retired people in every 100 interviewed. Once interviewers have filled their quota in certain age or gender groups, they are required to become more selective in whom they approach in order to fill the gaps in their quotas.

The quota method can only be used when background information on the target population is known – as with community surveys. In most user surveys this information is not known so the strict following of random sampling procedures must be relied upon.

Mail surveys

The initial list of people to whom the questionnaire is sent in a mail survey may be the whole population or a sample. If a sample is selected it can usually be done completely randomly because the mailing list for the whole population is usually available.

The respondents to a mail survey form a sample, but it is not randomly selected but self-selected. This introduces sources of bias similar to those in the uncontrolled self-completion site surveys discussed above. There is little that can be done about this except to make every effort to achieve a high response rate. In some cases information may be available on the population which can be used to weight the sample to correct for certain sources of bias. For example, in a national survey the sample could be weighted to correct for any geographical bias in response because the geographical distribution of the population would be known. If, for example, the survey is of an occupational association and the proportion of members in various grades is known from records, then this can be used for weighting purposes. But ultimately, mail surveys suffer from an unknown and uncorrectable element of bias caused by non-response. All surveys experience non-response of course, but the problem is greater with mail surveys because the level of non-response is usually greater.

SAMPLE SIZE

There is a popular misconception that the size of a sample should be decided on the basis of its relationship to the size of the population – for example that a sample should be five per cent or 10 per cent of the population. *This is not so.* What is important is the absolute size of the sample, regardless of the size of the population. For example, a sample size of 1000 is equally valid, provided proper sampling procedures have been followed, whether it is a sample of British adults (population 50 million), the residents of London (population seven million), the residents of Brighton (population 100 000) or the students of a university (population, say, 10 000).

It is worth repeating that: it is the *absolute size of the sample* which is important, not its size relative to the population.

On what criteria therefore should a sample size be determined? The criteria are basically three-fold:

- the required level of precision in the results
- the level of detail in the proposed analysis
- the available budget

The idea of the level of precision can be explained as follows. The question is to what extent the findings from a sample precisely reflect the population. For example, if a survey was designed to investigate holiday-making and it was found that 50 per cent of a sample of 500 people took a holiday in the previous year, how sure can we be that this finding – this *statistic* – is true of the population as a whole? How sure can we be, despite all efforts taken to choose a representative sample, that the sample is not in fact unrepresentative, and that the real percentage of holiday-taking in the population is in fact, say, 70 per cent or 30 per cent?

This question is answered in terms of probabilities. If the true value is around 50 per cent then, with random sampling, the probability of drawing a sample which was so wrong that no one in the sample had been on holiday would be very remote – almost impossible one might say. On the other hand the probability of coming up with say 48 or 49 per cent or 51 or 52 per cent would, one would think, be fairly high. The probability of coming up with 70 or 30 per cent would be somewhere in between.

Statisticians have examined the likely pattern of distribution of all possible samples of various sizes drawn from populations of various sizes and established that, when a sample is randomly drawn, the sample value of a statistic has a certain probability of being within a certain range either side of the real value of the statistic. That range is plus or minus twice the 'standard error' of the statistic. The size of the standard error depends on the size of the sample and is unrelated to the size of the population. A properly drawn sample has a 95 per cent chance of producing a statistic with a value which is within two standard errors of the true population value so, conversely, there is a 95 per cent chance that the true population value lies within two standard errors of the sample value. This means that, if 100 samples of the same size were drawn, in 95 cases we would expect the statistic to be within two standard errors of the population value; in five cases we would expect it to be outside the range. Since we do not generally know the population value, we have to rely on this theoretical statement of probability about the likely accuracy of our finding: we have a 95 per cent chance of being approximately right and a five per cent chance of being wrong.

This two standard error range is referred to as the '95 per cent confidence interval' of a statistic. The relationship between standard errors and level of probability is a property of the 'normal curve' – a bell-shaped curve with certain mathematical properties which we are not able to pursue here. The idea of a normal curve and 95 per cent confidence intervals is illustrated in Figure

Figure 12.1   Normal curve and confidence intervals

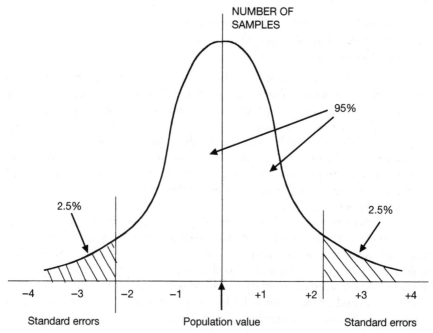

12.1. The general idea of probabilities related to the properties of certain types of 'distribution' is pursued in more detail in Chapter 14.

Tables have been drawn up by statisticians which give the confidence intervals for various statistics for various sample sizes, as shown in Table 12.2. Down the side of the table are various sample sizes, ranging from 50 to 10 000. Across the top of the table are statistics which one might find from a survey – for example, 20 per cent play tennis. The table shows 20 per cent together with 80 per cent because if it is found that 20 per cent of the sample play tennis, then clearly 80 per cent *do not* play tennis. Any conclusion about the accuracy of the statistic 20 per cent also applies to the corresponding statistic 80 per cent. In the body of the table are the *confidence intervals*.

An example of how the table is interpreted is as follows: suppose we have a sample size of 500 and we have a finding that 30 per cent of the sample have a certain characteristic – say, have been away on holiday in the previous summer (so 70 per cent have *not* been on holiday). Reading off the table, for a sample size of 500, we find that a finding of 30 per cent (and 70 per cent) is subject to a confidence interval of plus or minus 4.0. So we can be fairly certain that the population value lies in the range 26.0 per cent to 34.0 per cent.

An important point should be noted about these confidence intervals: to halve the confidence interval it is necessary to quadruple the sample size. In the example above, a sample of 2000 people (four times the original sample) would give a confidence interval of plus or minus 2.0 per cent (half the original

Table 12.2   Confidence intervals related to sample size

Sample size	Percentages found from sample ('results')					
	50%	40 or 60%	30 or 70%	20 or 80%	10 or 90%	5 or 95%
50	13.9	13.6	12.7	11.1	8.3	*
80	11.0	10.7	10.0	8.8	6.6	*
100	9.8	9.6	9.0	7.8	5.9	4.3
150	8.0	7.8	7.3	6.4	4.8	3.5
200	6.9	6.8	6.3	5.5	4.2	3.0
250	6.2	6.1	5.7	5.0	3.7	2.7
300	5.7	5.5	5.2	4.5	3.4	2.5
400	4.9	4.8	4.5	3.9	2.9	2.1
500	4.4	4.3	4.0	3.5	2.6	1.9
750	3.6	3.5	3.3	2.9	2.1	1.6
1000	3.1	3.0	2.8	2.5	1.9	1.3
2000	2.2	2.1	2.0	1.7	1.3	1.0
4000	1.5	1.5	1.4	1.2	0.9	0.7
10 000	1.0	1.0	0.9	0.8	0.6	0.4

*Confidence interval >5.0. For formula to calculate confidence interval, *see* Appendix 14.2.

confidence interval). The cost of increasing the precision of surveys by increasing the sample is therefore very high.

Note that for smaller samples the confidence intervals become very large. For instance, for a sample of 50 and a finding of 50 per cent the interval is plus or minus 13.9 per cent, meaning that the confidence interval can only be estimated to be within the range 36.1 to 63.9 per cent. For some statistics, for the smaller sample sizes, the confidence intervals are not calculable because the total margin of error is larger than the original statistic.

It should be noted that these confidence intervals apply only for samples which have been drawn using random sampling methods; other methods, such as multi-stage sampling, tend to produce larger confidence intervals (Hoinville and Jowell, 1978, p. 68).

The implications of the first criterion for deciding sample size – the required level of precision – now become clear. A sample size of, say, 1000 would give a confidence interval for a finding of 50 per cent of plus or minus 3.1 per cent. If that margin of error was not considered acceptable then a larger sample size would be necessary. Whether or not it is considered acceptable would depend on the uses to which the data were to be put and is related to the type of analysis to be done, as discussed below.

The confidence intervals in Table 12.2 illustrate further the second criterion concerning the choice of sample size – the type of analysis to be undertaken. If many detailed comparisons are to be made, especially concerning small proportions of the population, then the sample size may preclude very meaningful analysis. For instance, suppose a survey is conducted with a sample of 200 and it is found that 20 per cent of respondents went bowling and 30 per cent played tennis. The 20 per cent is subject to a margin of error of plus or minus 5.5 per cent and the 30 per cent is subject to a margin of plus or minus 6.3 per cent. Thus it is estimated that the proportions playing the two activities are as follows:

Bowling: between 14.5 and 25.5%.　　Tennis: between 23.7 and 36.3%.

The confidence intervals overlap, so we cannot conclude that there is any 'significant' difference in the popularity of the two activities, despite a 10 per cent difference given by the survey. This is likely to be very limiting in any analysis. If the sample were 500 the confidence intervals would be 3.5 per cent and 4.0 per cent respectively, giving estimates as follows:

Bowling: between 16.5 and 23.5%.　　Tennis: between 26.0 and 34.0%.

In this case the confidence intervals do *not* overlap and we can be fairly certain that tennis *is* more popular than bowling.

The detail of the analysis, the extent of subdivision of the sample into subsamples, and the acceptable level of precision will therefore determine the necessary size of the sample. By and large this has nothing to do with the overall size of the original population, although there is a likelihood that the larger the population the greater its diversity and therefore the greater the need for subdivision into sub-samples.

A further point to be noted is that it could be positively wasteful to expend resources on a large sample when it can be shown to be unnecessary. For example, a sample of 10 000 gives estimates of statistics with a maximum confidence interval of ±1.0 per cent. Such a survey could cost as much as £200 000 to conduct. To halve that confidence interval to ±0.5 per cent would mean quadrupling the sample size to 40 000 at an additional cost of £600 000. There can be very few situations where such expenditure would be justified for such a small return.

Ultimately then, the limiting factor in determining sample size will be the third criterion, the resources available. Even if the budget available limits the sample size severely it may be decided to go ahead and risk the possibility of an unrepresentative sample. If the sample is small however, the detail of the analysis will need to be limited. If resources are so limited that the validity of quantitative research is questionable, it may be sensible to consider qualitative research, which may be more feasible. Alternatively the proposed research can be seen as a 'pilot' exercise, with the emphasis on methodology, preparatory to a more adequately resourced full-scale study in future.

How should the issue of sample size and confidence intervals be referred to in the report on the research? In some scientific research complex statistical tests are considered necessary in reporting statistical results from surveys. In much social science research, and leisure and tourism research in particular, requirements are less rigorous. This is true to some extent in academic research, but is markedly so in the reporting of applied research. While it is necessary to be aware of the limitations imposed by the sample size and not to make comparisons which the data cannot support, explicit reference to such matters in the text of a consultancy report is rare. A great deal of statistical jargon is not generally required: the lay reader expects the researcher to do a good job and expert readers should be given enough information to check the analysis in the report for themselves. It is recommended that an appendix be included in reports indicating the size of the sampling errors. Appendix 12.1 presents a possible format.

In academic journals the rules are somewhat different and there is an expectation that statistical tests be 'up front'. The variety of tests available is pursued in Chapter 14.

WEIGHTING

In this and previous sections situations where weighting of survey or count data may be required have been indicated. In Chapter 13 the procedures for implementing weighting using the SPSS computer package are outlined. Here the principles involved are discussed. Take the example of the data shown in Table 12.3.

In the sample of 45 interviews the number of interviews is spread fairly evenly through the day, whereas more than half the users visit around the middle of the day (this information probably having been obtained by

Table 12.3 Interview or usage data (hypothetical)

Time	No. of interviews	%	Actual no. of users (counts)	%
9–11 a.m.	10	22.2	25	5.7
11.01 a.m.–1 p.m.	12	26.7	240	55.2
1.01–3 p.m.	11	24.4	110	25.3
3.01–5 p.m.	12	26.7	60	2.7
Total	45	100.0	435	100.0

observation or counts). This can be a source of bias in the sample, since the mid-day users may differ from the others in their characteristics or opinions and they will be under-represented in the sample. The aim of weighting is to produce a weighted sample with a distribution similar to that of the actual users.

One approach is to 'gross up' the sample numbers to reflect the actual numbers – for example, the 9–11 a.m. group is weighted by $25 \div 10 = 2.5$, the 11 a.m.–1 p.m. group is weighted by $240 \div 12 = 20$, and so on, as shown in Table 12.4.

The weighting factors can be fed into the computer for the weighting to be done automatically, as discussed in Chapter 13. The initial weighting factors are equal to the user number divided by the sample number for that time period. The weighted sample therefore is made to resemble the overall user numbers. It should be noted however, that the sample size is still 45, not 435! If statistical tests are to be carried out then it would be advisable to divide the weighting factors by 435/45 to bring the weighted sample total back to 45.

In this example the basis of the weighting relates to the pattern of visits over the course of the day, which happened to be information which was available in relation to this particular type of survey. Any other data available on the population could be used. For example, if age structure is available from the census, then age groups rather than time periods might be used.

Table 12.4 Weighting

Time	No. of interviews (A)	No. of users (B)	Weighting factors (C)	Weighted sample no. (D)
Source:	Survey	Counts	B/A	C × A
9–11 a.m.	10	25	2.5	25
11.01 a.m.–1 p.m.	12	240	20.0	240
1.01–3 p.m.	11	110	11.0	110
3.01–5 p.m.	12	60	5.0	60
Total	45	435		435

QUESTIONS AND EXERCISES

1 Examine either a published research report or a journal article related to an empirical study and identify the procedures used to ensure a random sample.

2 Using the report in exercise 1, produce confidence intervals for a range of percentage statistics occurring in the report.

3 In the example comparing bowling and tennis on page 212 above, what would the confidence intervals be if the sample size was 4000?

4 Examine the results from a national recreation participation survey or a domestic or international tourism survey and produce confidence intervals for a number of the key findings.

FURTHER READING

Sampling and the statistical implications of sampling are addressed in numerous statistics textbooks. *See also*: Hoinville and Jowell (1978, ch. 4); Kidder (1981).

APPENDIX 12.1
SUGGESTED APPENDIX ON SAMPLE SIZE AND CONFIDENCE INTERVALS

This is a suggested wording for an appendix or note to be included in research reports based on sample data. Suppose the survey has a sample size of 500.

Statistical note

All sample surveys are subject to a margin of statistical error. The margins of error, or 'confidence intervals', for this survey are as follows:

Finding from the survey	95% confidence interval
50%	± 4.4%
40/60%	± 4.3%
30/70%	± 4.0%
20/80%	± 3.5%
10/90%	± 2.6%
5/95%	± 1.9%

This means, for example, that if 20 per cent of the sample are found to have a particular characteristic, there is an estimated 95 per cent chance that the true population percentage lies in the range 20 ± 3.5, i.e. between 16.5 and 23.5 per cent.

These margins of error have been taken into account in the analyses in this report.

CHAPTER 13

Survey analysis

INTRODUCTION

This chapter outlines the use of a computer package for analysing data from questionnaire surveys. The chapter is organised as a step by step manual for operating the *Statistical Package for the Social Sciences* (SPSS) computer package and it is envisaged that the reader will have access to a computer with SPSS available on it, so that the various procedures described here can be tried out in practice.[1]

SPSS for Windows is the version of the package which is available for IBM-compatible personal computers using the Microsoft Windows system. The system is fully described in the *SPSS for Windows User's Manual* (Norusis, 1993). A *Studentware* version of SPSS exists, which is less expensive than the full version described here, but the number of variables which it can handle is restricted to 50 and the range of analytical procedures included is limited. (It can handle all the procedures covered in this chapter, except multiple response.) Versions of SPSS also exist for Macintosh computers and for mainframe computers. SPSS is one of the most commonly used statistical packages; others include *Minitab*, *BMD* (Biomedical Data analysis), *SAS* (Statistical Analysis System) and *Turbostats*.

A full list of SPSS procedures can be found in the SPSS manual. In this chapter four main procedures only are described:

- *Frequencies*, which involves counts and percentages of individual variables
- *Crosstabs*, the cross-tabulation of two or more variables
- *Means*, obtaining means or averages of appropriate variables
- *Graphics*, the production of graphics

Further procedures are covered in Chapter 14. The areas covered in this chapter and Chapter 14 are summarised in Figure 13.1.

This chapter deals with the analysis of data from questionnaire surveys. But it should be noted that SPSS can be used to analyse data from other sources also. And although the package is ideally suited to dealing with numerical data it can also handle non-numerical data. Any data organised on the basis of *cases* and a common range of *variables* for each case can be analysed using the package (*cases* and *variables* are defined below).

This chapter does not deal with procedures for logging into a computer, file handling, or the use of Windows in general, but some notes on the basics of Windows are included in Appendix 13.1. The chapter does not deal with the

Figure 13.1 **Survey analysis overview**

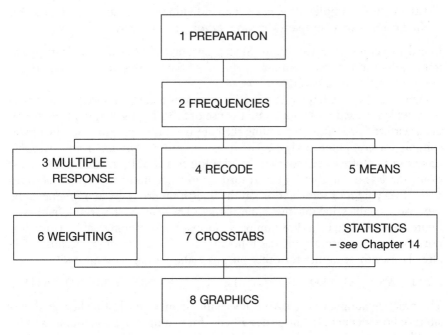

installation of the SPSS software on to the computer; it is assumed that SPSS for Windows is already installed on a computer available to the reader.

The information in the chapter provides an introduction to the basics only. It is envisaged that most readers will have access to a teacher or tutor to assist as problems arise and will also have access to the full SPSS manual for more advanced or detailed issues. In higher education institutions SPSS, as with other computer packages, is generally made available in computer laboratories on licence; copies of the official manuals are usually available in the university computer centre or the library.

Further training is available in SPSS, and other survey packages, through universities, commercial computer training organisations and the SPSS company itself in major centres around the world.

DEFINING VARIABLES

Variables and variable names

SPSS deals with data which are organised in terms of *cases* and *variables*.

- A *case* is a single example of the phenomenon being studied and on which data have been collected – for example, an individual member of a community, an employee of a company, a leisure or tourism organisation, or a country.

- A *variable* is an item of data relating to a case, which can take on different values – for example, the *gender* of an individual; the *salary* of an employee, the *turnover* of a company, the *population* of a country.

In order to communicate with the SPSS program it is necessary to identify each item of data in the questionnaire. An item of data is referred to as a *variable* and is identified by a *variable name*.

Figure 10.14, in Chapter 10 (p. 185), contains a copy of a simple questionnaire which is used to demonstrate the use of SPSS in this chapter. Chapter 10 dealt with the procedure for coding the data from this questionnaire in a form suitable for computer analysis. The questionnaire is *annotated with variable names* in the 'office use' column. In addition to variables related to the questions, there is a variable qno to record a reference number for the questionnaire. Every item of information on the questionnaire is given a *unique* name (no two variables having the same name). The length of variable names is limited to eight letters and/or numbers (no spaces), beginning with a letter. It is not permitted to use any of the following for variable names, because SPSS already uses these names for other purposes and would get confused!

ALL   AND   BY   EQ   GE   GT   LE   LT   NE   NOT   OR   TO   WITH

The practice adopted here is to use variable names which are shortened versions of how the item might be described – for example crse for course, and lib for library. An alternative way of labelling variables is to use a generalised name such as var for variable; so a questionnaire with five variables would have variable names: var01, var02, var03, var04, var05. In fact SPSS has a system of 'default' variable names already set up in this form, which can be used instead of the customised names used here.

Multiple response

Questions 2 and 6 in Figure 10.14 are *multiple-response* questions. Question 2 is a *multiple-response – dichotomous* variable, because each answer category is essentially a yes/no, dichotomous variable. One respondent could tick all four boxes, so each is a separate variable. Question 6 is a *multiple-response – categories* variable. It is a multiple-response question because it is open-ended and respondents might give any number of answers. In this case the designer of the questionnaire has assigned three variables to record the answers (sug1, sug2 and sug3), on the assumption that a maximum of three answers would be given by any one respondent. Not all respondents will necessarily give three answers. Some may, however, give more than three answers, in which case it would not be possible to record the fourth and any subsequent answers. If more than a handful of respondents give more than three answers then a fourth variable (sug4) would need to be added. The decision on how many answers to allow for must depend on examination of the survey returns. The coding for question 4, an open-ended question, would need to be devised as discussed in Chapter 10. The variables sug1, sug2 and sug3 have the same coding system.

AN SPSS SESSION

Starting up

Starting up an SPSS session involves just two steps, as shown in Figure 13.2. A copy of the *Newdata* screen which appears when step 2 is implemented is shown in Figure 13.3. The table presented is blank except for the 'default' variable names (var001, var002, etc.) across the top. You can move around this spreadsheet-style window (your current position being indicated by the highlighted cell) using the arrow keys on the keyboard or a mouse. At the start column 1, row 1 is highlighted.

Creating a data file

The first task is to create a *data file*. Later we will also encounter *output files* and *graphics files*. Details of these three different types of file and the *naming conventions* used when they are stored on hard disk or floppy disks are given in Figure 13.4. Further details of these files are given at appropriate points below. The *data file* provides information about a particular questionnaire to the computer and includes the data to be analysed. Once created, it is saved on a floppy disk or hard disk for future use.

Defining variables

In SPSS variables are defined by:

- *Variable name:* as discussed above. All variables *must* have names.
- *Variable label:* a longer version of the variable name to explain more fully what the variable is. This is *optional.*
- *Value labels:* labels explaining what each code stands for. This is *optional,* and is not required at all for numerical variables, such as the questionnaire number and cost (question 4).

The first task in establishing a data file is to tell the computer what variables are in the questionnaire, and the labels which are to be attached to them. This is covered in Figure 13.2, steps 3 to 10, which create a window which looks as shown in Figure 13.5.

The data window will now look as shown in Figure 13.5. Only the variable *names* are visible on the screen, but in Figure 13.5 the full list of **Variable Labels** and **Value Labels** entered for the example questionnaire is also shown. Variable labels and value labels can be checked by selecting **Utilities** (at the top of the screen) then **Variables**.

Saving files to disk

The data file should be saved (step 11) on to a floppy disk or hard disk periodically while entering information – say every 10 minutes or so. The most

Figure 13.2   An SPSS session

Starting up

1 From Windows, select the SPSS icon using the mouse.
2 You are presented with a blank 'Newdata' *window* (*see* Fig. 13.3).

Creating a data file

3 Select **Data** with the mouse, then select **Define Variables**.
4 In the **Variable Name** box, type qno over the top of the existing default name var001.
5 Then select **OK**. This is all that needs to be done for qno.
6 Move the highlight one space to the right and repeat steps 3 and 4 for the next variable name – crse.
7 Then select **Labels..** and enter a **Variable Label** (e.g. for variable crse: insert the variable label: **Course enrolled**).
8 Select **Value Labels**. Enter the values/codes and labels as follows:
   ● enter the code or value in the **Value** box and press the Tab key
   ● enter the corresponding label in the **Value Label** box
   ● select **Add** – the value and label appear in the box
     (e.g. for the variable crse: 1 U/grad 2 Grad.dip. 3 Masters 4 Other).
9 Select **Continue** then **OK**.
10 Repeat steps 6–9 for every variable; the result should appear as in Fig. 13.5.

Saving the data file to disk

11 Save the data file to disk as follows:
   ● Select **File**
   ● Select **Save**
   ● Enter a file name – with disk drive at the beginning and **.sav** as suffix, as shown in Fig. 13.4 – e.g. **a:\student.sav** (on the a: drive) or **b:\student.sav** (on the b: drive).

Restarting (with an existing file)

12 Select **File**, then **Open**, then **Data**.
13 Type in the data file name, e.g. **a:\student.sav**, or
   select the a: drive (or b: or c: drive) on the **Open Data** window, then select **OK** and the computer will list all the **.sav** files on the disk, and the required file can be selected.

Adding data

14 Enter data.

Figure 13.3 'Newdata' blank window

SPSS for Windows	▲▼

File Edit Data Transform Statistics Graphs Utilities Window Help

!Output ▲▼

Newdata ▲▼ ▲

	var001	var002	var003	var004	var005	var006	var007
1							
2							
3							
4							
5							
etc							

Figure 13.4 SPSS files

File type	Function/content	Naming convention			
		File suffix	Example 1	Example 2	Example 3
Data file	Contains details of questionnaire and survey data	.sav	student.sav	sport1.sav	smith.sav
Output files	Contains results (tables, analyses) from an SPSS session	.lst	student.lst	sport1.lst	smith.lst
Graphics files	Contains graphical output (bar charts, pie charts etc.) from an SPSS session	.cht	student.cht	sport1.cht	smith.cht

up-to-date version of the file replaces the last saved file on the disk. This ensures that, if anything happens to the computer (for example, a power cut), the data entered have been saved to disk and are not lost.

The preparation of a data file can be stopped and resumed once the latest version of the file has been saved. Restarting procedures are shown in steps 12 and 13 in Figure 13.2.

Using a template

Labels for a number of variables with the same labels can be added more quickly by using a *template*, as outlined in Figure 13.6.

Figure 13.5　Newdata window with variable names and labels

Newdata

qno	crse	lib	cant	comp	scs	rep	access	curr	fees	park	cost	text	lect	assgn	sug1	sug2	sug3
1																	
2																	
3																	
4																	
5																	

Variable labels and value labels

		Library use	Canteen use	Computer service	Student counselling service use	Reputation – rank	Ease of access – rank	Curriculum – rank	Fees – rank	Parking – rank	Course costs, £	Textbook	Lecturer	Assess-ment	Suggestion 1	Suggestion 2	Suggestion 3
Variable labels	–	Course enrolled															
Value labels	–	1 U/grad 2 Grad.dip 3 Masters 4 Other	1 Yes 0 No			No value labels – ranks					No value labels	1 Not important 2 Important 3 Very important			1 Content 2 Structure 3 Delivery 4 Lecturer 5 Skills etc.		

Figure 13.6 Using a template

1 If a number of variables have the same values and labels, use the *Template* facility to avoid having to repeatedly enter the same values – e.g. in the case of <u>lib</u> to <u>scs</u> or <u>text</u>, <u>lect</u> and <u>assgn</u>. If the variables are contiguous, highlight them all by 'dragging' the mouse along the first row of the variables – the variables are blocked in black. Select **Data** with the mouse and then **Template**.

2 On the **Template** window, you can leave the name as DEFAULT or give the template a name if you are likely to use a number of templates (e.g. **temp1**, **temp2**, etc.). Select **Value Labels** and **Column format**. Select **Define**, then **Value Labels**, as in steps 6–7. (If you want to name the template, change the name and select **Add**.)

3 Select **Continue** then select **OK** to apply the template values to the highlighted variables.

Note: A template, once defined, can be called up again and applied to other variables – e.g. when, as is often the case, a number of variables throughout a questionnaire have the same value/label, such as: 1/0 for Yes/No.

Entering data

The actual data from the survey can now be entered – one line of data per questionnaire. Thus the data from 15 questionnaires would appear as shown in Figure 13.7.

Decimal places may appear on the screen. This will not affect the analysis, but can be annoying. The decimal places can be altered for variables individually by selecting <u>D</u>ata then **Type**, and specifying **decimal places 0**. Or it can be done for all the variables via **Edit** and **Preferences**. (The change will come into force only when you have saved the data file and started another SPSS session.)

Instead of the numbers/codes being displayed in the data file window, the labels can be displayed if you prefer (for example, Yes, No, instead of 1 and 0). To do this, select <u>U</u>tilities then **Value Labels**. The result is shown in Figure 13.8. To revert to numerical display repeat this process.

Using a word processor or spreadsheet to enter data

If access to a computer with the SPSS program is limited, the actual *data* (step 14 of Figure 13.2 above) can be entered on another computer, using a normal word processor or spreadsheet program. The procedures for doing this are set out in Figure 13.9.

Figure 13.7 Data from 15 questionnaires

Data file: a:\student.sav

qno	crse	lib	cant	comp	scs	rep	access	curr	fees	park	cost	text	lect	assgn	sug1	sug2	sug3
1	2	1	1	0	0	1	4	2	3	5	100	3	3	1	1		
2	2	1	1	1	0	1	4	2	3	5	50	2	3	1	2	1	
3	3	1	0	0	0	2	5	1	3	4	250	2	2	2	3	4	
4	4	0	0	0	0	2	3	1	4	5	25	3	2	2	1	2	4
5	3	1	0	0	1	1	4	3	2	5	55	3	3	1			
6	3	1	1	1	0	2	4	1	3	5	40	2	3	1	2		
7	2	1	0	0	0	3	2	1	4	5	150	2	3	2	3		
8	2	1	0	1	0	3	4	2	1	5	250	1	2	2	4	5	
9	4	0	1	0	0	1	5	2	3	4	300	2	3	2			
10	3	1	1	0	0	2	3	1	5	4	100	1	2	1	1	1	
11	3	1	1	0	1	2	3	1	4	5	75	2	2	1	2	3	
12	2	1	0	1	0	1	4	3	2	5	50	2	3	1			
13	1	1	0	1	0	1	5	2	3	4	55	2	3	2	1	2	
14	3	1	1	0	0	2	4	1	3	5	75	3	3	2	4		
15	1	1	1	0	0	3	2	1	5	4	150	3	3	1	1	2	5

Figure 13.8   Data file with value labels displayed

Data file: a:\student.sav

qno	crse	lib	cant	comp	scs	rep	access	curr	fees	park	cost	text	lect	assgn	sug1	sug2	sug3
1	Grad/dip	Yes	Yes	No	No	1	4	2	3	5	100	Very im	Very im	Not im	Cont		
2	Grad/dip	Yes	Yes	Yes	No	1	4	2	3	5	50	Import	Very im	Not im	Structure	Cont	
3	Masters	Yes	No	No	No	2	5	1	3	4	250	Import	Import	Import	Deliv	Lect	
4	Other	No	No	No	No	2	3	1	4	5	25	Very im	Import	Import	Cont	Structure	Lect
5	Masters	Yes	No	No	Yes	1	4	3	2	5	55	Very im	Very im	Not im			
6	Masters	Yes	Yes	Yes	No	2	4	1	3	5	40	Import	Very im	Not im	Structure		
7	Grad/dip	Yes	No	No	No	3	2	1	4	5	150	Import	Very im	Import	Deliv		
8	Grad/dip	Yes	No	Yes	No	3	4	2	1	5	250	Not im	Import	Import	Lect	Skills	
9	Other	No	Yes	No	No	1	5	2	3	4	300	Import	Very im	Import			
10	Masters	Yes	Yes	No	No	2	3	1	5	4	100	Not im	Import	Not im	Cont	Cont	
11	Masters	Yes	Yes	No	Yes	2	3	1	4	5	75	Import	Import	Not im	Structure	Deliv	
12	Grad/dip	Yes	No	Yes	No	1	4	3	2	5	50	Import	Very im	Not im			
13	U/grad	Yes	No	Yes	No	1	5	2	3	4	55	Import	Very im	Import	Cont	Structure	
14	Masters	Yes	Yes	No	No	2	4	1	3	5	75	Very im	Very im	Import	Lect	Structure	
15	U/grad	Yes	Yes	No	No	3	2	1	5	4	150	Very im	Very im	Not im	Cont	Structure	Skills

Figure 13.9 Using a word processor or spreadsheet to prepare data

---

Word processor

1 The data can be prepared using a word processor, but the variable names and the variable and value labels must be added using SPSS. Type the data into a word processor file or document, with a TAB between each variable. Save in DOS or ASCII format using the procedure specified in the word-processor package. When saving the file, preferably name it using a **.dat** suffix – e.g. **a:\student.dat**

2 In SPSS Windows, select **File** and then **Read ASCII Data**. Enter name of file (e.g. **a:\student.dat**) and ENTER. Enter names for each variable as requested. Then select **OK**. Data appear in window, with the default variable names (var001, var002, etc.). Now insert variable names and labels and value labels.

Spreadsheet

1 Data can be prepared using a spreadsheet, but variable labels and value labels must be added using SPSS. Prepare the spreadsheet with one column for each variable and one row for each questionnaire. Put the variable names along the first row of the spreadsheet. The saved file will have a suffix **.wk1** or **.wk2** (Lotus) or **.wks** (Excel) – e.g. **student.wk1** or **student.wks**.

2 To import the spreadsheet into SPSS, start up SPSS as in steps 1–2 in Fig. 13.2. Select **File** then **Open**, then **Data**. Type in the file name, with drive – e.g. **a:\student.wk1**. Select **Lotus** and **Read Variable Names**, then select **OK**.

3 The data and variable names should appear in the **Newdata** window. Now go to step 6 in Fig. 13.2 to add variable labels and value labels.

4 *Updating:* If you have added more data to your file on the spreadsheet and wish to add to the SPSS file, proceed as follows. Import the updated file into SPSS, as in step 2 above. Now go to **File**, select **Apply Data Dictionary** and enter the previous SPSS (e.g. **student.sav**) name as requested, then **Continue**. The labels etc. will all now apply to the new data. Save under the old or a new name – e.g. **student2.sav.**

SURVEY ANALYSIS: INTRODUCTION

In Chapter 1 it was noted that research might be of three kinds: descriptive, explanatory and evaluative. Before considering the process of analysing questionnaire survey data, these types of research and their relationship to survey analysis by SPSS are discussed in turn below.

Descriptive research

Descriptive research usually involves the presentation of information in a fairly simple form. Of the SPSS procedures described here, the two most appropriate for descriptive research are *Frequencies* and *Means*. *Frequencies* presents counts and percentages for single variables. *Means* presents averages for those numerical variables.

The questionnaire used in this chapter to illustrate the use of SPSS involves mostly descriptive elements. However, it could have other dimensions, as discussed below.

Explanatory research

Descriptive data do not, of themselves, *explain* anything. To *explain* the patterns in data it is necessary to consider the question of *causality* and how data analysis can address the issue of whether A is caused by B. In Chapter 2 it was noted that to establish causality it was necessary to fulfil four criteria: association, time priority, non-spurious relation and rationale.

1 *Associations* between variables can be explored using such SPSS procedures as *crosstabs* and *regression* (discussed in Chapter 14).
2 *Time priority* – establishing that for A to be the cause of B then A must take place *before* B – is sometimes testable in social science research and is sometimes obvious, but is generally more appropriate for the conditions of the natural science laboratory.
3 *Non-spurious* relationships are those which 'make sense' theoretically (that is that the relationship between A and B is not mediated by a third variable C), and are not just a 'fluke' of the data. This can be approached using SPSS. For example, if A is related to B (for example, income related to leisure or tourism expenditure) for the whole sample, and the two variables are also related in a similar way for, say, men and women separately, and for other sub-groups – even random sub-samples – this suggests a non-spurious relationship (see discussion of reliability below).
4 *Rationale*, or theory, is of course not produced by SPSS but should be integral to the research design. As indicated in Chapter 2, the research may be deductive in nature, with pre-established hypotheses which are tested by the data analysis, or it may be inductive in nature, in which case development of theory and explanation building take place to a greater or lesser extent as part of the data analysis process. Either way, *explanation*, or the establishment of causality, is not complete without some sort of rational explanation of the relationships found.

The example questionnaire offers only limited scope for *explanatory* research. For example, differences in attitudes between the various groups – undergraduate and postgraduate for example – may reflect varying needs of the two groups and a very different set of expectations from education.

The particular procedures which are appropriate for explanatory analysis and which are covered in this chapter are *Crosstabs* and *Means*. However, it should be stressed that the fact that two variables are *related* in some way does not, of itself, indicate *causality*. For example it may be found that there is a relationship between expenditure on books and level of income. But this does not necessarily mean that there is a *causal* relationship between level of income and book-buying. While such a relationship found in a student survey might be based on causality, in the wider community, the determining factor in book-buying is more likely to be *education* level rather than income level, and a community survey would merely be picking up the fact that there is generally a positive relationship between income level and education level. It is *theory* that leads to conclusions about causality; data alone cannot be relied upon (see Hellevik, 1984).

As discussed in Chapter 2, it is also desirable to establish the *consistency* or reliability of associations between variables. While SPSS procedures are well suited to establishing the magnitude and strength of associations the question of the consistency of associations is more complex. In the social sciences, unlike the natural sciences, it is not always possible to replicate research to establish consistency. While reference to the literature can be relevant in this respect, in fact, the changing nature of human behaviour over time and space means that consistency with previous research findings is by no means a guarantee of validity.

Evaluative research

Evaluative research basically involves comparisons. Are the survey findings higher or lower than some external benchmark? The external benchmarks may be established performance standards (for example, a leisure centre being required to have at least x per cent of attendances by young people or a hotel to have a y per cent level of occupancy) or simply comparisons with previous years' figures or with comparable programmes elsewhere. The analysis called for is therefore relatively simple, is generally descriptive in nature and is easily facilitated by SPSS.

The example questionnaire does not appear to be related to research of an evaluative nature. However, it can be seen that the intended use of the results could well be evaluative – for example, a low level of use of one of the services listed in question 2 would imply that the service is not performing well in meeting the needs of students.

Overlaps

Analysis does not always fall exclusively into one of the above three modes. For example, in presenting a descriptive account of the example student questionnaire survey results, it would be natural to provide a breakdown of the participation patterns and preferences of the four graduate and undergraduate student groups included (provided the sample size was large enough). This would involve the use of *Crosstabs* and/or *Means*). While this account would be descriptive in form, it would begin to hint at explanation, in that any differences in the groups' patterns of behaviour or opinions would seem to call for explanation; the analysis would be saying 'these groups are different' and would be implicitly posing the question 'why?'

The relationships between the various types of research discussed and SPSS analysis procedures are summarised in Figure 13.10.

Figure 13.10   Research types and SPSS procedures

- *Descriptive:* Frequencies, Means

- *Explanatory:* Crosstabs, Compare Means

- *Evaluative:*   Frequencies (compared with targets or benchmarks)
                  Crosstabs (comparing groups)
                  Means (compared with some benchmark or target)

RELIABILITY

In Chapter 2 reference was made to questions of validity and reliability. It has been noted that some attempt at testing validity – whether the data are measuring what they are intended to measure – can be achieved in the design of questionnaires. Reliability – whether similar results would be obtained if the research were replicated – is again a difficult issue in the social sciences, but an approach can be made at the analysis stage. If the sample is large enough, one approach to testing reliability is to split the sample into two or more subsamples on a random basis and see if the results for the sub-sample are the same as for the sample as a whole. This can be achieved in SPSS: this procedure is not covered here but full details are given in the SPSS manual.

STARTING AN SPSS ANALYSIS SESSION

The data file may already be on screen (as in Figure 13.7) if you have just completed typing in your data. If not, you need to open the file as shown in steps 12 and 13 in Figure 13.2. Once a disk drive has been specified (for example, a: or b:) the computer will continue to use that drive until you change it.

FREQUENCIES

One variable

Frequencies is the simplest form of descriptive analysis: it merely produces counts and percentages for individual variables – for instance, the numbers and percentages of respondents registered in each type of course (crse).

It is advisable to begin the analysis of a data set by running *Frequencies* for one variable, so that the computer can read through the data and establish that there are no serious problems with the data. The steps to obtain a table of the number of students enrolled in different types of course are set out in Figure 13.11, together with the resultant output.

Figure 13.11 Frequencies for one variable

Procedures

1 Select **Statistics**.
2 Select **Summarize**.
3 Select **Frequencies**.
4 Select the variable of interest (crse) by highlighting and clicking on the 'right arrow' box.
5 The variable name appears in the **Variables:** box.
6 Select **OK:** the results appear in the **Output** window, as shown below

After checking the table, if you wish to save it to disk:

7 Select **File**.
8 Then **Save SPSS Output**.
9 Enter an appropriate file name with drive and suffix **.lst** – e.g. **a:\student.lst**.

Output

CRSE   Course

Value Label	Value	Frequency	Per cent	Valid per cent	Cum per cent
Undergrad.	1	2	13.3	13.3	13.3
Grad. Dip.	2	5	33.3	33.3	46.7
Masters	3	6	40.0	40.0	86.7
Other	4	2	13.3	13.3	100.0
	Total	15	100.0	100.0	

Valid cases   15   Missing cases   0

Notes

- *Values* are the codes (1 to 4) for the variable crse.
- *Frequency* is a count of the numbers of respondents or students falling into each category, adding up, in this case, to 15, the sample size.
- *Per cent* converts this into percentages.
- *Valid per cent* is explained below, under 'missing values'.
- *Cum per cent* adds percentages cumulatively – which may be useful for a variable like age, expenditure or income, but is not particularly useful for the variable crse.

Presentation note

The format of the output table in Figure 13.11 is not suitable for inclusion in a research report. It must be edited or retyped for inclusion in a report – *see* Presentation of results below.

Frequencies for a number of variables

If the single variable table has worked satisfactorily, frequency tables for all the variables can be obtained by the same procedure as above, but selecting all the variables (except qno). At step 4 (in Figure 13.11) just block in all the variables in the 'dialogue' box and transfer them to the right-hand box for analysis. This runs frequency tables for all variables and is a common initial instruction in survey analysis: it is a good way of obtaining an overview of the results, and checking that all is well with the data. The results of this exercise for the example questionnaire are in Appendix 13.2.

Missing values

What happens when questions are not answered, either by error or design, and the particular column or columns in the data file are left blank? This can be seen in Questions 6(1) to 6(3) in Appendix 13.2. When there is no answer for a question or variable, the computer calls them 'missing values' and they are listed with a 'Value' of a full stop in the table. In the *Per cent* column missing values are included, but in the *Valid per cent* column they are excluded. In any particular situation, the question of which set of percentages to use – the one including the missing values (*Per cent*) or the one excluding them (*Valid per cent*) – is a matter of judgement.

Checking for errors

After obtaining the *Frequencies* printout for all variables it is necessary to check through the results to see if there are any errors. This could be, for example, in the form of a non-valid code or an unexpected missing value. The error must be traced in the data file and corrected, perhaps by reference back to the original questionnaire. The data must then be corrected on the data file and the *Frequencies* table for that variable run again. *The corrected data file should then be saved to disk.*

MULTIPLE RESPONSE

It has been noted that questions 2 and 6 in Figure 10.14 are *multiple-response* questions. It can be seen from Appendix 13.2 that the normal *Frequencies* procedure produces output for these questions in a rather inconvenient format – four tables for question 2 and three tables for question 6. SPSS will combine multiple responses into one table. The SPSS procedure *Multiple Response* is operated as shown in Figure 13.12. The difference between dichotomous and category multiple-response variables in explained on page 218.

RECODE

Recode with numerical non-pre-coded variables

As the name implies, *Recode* is a procedure which can be used to change the codes of variables. This applies particularly to numerical variables such as <u>cost</u> in the example questionnaire. This variable is a numerical variable, which is not 'pre-coded': the *actual* expenditure was recorded rather than a group code. The advantage of not having the variable pre-coded is that it is possible to be flexible about what groupings are required and it is possible, as shown below, to use such procedures as *Means*. This is not generally possible with pre-coded variables.

Because <u>cost</u> is not pre-coded, the *Frequencies* output lists every single level of expenditure given by respondents, as shown in Appendix 13.2. In a large survey this could become hundreds, and would be unmanageable for cross-tabulation. A *Recoded*, grouped, version of the expenditure variable can be produced. The method is demonstrated, using the variable <u>cost</u>, in Figure 13.13.

Recode with pre-coded variables

It is also possible to change the groupings of pre-coded variables using *Recode*. For instance, analysis could be conducted comparing undergraduates and postgraduates as two groups, by recoding postgraduates into one group. This is illustrated in the second part of Figure 13.13.

MEANS

A *mean* is the same as an *average*. It is often useful to be able to produce means – for instance mean ages, incomes, time spent. Means can only be produced for numerical data. Means *cannot* be produced for coded variables where the codes represent qualitative categories and not quantities.

Two procedures are available in SPSS for producing means, as shown in Figure 13.14. Method 1 shows that average course expenditure among the sample is £115. Note that this is purely *descriptive*. Method 2 produces means for sub-groups as well as for the whole sample. For example, in Figure 13.14 the mean costs are shown for students on different courses. Note that this moves into the area of *explanation*, since it reveals that different courses lead to different levels of expenditure.

Figure 13.12 Multiple response

Procedures

1 Select **Statistics**.
2 Then **Multiple Response**.
3 Then **Define Sets**.

Multiple response – dichotomous	Multiple response – categories
4 Put lib, cant, comp, scs in the **Variables in Set** box.	4 Put sug1, sug2, sug3 into the **Variables in Set** box.
5 Under the **Variables are coded as..** box, select **Dichotomies**.	5 Under **Variables are coded as..**, select **Categories**.
6 Enter **1** in the **Counted value** box (then TAB).	6 Enter **Range** 1 through 5.
7 Give the 'set' a **Name** – e.g. services.	7 Add **Name**, e.g. sug.
8 Add a **Label** – e.g. Services used.	8 Add **Label**, e.g. Suggestions.
9 Select **Add**.	9 Select **Add**.
10 A new variable, $services is listed automatically.	10 A new variable $sug is listed automatically.
11 Select **Close**.	11 Select **Close**.

To produce a table

12 Select **Statistics**.
13 Select **Multiple Response**.
14 Select **Frequencies** and use the new variable.

Output

Dichotomous

Group $services Services used (Value tabulated = 1)

Dichotomy label	Name	Count	Per cent of responses	Per cent of cases*
Library	LIB	13	46.4	92.9
Canteen	CANT	8	28.6	57.1
Computer service	COMP	5	17.9	35.7
Student counselling	SCS	2	7.1	14.3
Total responses		28	100.0	200.0

1 missing cases; 14 valid cases

Categories

Group $sug Suggestions

Category label	Code	Count	Per cent of responses	Per cent of cases
Content	1	7	31.8	58.3
Structure	2	6	27.3	50.0
Delivery	3	3	13.6	25.0
Lecturer	4	4	18.2	33.3
Skills etc.	5	2	9.1	16.7
Total responses		22	100.0	183.3

3 missing cases; 12 valid cases

*NB. Per cent differs from Appendix 13.2 because of exclusion of non-respondents.

Figure 13.13   Recode

For a non-pre-coded/numerical variable

The aim is to recode the variable <u>cost</u> as follows:

Proposed groups	New code	Value labels
0–50	1	£0–50
51–100	2	£51–100
101–200	3	£101–200
201+	4	£201 and over

Procedures

1 Select **Transform**.
2 Select **Recode**.
3 Select **Into Different Variable**.
4 Select the variable to be recoded (<u>cost</u>) and transfer to the box labelled **Numeric variable > Output variable**.
5 Select **Old and New Values**.
6 Select **Range**.
7 Enter **1** to **50** (Press TAB), enter **1** against **Value** (TAB), then **Add**.
8 Enter **51** to **100** (TAB), enter **2** against **Value** (TAB), then **Add**.
9 Enter **101** to **200** (TAB), enter **3** against **Value** (TAB), then **Add**.
10 Select **Range through Highest**.
11 Enter **201** (TAB), enter **4** against **Value** (TAB), then **Add**. The '**Old – New**' box now contains:

> 1 thru 40 -> 1
> 51 thru 100 -> 2
> 101 thru 200 -> 3
> 201 thru highest -> 4

12 Select **Continue**.
13 Under **Output Variable**, add a name (e.g. <u>costr</u>) and label (e.g. <u>Cost Recoded</u>).
14 Select **Change**, then **OK**. The new variable appears on the data screen.
15 Add **Value Labels** now, via **Data**, as for any variable.
16 **Save** the data file with the new variable, if you want to use it again.
17 Produce a **Frequencies** table for <u>costr</u> in the usual way.

For a pre-coded variable

Example: recode the variable <u>crse</u>:

From	To
1 Undergraduate	1 Undergraduate
2 Grad. Diploma	2 Other
3 Masters	
4 Other	

Procedures

1 Do steps 1–5 above.
2 Value 1 retains old value.
3 Recode values 2–4 as 2.
4 Do steps 12 to 17 above.

Figure 13.14 Means

Method 1 Procedure – using 'Frequencies'

1 Select **Statistics**.
2 Select **Summarize**.
3 Select **Frequencies**.
4 Select <u>cost</u>.
5 Within the **Frequencies** box, select **Statistics** at the bottom of the screen.
6 Select **Mean**.
7 Select **Continue**.
8 Select **OK** to run the **Frequencies** in the normal way.

Output

COST   Course costs, £

Value label	Value	Frequency	Per cent	Valid per cent	Cum Per cent
	25	1	6.7	6.7	6.7
	40	1	6.7	6.7	13.3
	50	2	13.3	13.3	26.7
	55	2	13.3	13.3	40.0
	75	2	13.3	13.3	53.3
	100	2	13.3	13.3	66.7
	150	2	13.3	13.3	80.0
	250	2	13.3	13.3	93.3
	300	1	6.7	6.7	100.0
	Total	15	100.0	100.0	

Mean   115.000

Valid cases   15   Missing cases   0

Method 2 Procedure – Using 'Means'

1 Select **Statistics**, then **Compare Means**, then **Means**.
2 Select <u>crse</u> and put it into the **Independent list** box.
3 Select <u>exp</u> and put it into the **Dependent list** box.
4 Select **OK**.

Output

Description of Subpopulations

Summaries of   COST Course costs, £   by Levels of   CRSE   Course

Variable	Value	Label	Mean	Std Dev	Cases
For entire population			115.0000	87.0755	15
CRSE	1	Undergrad.	102.5000	67.1751	2
CRSE	2	Grad. Dip.	120.0000	83.6660	5
CRSE	3	Masters	99.1667	76.6431	6
CRSE	4	Other	162.5000	194.4544	2

Total Cases = 15.

ATTITUDE AND LIKERT SCALES

Means are an appropriate form of analysis when using attitude or 'Likert' type scales. The scores of 1 to 3 in question 5 in Figure 10.14 can be treated as numerical indicators of the level of importance respondents attach to text-books, the lecturer and ease of assignments.

For example, using the *Method 1* on text, lect and assgn produces means as shown in Figure 13.15. The means can be interpreted as 'scores' on impor-tance. In the example, a knowledgeable lecturer is seen as most important, fol-lowed by the textbook then the ease of assignments, which is seen as not at all important. Means can also be used in relation to ranked variables, as in ques-tion 3 of Figure 10.14.

PRESENTATION OF RESULTS: STATISTICAL SUMMARIES

The layout of the tables produced by SPSS contains more detail than is neces-sary for most reports. It is recommended that a *statistical summary* be pre-pared for inclusion in any report, rather than include a copy of the SPSS printout. The summary must be prepared with a word processor, either typing it out afresh or editing the saved *output* file. For example, the output from the *Frequencies* analysis for all variables could be summarised as in Figure 13.15.

Notes

1 The results from the *Multiple Response* variables lib to scs and sug1 to sug3 are presented in single tables in Figure 13.15.
2 The average cost and the scores for the attitude variables come from the *Means* procedure discussed above.
3 It is generally not necessary to include frequency counts as well as percent-ages in reports, as long as the sample size is indicated, so that, if needed, any reader can work out the raw numbers for themselves.

CROSS-TABULATION

Introduction

After *Frequencies*, the most commonly used SPSS command is probably *Crosstabs*. This command relates two or more variables and marks the move from purely descriptive to explanatory analysis. The procedure and output are shown in Figure 13.16.

Note that, having been specified as the *row* variable, crse goes down the side, and, as the *column* variable, comp goes across the top. Specifying the two variables the other way round would produce a table with crse across the top and comp down the side.

Figure 13.15   Student survey 1996: statistical summary

Sample size	15
Type of course enrolled in	%
Undergraduate	13.3
Graduate diploma	33.3
Masters	40.0
Other	13.3
University services used in the last six months	
Library	86.7
Canteen	53.3
Union computer services	33.3
Student counselling service	13.3
Importance of factors in choosing a course	Average rank
(a) Good reputation	1.8
(b) Easy access	3.7
(c) Curriculum	1.6
(d) Level of fees	3.0
(e) Easy parking	4.7
Cost of books in the last year	%
£0–50	26.7
£51–100	26.7
£101–200	26.7
Over £200	20.0
Average cost	£115.00

Importance of factors in studying

	Very important %	Important %	Not important %	Mean score*
Good textbook	33.3	53.3	13.3	2.2
Knowledgeable lecturer	66.7	33.3	0.0	2.7
Easy assignments	0.0	46.7	53.3	1.5

(* 3 = very important; 2 = important; 1= not important)

Suggestions for improving the course	%
Comments on course contents	46.7
Comments on course structure	40.0
Comments on course delivery	20.0
Comments on lecturer	20.0
Comments on skills learned	13.3

Figure 13.16   Crosstabs

Procedures

1 Select **Statistics**.
2 Select **Summarize**.
3 Select **Crosstabs**.
4 Put crse into the **Columns** box.
5 Put pref into the **Rows** box.
6 Select **OK**.

Output

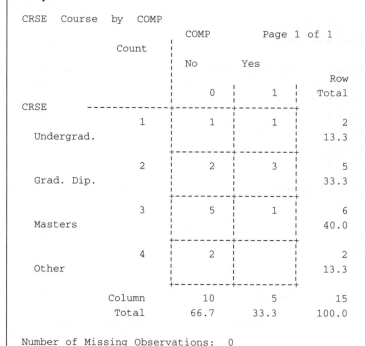

```
CRSE   Course   by   COMP
                          COMP           Page 1 of 1
                  Count :
                        :   No      Yes
                        :                          Row
                        :    0   :    1   :      Total
CRSE        ------------+--------+--------+
                    1   :    1   :    1   :        2
  Undergrad.        :        :        :       13.3
                        +--------+--------+
                    2   :    2   :    3   :        5
  Grad. Dip.        :        :        :       33.3
                        +--------+--------+
                    3   :    5   :    1   :        6
  Masters           :        :        :       40.0
                        +--------+--------+
                    4   :    2   :        :        2
  Other             :        :        :       13.3
                        +--------+--------+
              Column        10       5           15
              Total       66.7    33.3        100.0

Number of Missing Observations:   0
```

Percentages

In most cases we require percentages rather than just the raw figures. The procedure above only produces percentages for the row and column totals (which are the same as the percentages in the *Frequencies* tables for the individual variables). The cells in the body of the table contain only counts of the raw data, not percentages. To produce percentages in the body of the table it is necessary to specify the 'cell contents'. There are four relevant options:

- counts
- row percentages

- column percentages
- total percentages

The options specified in the *Crosstabs* command are as shown in Figure 13.17.

Figure 13.17 Crosstabs with percentages

Procedures

After step 5 in Fig. 13.16:

6 Select **Cells**.
7 Select one or more of the options.
6 Select **OK**.

Output (with row percentages)

```
CRSE    Course  by   COMP
                          COMP          Page 1 of 1
                 Count
                 Row Pct  ¦  No       Yes
                          ¦                      Row
                          ¦   0    ¦    1   ¦  Total
CRSE      -----------+--------+--------+
          1         ¦   1    ¦    1   ¦     2
  Undergrad.        ¦  50.0  ¦  50.0  ¦   13.3
                    +--------+--------+
          2         ¦   2    ¦    3   ¦     5
  Grad. Dip.        ¦  40.0  ¦  60.0  ¦   33.3
                    +--------+--------+
          3         ¦   5    ¦    1   ¦     6
  Masters           ¦  83.3  ¦  16.7  ¦   40.0
                    +--------+--------+
          4         ¦   2    ¦        ¦     2
  Other             ¦ 100.0  ¦        ¦   13.3
                    +--------+--------+
          Column       10        5         15
          Total       66.7      33.3      100.0

Number of Missing Observations:   0
```

WEIGHTING

The weighting of data to correct for biased samples is discussed in Chapter 12, where the procedure for calculating a weighting factor is discussed. The simplest way of introducing the weighting factor to the SPSS process is to add it as an additional variable. For example, the 'weighting' variable might be called <u>wt</u> and the weights entered into the data file like any other item of data.

To weight data, use the *weight* feature in **Transform**, specifying wt as the weighting variable. To save having to type in the weights for every respondent, SPSS provides a logical procedure. For example, if all Masters course students had to be given a weight of 1.3, it is possible to indicate this in the *weight* procedure. It is not intended to explain the detail of this procedure here. The reader is referred to the SPSS manual.

GRAPHICS

Graphical presentation of data is generally considered to be an aid to communication. Most people can see trends and patterns more easily in graphic form. Computer packages generally offer the following graphic formats:

- bar graph (or histogram)
- stacked bar graph
- pie chart
- line graph

Computers will produce all four formats from any one set of data. But all formats are not equally appropriate for all data: the appropriate type of graphic depends on the type of data or level of measurement involved.

Data can be divided into nominal, ordinal and ratio types. Nominal data are made up of *categories*, such as questions 1, 2 and 6 in the example questionnaire (Figure 10.14). While numerical codes are used for computer analysis, they have no numerical meaning – for example, code 2 is not 'half' of code 4 – the codes could equally well be A and B. It does not make sense to take an average or mean of the codes. Ordinal data reflect a ranking, as in question 3 of the example questionnaire; the 1, 2, 3 in this question represent the *order of importance*, but rank 3 cannot be interpreted as being three times as high as rank 1. It is, however, possible to take an average or mean – for example to speak of an 'average ranking'. Ratio data are fully numerical – as in question 4 of the example questionnaire. Numerical information such as age, expenditure, frequency of participation are ratio data. Here an answer of 4 is twice as high as an answer of 2 and averages or means are clearly appropriate.

The three data types lend themselves to different graphical treatment. The relationships between these types of data and permitted graphical types is summarised in Figure 13.18.

Bar graphs or histograms

The *bar graph* or *histogram* is perhaps the most commonly used in leisure and tourism research; because it deals with categories any numerical or ratio variable must first be divided into groups – as in the recoding of the cost variable from the example questionnaire.

Stacked bar graphs include information on two variables rather than one. They are the graphical equivalent of the crosstabulation.

Figure 13.18 Data types and graphics

Data type	Characteristics	Example questions in Fig. 10.14	Mean/ average possible	Types of graphic		
				Bar graph	Pie chart	Line graph
Nominal	Qualitative categories	1, 2, 6	No	Yes	Yes	No
Ordinal	Ranks	3, 5	Yes	Yes	Yes	No
Ratio	Numerical	4	Yes	Yes (grouped)	Yes (grouped)	Yes

Pie charts

The *pie chart* is just that – it divides something into sections like a pie. The categories making up the pie chart must therefore add up to some sort of meaningful total, often the total sample, or 100 per cent.

Line graph

The *line graph* is the most constrained in its usage and it is used more generally in research in the more quantified fields such as economics and the natural sciences. The line graph relates two numerical variables: the scales on both axes are generally continuous numbers, although this rule is sometimes broken for illustrative purposes, as in Figure 13.19(d).

SPSS graphics procedures

Graphics are easily produced in SPSS using the **Graphics** option and specifying the variable required. Examples of graphics output from SPSS are shown in Figure 13.19. It is not proposed to consider this option in detail here; readers should refer to the *SPSS for Windows* manual.

Note that consecutive graphics are held in a numbered separate 'window' on the graphics 'carousel'. Each graphic can be saved or printed out via **File** and **Print**. Each graphic can be saved to disk as a separate file. The file can be 'imported' into a Windows software package.

THE ANALYSIS PROCESS

The above is only a brief introduction to the mechanics of survey data analysis. While SPSS is capable of much more sophisticated analyses, mastery of the procedures presented here can provide a good basis for more ambitious programmes of analysis.

Figure 13.19   Examples of graphics output

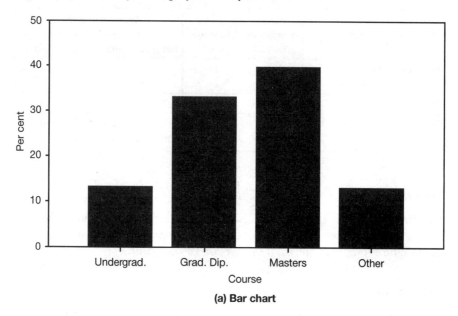

(a) Bar chart

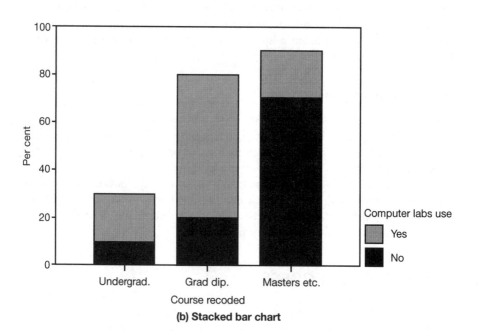

(b) Stacked bar chart

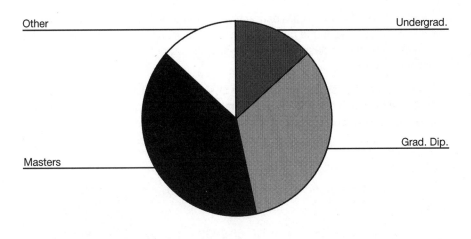

(c) Pie chart

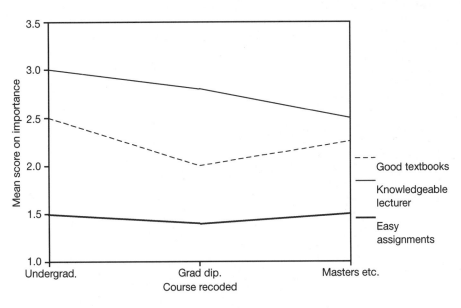

(d) Line graph

EXERCISES

1 Replicate the SPSS data file and analysis used in this chapter as an example. Copy the data used in the chapter or include your own data from questionnaires completed by fellow class members, or any other group of persons engaged in a tertiary course.

2 Create a data file for the questionnaire in either Case study 10.1 or Case study 10.2. Get friends or fellow class members to complete the questionnaire to provide data. Run a selection of frequency and cross-tabulation tables.

NOTE

1. This chapter relates to version 6.0 of SPSS, which works with Windows 3.1. Version 7.0 of SPSS is now available for Windows 95. The analytical procedures are similar to those for version 6.0, but the format of the output tables is significantly improved.

APPENDIX 13.1
SOME WINDOWS BASICS

- The instruction to 'select' something involves using the mouse to highlight the relevant box on the screen and clicking on the mouse to select, or pressing ENTER.

- A box is not available to be selected unless it is highlighted in **bold**; it cannot be selected if it is in grey. If it is in grey it means that you have not given all the necessary information for that process to be operated.

- Different 'windows' – for example, the data file, output file, etc. – can be imagined as being stacked behind each other like cards. They can be viewed by clicking on **Windows** at the top of the screen – which lists the 'windows' in operation. If 'Cascade' is selected, all the windows can be seen, stacked one behind the other. Any window can be brought to the front by clicking on any part of it which is visible.

- In any one session, the various tables which you run are tacked on to the end of the **output** window and you can scroll up and down that window to view what has already been done.

- 'Scroll' up and down any window by holding the mouse button down on the little arrows in the corner of the window.

- Expand or contract the size of the window by clicking on the larger arrows in the top right-hand corner of the screen.

- Print the contents of any window by selecting **File** then **Print**.

- Delete any section of the display by holding down the button on the mouse and 'blocking' it in. A block, which appears in black, can be deleted by selecting **Edit** and **Clear**. The highlighted block can also be printed.

- The contents of any file or 'window' can be saved to disk (via **File**). When you click on **File** SPSS offers to save whatever window is visible – for example, datafile window or output file window – and the menu list changes to reflect this (for example, **Save output** or **Save data**).

- As you exit from SPSS there is a 'failsafe' mechanism. If you have not saved any file or window since the last operation was performed on it SPSS asks you if you wish to save the file.

- Using **Save** saves the updated file under the existing name. **Save as . .** offers the opportunity to save the updated file under a different name.

- The output file is saved in ASCII and can be read or edited using a word processor.

APPENDIX 13.2
SPSS OUTPUT FILE (data from questionnaire in FIGURE 10.14)

Question 1

CRSE   Course

Value Label	Value	Frequency	Per cent	Valid per cent	Cum per cent
Undergrad.	1	2	13.3	13.3	13.3
Grad. dip.	2	5	33.3	33.3	46.7
Masters	3	6	40.0	40.0	86.7
Other	4	2	13.3	13.3	100.0
	Total	15	100.0	100.0	

Valid cases   15   Missing cases   0

Question 2a

LIB   Library use

Value Label	Value	Frequency	Per cent	Valid per cent	Cum per cent
No	0	2	13.3	13.3	13.3
Yes	1	13	86.7	86.7	100.0
	Total	15	100.0	100.0	

Valid cases   15   Missing cases   0

Question 2b

CANT   Canteen use

Value Label	Value	Frequency	Per cent	Valid per cent	Cum per cent
No	0	7	46.7	46.7	46.7
Yes	1	8	53.3	53.3	100.0
	Total	15	100.0	100.0	

Valid cases   15   Missing cases   0

Question 2c

COMP   Computer service use

Value Label	Value	Frequency	Per cent	Valid per cent	Cum per cent
No	0	10	66.7	66.7	66.7
Yes	1	5	33.3	33.3	100.0
	Total	15	100.0	100.0	

Valid cases   15   Missing cases   0

Question 2d

SCS   Student counselling service use

Value Label	Value	Frequency	Per cent	Valid per cent	Cum per cent
No	0	13	86.7	86.7	86.7
Yes	1	2	13.3	13.3	100.0
	Total	15	100.0	100.0	

Valid cases   15   Missing cases   0

Question 3a

REP   Reputation – rank

Value Label	Value	Frequency	Per cent	Valid per cent	Cum per cent
	1	6	40.0	40.0	40.0
	2	6	40.0	40.0	80.0
	3	3	20.0	20.0	100.0
	Total	15	100.0	100.0	

Valid cases   15   Missing cases   0

Question 3b

ACCESS   Easy access – rank

Value Label	Value	Frequency	Per cent	Valid per cent	Cum per cent
	2	2	13.3	13.3	13.3
	3	3	20.0	20.0	33.3
	4	7	46.7	46.7	80.0
	5	3	20.0	20.0	100.0
	Total	15	100.0	100.0	

Valid cases   15   Missing cases   0

Question 3c

CURR   Curriculum – rank

Value Label	Value	Frequency	Per cent	Valid per cent	Cum per cent
	1	8	53.3	53.3	53.3
	2	5	33.3	33.3	86.7
	3	2	13.3	13.3	100.0
	Total	15	100.0	100.0	

Valid cases   15   Missing cases   0

Question 3d

FEES   Level of fees - rank

Value Label	Value	Frequency	Per cent	Valid per cent	Cum per cent
	1	1	6.7	6.7	6.7
	2	2	13.3	13.3	20.0
	3	7	46.7	46.7	66.7
	4	3	20.0	20.0	86.7
	5	2	13.3	13.3	100.0
	Total	15	100.0	100.0	

Valid cases   15   Missing cases   0

Question 3e

PARK   Parking - rank

Value Label	Value	Frequency	Per cent	Valid per cent	Cum per cent
	4	5	33.3	33.3	33.3
	5	10	66.7	66.7	100.0
	Total	15	100.0	100.0	

Valid cases   15   Missing cases   0

Question 4

COST   Expenditure - £

Value Label	Value	Frequency	Per cent	Valid per cent	Cum per cent
	25	1	6.7	6.7	6.7
	40	1	6.7	6.7	13.3
	50	2	13.3	13.3	26.7
	55	2	13.3	13.3	40.0
	75	2	13.3	13.3	53.3
	100	2	13.3	13.3	66.7
	150	2	13.3	13.3	80.0
	250	2	13.3	13.3	93.3
	300	1	6.7	6.7	100.0
	Total	15	100.0	100.0	

Valid cases   15   Missing cases   0

Question 5a

```
TEXT      Textbook
```

Value Label	Value	Frequency	Per cent	Valid per cent	Cum per cent
Not import.	1	2	13.3	13.3	13.3
Important	2	8	53.3	53.3	66.7
Very import.	3	5	33.3	33.3	100.0
	Total	15	100.0	100.0	

Valid cases   15   Missing cases   0

Question 5b

```
LECT      Lecturer
```

Value Label	Value	Frequency	Per cent	Valid per cent	Cum per cent
Important	2	5	33.3	33.3	33.3
Very import.	3	10	66.7	66.7	100.0
	Total	15	100.0	100.0	

Valid cases   15   Missing cases   0

Question 5c

```
ASSGN     Easy assignments
```

Value Label	Value	Frequency	Per cent	Valid per cent	Cum per cent
Not import.	1	8	53.3	53.3	53.3
Important	2	7	46.7	46.7	100.0
	Total	15	100.0	100.0	

Valid cases   15   Missing cases   0

Question 6 (1)

```
SUG1      Suggestion 1
```

Value Label	Value	Frequency	Per cent	Valid per cent	Cum per cent
Content	1	5	33.3	41.7	41.7
Structure	2	3	20.0	25.0	66.7
Delivery	3	2	13.3	16.7	83.3
Lecturer	4	2	13.3	16.7	100.0
	.	3	20.0	Missing	
	Total	15	100.0	100.0	

Valid cases   12   Missing cases   3

Question 6 (2)

SUG2   Suggestion 2

Value Label	Value	Frequency	Per cent	Valid per cent	Cum per cent
Content	1	2	13.3	25.0	25.0
Structure	2	3	20.0	37.5	62.5
Delivery	3	1	6.7	12.5	75.0
Lecturer	4	1	6.7	12.5	87.5
Skills etc.	5	1	6.7	12.5	100.0
	.	7	46.7	Missing	
	Total	15	100.0	100.0	

Valid cases   8   Missing cases   7

Question 6 (3)

SUG3   Suggestion 3

Value Label	Value	Frequency	Per cent	Valid per cent	Cum per cent
Lecturer	4	1	6.7	50.0	50.0
Skills etc.	5	1	6.7	50.0	100.0
	.	13	86.7	Missing	
	Total	15	100.0	100.0	

Valid cases   2   Missing cases   13

CHAPTER 14

Statistical analysis

INTRODUCTION

This chapter provides an introduction to statistics, building on the outline of sampling theory in Chapter 12 and the introduction to the SPSS package in Chapter 13. It *is* only an introduction: it is not intended to be a complete course in statistics. There are many textbooks covering approximately the same ground as covered here, but in more detail and more depth, and reference to some of these texts is given in the Further Reading section. After dealing with some general concepts related to the statistical method, the chapter covers, in turn: the chi-square test, the *t*-test, analysis of variance, correlation and linear and multiple regression. In each case the SPSS procedures for carrying out the tests are described.

THE STATISTICS APPROACH

Before examining particular statistical tests, some preliminary concepts and ideas should be discussed, namely: the idea of probabilistic statements; the normal distribution; probabilistic statement formats; significance; the null hypothesis; and dependent and independent variables.

Probabilistic statements

In general, 'inferential statistics' seeks to make *probabilistic* statements about a *population* on the basis of information available from a *sample* drawn from that population. The statements are *probabilistic* because it is not possible to be absolutely sure that any sample is truly representative of the population from which it has been drawn, so we can only estimate the *probability* that results obtained from a sample are true of the population. The 'statements' can be descriptive, comparative or relational:

- *descriptive:* for example: 10 per cent of adults play tennis
- *comparative:* for example: 10 per cent play tennis, but 12 per cent play golf
- *relational:* for example: people with high incomes play tennis more than people with low incomes.

If they are based on data from samples, such statements cannot be made without qualification. The *sample* may indicate these findings, but it is not certain that they apply precisely to the population from which the sample is drawn, because there is always an element of doubt about any sample. Inferential statistics modifies the above example statements to be of the form:

- We can be 95 per cent confident that the proportion of adults that plays tennis is between 9 per cent and 11 per cent.
- The proportion of golf players is *significantly* higher than the proportion of tennis players (at the 95 per cent level of probability).
- There is a significant positive relationship between level of income and level of tennis playing (at the 95 per cent level).

The basis of probability statements: the normal distribution

Descriptive statements and 'confidence intervals' are discussed in general terms in Chapter 12 in relation to the issue of sample size. The probability or confidence interval statement is based on the *theoretical* idea of drawing repeated samples of the same size from the same population. The sample drawn in any one piece of research is only one of a large number of *possible* samples which *might* have been drawn. If a large number of samples *could* be drawn, such an exercise would produce a variety of results, some very unrepresentative of the population but most, assuming random sampling procedures are used, tending to produce results close to the true population values. Statistical theory – which we are unable to explore in detail here – is able to quantify this tendency, so that we can say that, in 95 or 99 out of a hundred of such samples, the values found from the sample will fall within a certain range either side of the true population value – hence the idea of 'confidence intervals' as discussed in Chapter 12.

The theory relates to the bell-shaped 'normal distribution' which would result if repeated samples were drawn and the values of a statistic (for example the proportion who play tennis) plotted, as shown in Figure 14.1. The 'normal curve' which would result if a very large number of samples was drawn was shown in Figure 12.1 in Chapter 12. The population value of a statistic (such as a percentage or average) lies at the centre of the distribution and the value of the statistic found from a sample in a particular research project is just one among the many sample possibilities.

This idea of levels of probability about the accuracy of sample findings based on the theoretical possibility of drawing many samples is common to most of the statistical procedures examined in this chapter.

Statement formats

It is customary in social research to use probability levels of 95 per cent or 99 per cent – and occasionally 90 per cent or 99.9 per cent. As probability estimates these can be interpreted exactly as in everyday language – for example when we say '90 per cent certain', '50:50' or 'nine times out of 10' we are making probabilistic statements. So if a finding is significant (*see* below) at the '99

Figure 14.1   Drawing repeated samples

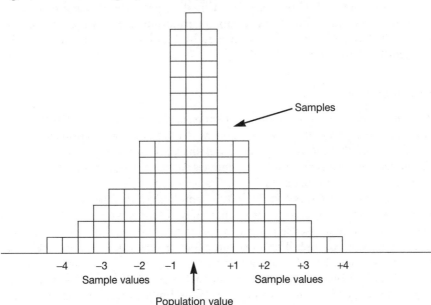

per cent level', we are saying that we believe that there is a 99 per cent chance that what we have found is true of the population – therefore there is a one per cent chance that what we have found is not true. If we can only say that something is significant at the 95 per cent level, we are less confident: there is a five per cent chance that what we have found is not true. Thus the terminology 'highly significant' is sometimes used in relation to findings at the 99 per cent level and 'significant' for the 95 per cent level.

In some cases, instead of the computer-generated results of statistical tests using these conventional cut-off points, they calculate the exact 'probability'. For example, it might be found that a result is significant at the 96.5 per cent level or the 82.5 per cent level. It is then left up to the researcher to judge whether such levels are acceptable.

Note also, that sometimes the result is expressed as one per cent and sometimes as 99 per cent, or five per cent rather than 95 per cent. A further variation is to express the probability as a *proportion* rather than a percentage – for example 0.05 rather than five per cent or 0.01 rather than one per cent. Similarly the exact calculations may be expressed as proportions, for example 0.035 rather than 3.5 per cent or 96.5 per cent. In the following, therefore, the three forms are equivalent:

5%	95%	0.05
1%	99%	0.01
0.1%	99.9%	0.001
3.5%	96.5%	0.035
7.5%	92.5%	0.075

In computer printouts from SPSS, if the probability is below 0.0005 it some-times comes out as .000 because it is printed only to three decimal places.

In some research reports and computer printouts results which are signifi-cant at the five per cent level are indicated by * and those significant at the one per cent level are indicated by **.

Significance

The second common feature of statistical tests and procedures is that they deal with the idea of *significance*. A *significant* difference or relationship is one which is *unlikely to have happened by chance*. So, for example, the bigger the difference between two sample percentages the more likely it is that the differ-ence is 'real' and not just a statistical chance happening.

For example, if it was found from a sample that 10.1 per cent of women played tennis and 10.2 per cent of men played tennis we would be inclined, even from a common-sense point of view, to say that the difference is not sig-nificant. This is because, if another sample were selected, it is quite likely that the figures would be different, and even the opposite way around: it is 'too close to call'. However, whether or not such a small difference is *statistically* significant depends on the sample size. If the findings were based on a small sample, say around 100 people, the difference would not be significant – the chances of getting a different result from a different sample would be high (and the statistical procedures outlined below would establish this). But if the sample were large – say several thousand – then it might be found to be statis-tically significant: that is, if the result is based on such a large sample we can be much more confident that it is 'real' and would be reproduced if another sample of similar size were drawn.

Statistical theory enables us to quantify and assess 'significance' – that is, to say what sizes of differences are significant for what sizes of sample.

Statistical significance should not, however, be confused with *social, theo-retical* or *managerial* significance. For example, if the above finding about men's and women's tennis-playing was based on a sample of, say, 10 000, it would be *statistically* significant, but this does not make the difference signifi-cant in any social sense. For all practical purposes, on the basis of such find-ings, we would say that men's and women's tennis-playing rates are the same. This is a very important point to bear in mind when reading research results based on statistics; large samples can produce many 'statistically significant' findings; but that does not necessarily make them 'significant' in any other way.

The null hypothesis

Another common feature of the statistical method is the idea of the *null hypoth-esis*, referred to by the symbol H_0. It is based around the idea of setting up two mutually incompatible hypotheses, so that only one can be true. For example either more people play tennis than golf or the number of people who play ten-nis is less than or equal to the number who play golf. If one proposition is true then the other must be untrue. The null hypothesis usually proposes that there is *no difference* between two observed values or that there is *no relationship* between two variables. There are therefore two possibilities:

H_0 – null hypothesis: there is *no* difference or *no* relationship.
H_1 – alternative hypothesis: there *is* a difference or a relationship.

Usually it is the *alternative* hypothesis, H_1, that the researcher is interested in, but statistical theory explores the implications of the *null* hypothesis.

The use of the null hypothesis idea can be illustrated by example. Suppose, in a study of leisure participation patterns, using a sample of 1000 adults, part of the study focuses on the relative popularity of golf and tennis. The null hypothesis would be that the participation levels are the same.

H_0 – tennis and golf participation levels are the same.
H_1 – tennis and golf participation levels are different.

Suppose it is found that 120 (12 per cent) play tennis and 120 (12 per cent) play golf. Clearly there is no difference between the two figures; they are consistent with the null hypothesis. The null hypothesis is accepted and the alternative hypothesis is rejected. In terms of the research categories discussed in Chapter 2, this is very much a *deductive* approach: the hypothesis is set up in advance of the analysis, possibly within a theoretical framework.

But suppose the numbers playing tennis were found to be 121 (12.1 per cent) and the number playing golf was 120 (12.0 per cent). Would we reject the null hypothesis and accept the alternative, that tennis and golf participation levels are different? From what we know of samples, clearly not: this would be too close to call. Such a small difference between the two figures would still be consistent with the null hypothesis. So how big would the difference have to be before we reject the null hypothesis? A difference of 5, 10, 15? This is where statistical theory comes in, to provide a test of what is and is not an acceptable difference. And it is basically what the rest of this chapter is all about: providing tests of the relationship between sample findings and the null hypothesis for different situations.

Dependent and independent variables

The terms *dependent variable* and *independent variable* are frequently used in statistical analysis. If there is a relationship between a dependent and an independent variable, the implication is that changes in the former are caused by changes in the latter: the independent variable influences the dependent variable. For example, if it is suggested that the level of holiday-taking is related to income level then level of holiday-taking is the *dependent* variable and income is the *independent* variable. Even though a certain level of income does not *cause* people to go on holiday, it makes more sense to suggest that level of income facilitates or constrains the level of holiday-taking, than to suggest the opposite. So it makes some sense to talk of holiday-taking being *dependent* on income. One variable can be dependent on a number of independent variables,

Figure 14.2   Dependent and independent variables

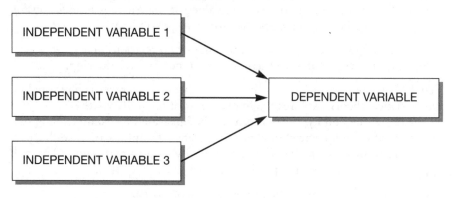

as illustrated in Figure 14.2. For example it may be hypothesised that holiday-taking is dependent on income *and* occupation *and* age.

WHAT TESTS?

The idea of levels of measurement, or types of data, was introduced in Chapter 13 (*see* page 240), when nominal, ordinal and ratio data were discussed. The higher the level of measurement the greater the range of analysis that can be carried out on the data. For example, it is possible to calculate means and averages of ordinal and ratio measures, but not of nominal measures. Consequently, different statistical tests are associated with different levels of measurement. The rest of this chapter sets out different statistical tests to be used in different situations, as summarised in Figure 14.3. The tests all relate to comparisons between variables and relationships between variables. The type of test to be used depends on the format of the data, the level of measurement and the number of variables involved.

   In what follows some fictitious data are used to illustrate the various tests. The data arise from a questionnaire survey similar to that used in Chapter 13, but with a larger sample and with the addition of age, gender, income and leisure participation variables. A list of the variables used is included as Appendix 14.1. As in Chapter 13, the examples have been created using SPSS for Windows, version 6.1.

CHI-SQUARE

Introduction

The chi-square test (symbol: χ^2, pronounced 'ky', to rhyme with 'sky') can be used in a number of situations, but its use is demonstrated here in relation to cross-tabulations of two *nominal* variables – the familiar tables produced from such packages as SPSS. When examining cross-tabulations it is possible to use

Figure 14.3 Types of statistical test

Task	Data format	No. of variables	Types of variable	Test
Relationship between 2 variables	Cross-tabulation of frequencies	2	Nominal	Chi-square
Difference between 2 means – paired	Means – whole sample	2	Ratio or ordinal	t-test – paired
Difference between 2 means – independent samples	Means – 2 sub-groups	2	1 Ratio or ordinal (means) 2 Nominal (2 groups only)	t-test – independent samples
Relationship between 2 variables	Means – 3+ sub-groups	2	1 Ratio or ordinal (means) 2 Nominal (3+ groups)	One-way analysis of variance
Relationship between 3+ variables	Means – cross-tabulated	3+	1 Ratio or ordinal (means) 2 Nominal (2+)	Factorial analysis of variance
Relationship between 2 variables	Individual measures	2	Ratio or ordinal (2)	Correlation
Linear relationship between 2 variables	Individual measures	2	Ratio or ordinal (2)	Linear regression
Linear relationship between 3+ variables	Individual measures	3+	Ratio or ordinal (3+)	Multiple regression
Relationships between large numbers of variables	Individual measures	Many	Ratio or ordinal	Factor analysis Cluster analysis

'common sense' and an underlying knowledge of the size of confidence intervals (as discussed in Chapter 12) to make an approximate judgement as to whether there is any sort of relationship between the two variables involved in the table. However, unless the pattern is very clear, it can be difficult to judge whether the overall differences are *significant*. The chi-square test is designed to achieve this.

Figure 14.4 shows the SPSS procedures to obtain a cross-tabulation with a chi-square test, and the resultant output. The example chosen relates the type of course in which a student is enrolled (<u>crser</u>) to gender (<u>gend</u>). The interpretation of this output is discussed below.

Null hypothesis

The null hypothesis is that *there is no difference in course enrolment patterns between male and female respondents*: that is:

H_0 – there is *no* relationship between course enrolment pattern and gender in the population.

H_1 – there *is* a relationship between course enrolment pattern and gender in the population.

Expected frequencies

The cells of the table include counts and column percentages, as discussed in relation to cross-tabulations in Chapter 13. But they also include *expected values*. These are the counts which would be expected *if the null hypothesis were true* – that is, if there was no difference between males and females in their pattern of course enrolment. In this case we have an equal number of men and women in the sample, so the expected values show a 50:50 split for each of the three types of course.

Note that the proposition being tested can therefore be expressed in three ways, as shown in Figure 14.5.

The value of chi-square

Chi-square is a statistic based on the sum of the differences between the counts (or *observed* values) and the *expected* values: the greater the aggregate difference, the greater the value of chi-square. However, if you simply add the differences between the observed and expected values in the table you will find that the positives cancel out the negatives, giving zero. Chi-square is therefore based on the sum of the *squared* values of the differences. For readers who are mathematically inclined, the formula for chi-square is shown in Appendix 14.2. Fortunately the SPSS package calculates the value of chi-square for us, so it is not necessary to know the details of the formula. It is sufficient to understand that chi-square is a statistical measure of the difference between the observed and expected values in the table.

Figure 14.4   Chi-square test

SPSS procedures

1 Select **Statistics**.
2 Select **Summarize**.
3 Select **Crosstabs**.
4 Select variables to be cross-tabulated (in this case <u>crser</u> and <u>gend</u>).
5 Select **Statistics** (within the **Crosstabs** box).
6 Select **Chi-square** then **Continue**.
7 Select **Cell Contents** (within the **Crosstabs** box).
8 Select **Observed** and **Expected** then **Continue**.
9 Select **OK**.

Output

CRSER course recoded by GEND Gender

```
              Count    GEND
              Exp Val  Male    Female   Row
                       1       2       Total
CRSER         ---------+-------+-------+
              1         9       4        13
   Undergrad            6.5     6.5     26.0%
                       +-------+-------+
              2         9       5        14
   Grad dip.           7.0     7.0     28.0%
                       +-------+-------+
              3         7      16        23
   Masters etc.       11.5    11.5     46.0%
                       +-------+-------+
              Column    25      25       50
              Total    50.0%   50.0%   100.0%
```

Chi-square	Value	DF	Significance
Pearson	6.58767	2	.03711
Likelihood ratio	6.75010	2	.03422
Mantel-Haenszel test for linear association	5.64941	1	.01746

Minimum expected frequency - 6.500

Number of missing observations: 0

Figure 14.5   Alternative expressions of hypotheses

Option 1	Option 2	Option 3
Null hypothesis (H_0): there is *no* relationship between course enrolment pattern and gender in the population.	Male and female enrolment patterns in the population are the same.	Observed and expected values are not significantly different.
Alternative hypothesis (H_1): there *is* a relationship between course enrolment pattern and gender in the population.	Male and female enrolment patterns in the population are different.	Observed and expected values are significantly different.

In the example in Figure 14.4, the value of chi-square is 6.58767. We are using the 'Pearson' value, devised by the statistician Pearson; the other values (likelihood ratio and Mantel-Haenszel test) do not concern us here. How should this be interpreted? We have noted that the greater the difference between the observed and expected values the greater the value of chi-square. Our null hypothesis is that there is *no* difference between the two sets of values. But clearly, we would accept some *minor* differences between two sets of values and still accept the null hypothesis: for example if the split between males and females among undergraduates was 6:7 or if the split between males and females among postgraduate diploma students was, say, 8:6. But just how big would the differences have to be before we would reject the null hypothesis and conclude that there *is* a difference between male and female enrolment patterns?

For a given size of table (in this case three cells by two) statisticians (like Professor Pearson) have been able to calculate the likelihood of obtaining various values of chi-square when the null hypothesis is true. As with the normal distribution discussed in Chapter 12, this is based on the theoretical possibility of drawing lots of samples of the same size. This is shown in Figure 14.6. It shows that, for a given table size, if the null hypothesis is true (observed and expected values are the same), some differences in observed and expected values can be expected from most samples drawn, so a range of values of chi-square can be expected. Most values of chi-square would be fairly small; larger values would occur, but only rarely – they are unlikely. As with the normal curve discussed in Chapter 12, it is customary to adopt either a five per cent or one per cent cut-off to decide what is considered to be 'unlikely'. Five per cent is used in the ensuing discussions. Therefore, any value of chi-square above the five per cent point is considered unlikely and *inconsistent* with the null hypothesis. So, if the value of chi-square is *above* the five per cent point we *reject* the null hypothesis; if it is *below* the five per cent point we *accept* the null hypothesis.

Figure 14.6   Distribution of chi-square assuming null hypothesis is true

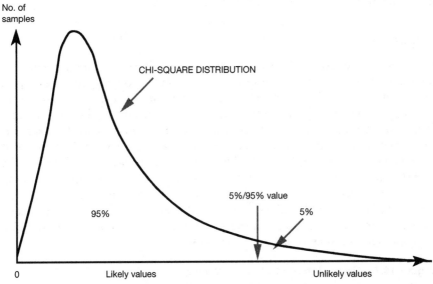

Value of chi-square when null hypothesis true

In Figure 14.4, the SPSS output tells us where the particular value lies on the likelihood scale or axis: under 'significance', it gives 0.03711 or 3.711 per cent. Our value of chi-square is therefore an unlikely one (it is below five per cent), so we reject the null hypothesis and conclude that there *is* a significant difference between the male and female enrolment patterns.

Degrees of freedom

The values of chi-square depend on the table size, which is indirectly measured by the *degrees of freedom*. Degrees of freedom are calculated by: the number of rows less one, multiplied by the number of columns less one. So, for the table in Figure 14.4, the 'degrees of freedom' are:

$$(2{-}1) \times (3{-}1) = 1 \times 2 = 2$$

This is shown in the SPSS output under 'DF'.

Expected frequencies rule

One rule for the application of chi-square is that not more than one-fifth of the cells of the table should have 'expected frequencies' of less than 5, and none should have an expected frequency of less than 1. The SPSS output indicates whether such cells exist; in the example the minimum expected frequency is 6.5, so there is no problem. Grouping of some of the values by recoding can be used to reduce the number of cells and thus increase the expected frequencies.

In fact this was done in the example, in that Masters and 'Other' courses were combined to form one category, 'Masters etc.'.

Reporting

How should the results of statistical tests such as chi-square be reported? One solution is to include the results of the test in a table in the report, for example, as in Figure 14.7. The commentary might then merely say: 'The relationship between enrolment patterns and gender was significant at the five per cent level'. Another approach is to include the test results in the text, for example: 'The relationship between enrolment patterns and gender was significant at the five per cent level ($\chi^2 = 6.6$, 2 DF)'. A third approach, which makes the statistics less intrusive, is to include a note in the report or paper indicating that all tests were conducted at the five per cent level, and possibly that test values are included in the tables, or are listed in an appendix, or even excluded altogether for non-technical audiences. A fourth approach is to use the * and ** approach as discussed above (*see* p. 254).

Figure 14.7 Presentation of chi-square test

Table x: Enrolment pattern by gender			
Level of course	Per cent enrolled		
	Male	Female	Total
Undergraduate	36.0	16.0	26.0
Graduate diploma	36.0	20.0	28.0
Masters etc.	28.0	64.0	46.0
Total	100.0	100.0	100.0
Sample size	25	25	50

$\chi^2 = 6.59$ DF 2, significant at the 5% level.

COMPARING TWO MEANS: THE *t*-TEST

Introduction

So far we have dealt only with proportions or percentages, either singly or in cross-tabulations; but many research results are in the form of averages – for example, the average age of a group of participants in an activity, the average holiday expenditure of visitors from different countries or the average score of a group on a Likert scale. In statistical parlance an average is referred to as a *mean*. Means can only be calculated for *ordinal* and *ratio* variables, not nominal variables.

The simplest form of analysis is to compare two means, to see whether they are significantly different. For example, we might want to test whether the average age of the golf players in a sample is significantly different from that of the tennis players, or whether the average amount spent on holidays by a group of people is greater or less than the amount spent on the arts and entertainment. In this situation the null hypothesis is expressed as follows:

- H_0 – null hypothesis: there is *no* difference between the means.
- H_1 – alternative hypothesis: there *is* a difference between the means.

For this situation, rather than chi-square, a statistic referred to as '*t*' is calculated. This is based on a formula involving the sample size and the two means being compared (*see* Appendix 14.2). If there is *no difference* between two means in the population (H_0) then, for a given sample size, t has a known 'distribution' of likely values (*see* Figure 14.8): high values are rare, so if the value from a sample is high – in the top five per cent of values for that sample size – then we reject H_0 and accept H_1; that is, we conclude that there *is* a significant difference at the five per cent level of probability respectively.

There are two situations where we might want to compare means:

1 To compare the means of two variables which apply to the whole sample – for example, comparing the average amount spent on holidays with the average amount spent on the arts and entertainment (for everybody in the sample). This is known as a *paired samples test*.
2 To compare the means of one variable for two sub-groups – for example, comparing the average age of men in the sample with that of women. The sample is divided into two sub-groups, men and women; this is known as a *group* or *independent samples* test.

Figure 14.8 Chi-square and *t* distributions

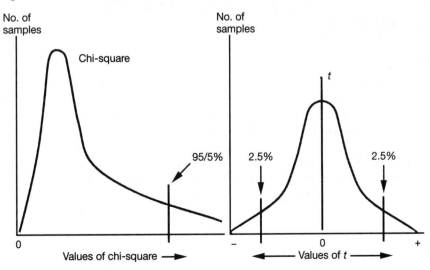

1 Paired samples test

Figure 14.9 gives two examples of the paired samples test. The SPSS output provides a range of statistics with which we are not concerned here; the items in which we are interested are underlined. Example 1 compares the frequency of playing sport with the frequency of visiting national parks. The sample plays sport on average 12.2 times in three months and visits national parks on average 9.8 times in three months. The value of t is 1.25 and its (2-tail) significance is 0.219 or 21.9 per cent. The result is consistent with the null hypothesis (0.219 is much higher than 0.05), so we accept that there is no significant difference between the level of sport playing and the level of visits to national parks. The second example refers to visiting national parks and going out for a meal. In this case the value of t is 2.43 and its significance level is 0.019, which is below 0.05, so we reject the null hypothesis and conclude that there is a significant difference between the frequency of visiting national parks and going out for meals.

The t-test output from the computer refers to the *2-tail significance* – this is because, unlike chi-square, the test involves both ends of the distribution, as shown in Figure 14.8; the value of t can be negative or positive. The interpretation is, however, the same.

2 Independent samples test

Figure 14.10 compares levels of expenditure on books by male and female students. For males expenditure is £110 and for females it is £138.60. In this case t has a value of -1.25 and a significance level of 0.219. Since 0.219 is above 0.05, this is consistent with the null hypothesis, so we accept that there is no significant difference between the two expenditure figures.

A NUMBER OF MEANS: ONE-WAY ANALYSIS OF VARIANCE

Introduction

The t-test was used to examine differences between means two at a time. *Analysis of variance* (ANOVA) is used to examine *more than two* means at a time. This begins to resemble the cross-tabulation process, but with *means* appearing in the cells of the table instead of sample numbers, as shown in the example table in Figure 14.11. Here the question which we seek to answer with ANOVA is whether the mean course expenditures for the different groups of course members are different from the overall mean – that is, whether expenditure is related to type of course enrolment.

Figure 14.9   Comparing means: *t*-test: paired samples

SPSS procedures

1 Select **Statistics**.
2 Select **Compare Means**.
3 Select **Paired Samples *t*-Test**.
4 Select the *two variables* to be compared
   (they appear first in the **Current Selections** box, then are transferred to
   the **Paired variables** box).
5 Select **OK** to obtain *t*-test.

SPSS Output

```
        - - - t-tests for paired samples - - -
```

Example 1: Sport vs National Parks

Variable	Number of pairs	Corr	2-tail Sig	Mean	SD	SE of Mean
SPORT Play sport				12.2000	13.095	1.852
	50	.274	.054			
NPARK Visit national park				9.8000	8.804	1.245

Paired Differences						
Mean	SD	SE of Mean	*t*-value	df	2-tail Sig	
2.4000	13.631	1.928	1.25	49	.219	
95% CI (-1.475, 6.275)						

Example 2: National Parks vs Meals Out

Variable	Number of pairs	Corr	2-tail Sig	Mean	SD	SE of Mean
NPARK Visit national park				9.8000	8.804	1.245
	50	-.044	.759			
MEAL Go for meal				6.5400	3.157	.446

Paired Differences						
Mean	SD	SE of Mean	*t*-value	df	2-tail Sig	
3.2600	9.484	1.341	2.43	49	.019	
95% CI (.564, 5.956)						

Figure 14.10   Comparing means: *t*-test: independent samples

---

SPSS procedures

1 Select **Statistics**.
2 Select **Compare Means**.
3 Select **Independent Samples *t*-Test**.
4 Select the variable whose mean you want.
5 Select **Grouping variable**, which will be used to divide the sample into two groups (in the example: gend).
6 Select **Define groups**, then select the values used to divide the sample into two groups (in the example: 1 and 2).
7 Select **OK** and the two values appear in brackets following the name of the grouping variable (e.g. gend[1,2]).
8 Select **OK** to obtain *t*-test.

Example: Course cost by gender

```
t-tests for independent samples of  GEND   Gender
```

Variable	Number of Cases	Mean	SD	SE of Mean
COST Course costs, £ p.a.				
Male	25	110.0000	77.607	15.521
Female	25	138.6000	84.613	16.923

```
Mean Difference = -28.6000
```

Levene's Test for Equality of Variances: F= .431 P= .514

```
t-test for Equality of Means
```

Variances	*t*-value	df	2-Tail Sig	SE of Diff	95% CI for Diff
Equal	-1.25	48	.219	22.963	(-74.781, 17.581)
Unequal	-1.25	47.65	.219	22.963	(-74.781, 17.581)

NB: If, in *Levene's Test*, P is greater than 0.05 use the *Equal t*-test; if P is 0.05 or less, use the *Unequal* test. In the example the two tests are the same, but they can vary.

Null hypothesis

The null hypothesis is therefore: *that all the means are equal to the overall mean.* How different must the group means be from the overall mean before we reject this hypothesis?

Figure 14.11   Comparing a range of means

SPSS procedures

1 Select **Statistics**.
2 Select **Compare Means**.
3 Select **Means**.
4 Select variable for which mean is required (<u>inc</u> in the example) and put in
  the **Dependent list** box.
5 Select variable for grouping (<u>crser</u> in example) and put in the
  Independent list box.
6 Select **OK**.

SPSS output

```
            - - Description of Subpopulations - -

Summaries of      INC          Income pa
By levels of      CRSER        Course recoded
```

Variable	Value	Label	Mean	Std Dev	Cases
For entire population			14.2000	4.4493	50
CRSER	1	Undergrad	12.5385	2.6651	13
CRSER	2	Grad dip.	12.9286	3.4073	14
CRSER	3	Masters etc.	15.9130	5.2563	23

```
  Total Cases = 50.
```

Variance

Whether or not the means are in effect from *one* population (with *one* mean) or from *different* sub-populations (with *different* means) depends not only on the differences between the means but also on their 'spread', or *variance*. Figure 14.12 shows four examples of three means, with the associated 'spread' of cases around each mean. In Example A, the means are well spaced and there is very little overlap in the cases, whereas in Example C the means are closer together and there is considerable overlap. In Example B the means are spaced as in A, but the spread around the means is greater and so overlap is considerable. Example D presents the worst case of overlap. So we might expect to find that for Example A there *is* a significant difference between the means, while for Example D there is not. Examples B and C raise doubts because of the overlaps. (Note that a visual presentation of this type of information, although in a different format, can be obtained using the *Boxplot* feature within the *Graphics* procedure of SPSS.)

The 'spread' of sample values is referred to as the *variance* and can be measured by adding up the differences between the scores of individual

Figure 14.12   Comparing means and variance

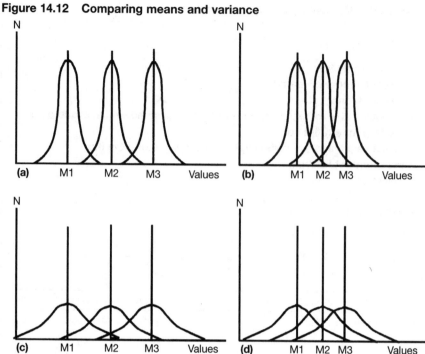

observations or cases and the mean score. The formula for calculating variance is shown in Appendix 14.2.

Analysis of variance

Thus whether or not the means are significantly different from the overall means depends on:

(a) the spread of the separate sub-group means around the overall mean – the *between groups* variance; and

(b) the spread of sub-group observations around the means of each of the sub-groups – the *within groups* variance.

The greater the *between groups* variance the *greater* the likelihood of significant difference. The greater the *within groups* variance the *less* the likelihood of significant difference. Analysis of variance is based on the ratio of these two measures, which produces a statistic referred to as 'F'.

As with the other statistics examined, values of F for a given number of degrees of freedom (based on sample sizes and number of groups) have a known probability distribution in the null hypothesis situation. High values are unlikely and result in the rejection of the null hypothesis.

SPSS procedures and output

SPSS procedures and examples of output are shown in Figure 14.13. For 'between groups' and 'within groups' the output shows the degrees of freedom (DF), the 'sum of squares', the 'mean squares' (variance), the F ratio and the F probability. In Example 1 the F ratio is 1.3915 and the F probability is 0.2588. The latter is greater than 0.05, so the null hypothesis is accepted and it is concluded that there is no significant difference between the means: that is, expenditure is not related to course type. In Example 2, the F probability is 0.0118, which is less than 0.05, so in this case the null hypothesis is rejected and it is concluded that there *is* a relationship between age and course type.

A TABLE OF MEANS: FACTORIAL ANALYSIS OF VARIANCE

Introduction

As with one-way analysis of variance, factorial analysis of variance deals with *means*. But while one-way analysis of variance deals with means of groups determined on the basis of *one* variable, factorial analysis of variance is designed for sets of means grouped by more than one classifying variable, or 'factor'. An example is shown in Figure 14.14, examining frequency of theatre-going by course type and gender. It can be seen that, while there is little difference in frequency of attendance by course or between male and female students, when the two variables are put together, considerable differences emerge. Analysis of variance examines this 'cross-tabulation of means' and determines whether the differences revealed are significant. As with the one-way analysis of variance, the procedure examines the differences between group means and the spread of values within groups.

Null hypothesis

The null hypothesis is that there is no interaction between the variables – that the level of theatre-going of the students in the various courses is not affected by gender. A table of 'expected values' consistent with the null hypothesis could be produced as for the chi-square example, but the values would be means rather than numbers of cases.

SPSS factorial analysis of variance

Figure 14.15 shows the results of a factorial analysis of variance on the above data. The underlined F probabilities in the 'main effects' part of the output indicate that neither the relationship between theatre-going and course nor that between theatre-going and gender is significant on its own. However, when both variables are taken into account, in the '2-way interactions' part of the table, the F probability is 0.009, which is less than 0.05.

Figure 14.13   One-way analysis of variance

SPSS procedures

1 Select **Statistics**.
2 Select **Compare Means** (*not* ANOVA).
3 Select **Oneway ANOVA** in the 'dialogue box'.
4 Select variable for which mean is required (inc in Example 1 below, age in Example 2: place in **Dependent List** box.
5 Select variable which determines sub-groups (crser in examples below) and place in the **Factor** box.
6 Select **Define Range** and enter the range of values of the sub-groups (1 to 3 in examples).
7 Select **OK** (values appear in brackets – e.g. crser[1,3]).
8 Select **OK** to obtain output.

SPSS output

Example 1 Income by course

```
        - - - - -  O N E W A Y  - - - - -

     Variable   INC        Income pa
  By Variable   CRSER      Course recoded

              Analysis of Variance
```

Source	DF	Sum of Squares	Mean Squares	F Ratio	F Prob.
Between Groups	2	66.6345	33.3172	1.3915	.2588
Within Groups	47	1125.3655	23.9439		
Total	49	1192.0000			

Example 2 Age by course

```
        - - - - -  O N E W A Y  - - - - -

     Variable   AGE        Age
  By Variable   CRSER      Course recoded

              Analysis of Variance
```

Source	DF	Sum of Squares	Mean Squares	F Ratio	F Prob.
Between Groups	2	204.2060	102.1030	4.8897	.0118
Within Groups	47	981.4140	20.8811		
Total	49	1185.6200			

Figure 14.14   A table of means

SPSS procedures

1 Select **Statistics**.
2 Select **Compare Means**.
3 Select **Dependent** variable (theatre in the example).
4 Select **Independent** variable (crser in the example).
5 Define **Range** (in the case of crser it is 1,3).
6 Select **OK** to obtain analysis.

SPSS output

```
              - - Description of Subpopulations - -

Summaries of      THEATRE
By levels of      CRSER       Course recoded    GEND      Gender
```

Variable	Value	Label	Mean	Std Dev	Cases
For entire population			2.6800	2.2446	50
CRSER	1	Undergrad	2.6154	2.0631	13
GEND	1	Male	3.1111	1.8333	9
GEND	2	Female	1.5000	2.3805	4
CRSER	2	Grad dip.	2.9286	2.4326	14
GEND	1	Male	1.5556	1.1304	9
GEND	2	Female	5.4000	2.1909	5
CRSER	3	Masters etc.	2.5652	2.3125	23
GEND	1	Male	2.0000	2.1602	7
GEND	2	Female	2.8125	2.4005	16

```
   Total cases = 50.
```

How the above might be presented in a report

Table: Frequency of visiting theatre, by course and gender			
	Mean number of visits in three months		
Course	Male	Female	Total
Undergraduate	3.1	1.5	2.6
Graduate diploma	1.5	5.4	2.9
Masters etc.	2.0	2.8	2.6
Total	2.2	3.1	

Use Fig. 13.14, Method 2 to obtain column totals.

Figure 14.15   Factorial analysis of variance

This relates to data in Fig. 14.14.

SPSS procedures

1 Select **Statistics**.
2 Select **ANOVA Models**.
3 Select **Simple Factorial**.
4 Select the **Dependent** variable – the one for which the means are to be calculated and used (theatre in the example).
5 Select the **Factors** – the two variables affecting the dependent variable (crser and gend in the example).
6 Select **Define Ranges** and enter values (in the example, crser is 1,3 and gend is 1,2).
7 Select **OK** to obtain analysis.

SPSS output

```
    * * *   A N A L Y S I S    O F    V A R I A N C E   * * *

THEATRE    by    CRSER    Course recoded and GEND    Gender

UNIQUE sums of squares (All effects entered simultaneously)
```

Source of Variation	Sum of Squares	DF	Mean Square	F	Sig of F
Main Effects	20.412	3	6.804	1.595	.204
CRSER	11.182	2	5.591	1.310	.280
GEND	10.571	1	10.571	2.477	.123
2-Way Interactions	44.966	2	22.483	5.269	.009
CRSER GEND	44.966	2	22.483	5.269	.009
Explained	59.131	5	11.826	2.772	.029
Residual	187.749	44	4.267		
Total	246.880	49	5.038		

```
50 cases were processed.
0 cases (.0 per cent) were missing.
```

The null hypothesis is therefore rejected and it is concluded that the interaction between gender and course type with regard to theatre-going is significant.

CORRELATION

Introduction

Correlation can be used to examine the relationships between two or more *ordinal or ratio* variables. If two phenomena are related in a systematic way they are said to be *correlated*. They can be:

- *positively* correlated (as one variable increases so does the other);
- *negatively* correlated (as one variable increases the other decreases); or
- *un-correlated* (there is no relationship between the variables).

It is often helpful to think of correlation in visual terms. Relationships between income (or age) and the four variables are shown in Figure 14.16, illustrating a variety of types of correlation. The graphics were produced using the SPSS graphics **Scatterplot** procedure. Each dot represents one person (or 'case' or 'observation').

Correlation coefficient (*r*)

Correlation can be measured by means of the *correlation coefficient*, usually represented by the letter *r*. The coefficient is:

- 0 if there is no relationship between two variables;
- +1.0 if there is perfect positive correlation between two variables;
- −1.0 if there is perfect negative correlation between two variables;
- between 0 and +1.0 if there is *some* positive correlation;
- between 0 and −1.0 if there is *some* negative correlation.

The closer the coefficient is to 1.0, the greater the correlation: for example, 0.9 is a *high positive* correlation, 0.2 is a *low positive* correlation and −0.8 is a *high negative* correlation.

The correlation coefficient is calculated by measuring how far each data point is from the mean of each variable and multiplying the two differences. In Figure 14.17 it can be seen that the result will be a positive number for data points in the top right-hand and bottom left-hand quadrants (B and C) and negative for data points in the other two quadrants (A and D). The calculations are shown for two of the data points by way of illustration. If most of the data points are in quadrants B and C a positive correlation will result, while if most of the data points are in A and D a negative correlation will result. If the data points are widely scattered in all four quadrants, then the negatives cancel out the positives, resulting in a low value for the correlation. This explains in very broad terms the basis of the positive and negative correlations, and

Figure 14.16 Relationships between variables

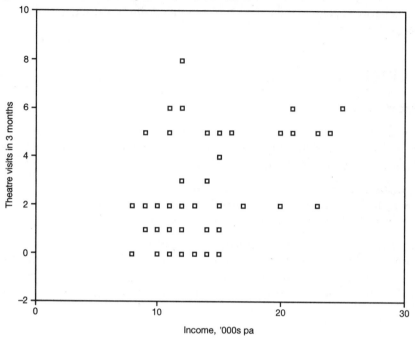

(a) Theatre-going increases with income – a fairly positive correlation (0.400)

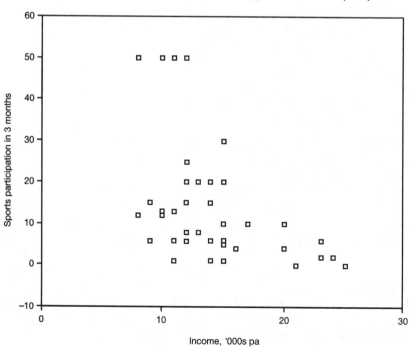

(b) Sport participation declines with income – a fairly strong negative correlation (–0.439)

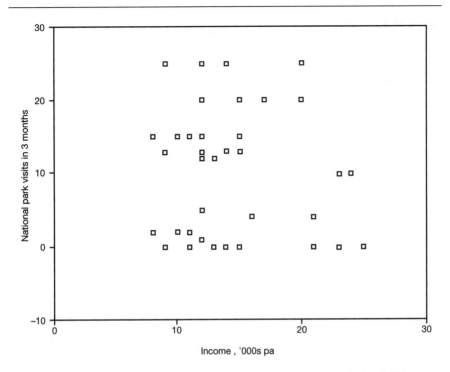

(c) National park visiting is not related to income – almost zero correlation (0.024)

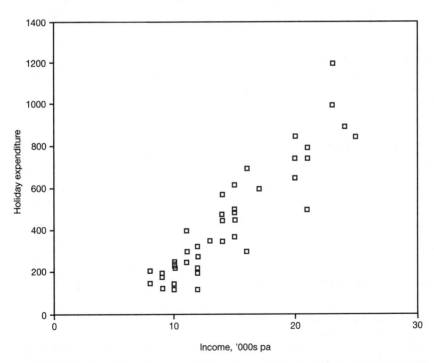

(d) Holiday expenditure increases with income – a very strong positive correlation (0.915)

Figure 14.17   Correlation

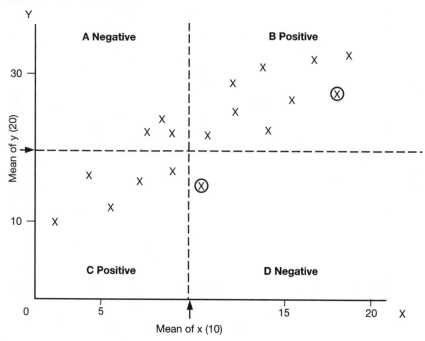

Notes: For circled point in sector B: x = 18, y = 26, product = (18−10) × (26−20) = 8 × 6 = 48.
For circled point in sector D: x = 12, y = 18, product = (12−10) × (18−20) = 2 × (−2) = −4.

high and low correlations. It is beyond the scope of this book to explain how the 'perfect' correlation is made to equal one, but, for those with the requisite mathematics, this can be deduced from the formula for *r*, which is given in Appendix 14.2.

Significance of *r*

The *significance* of a correlation coefficient depends on its size and the sample size and is assessed by means of a *t*-test (*see* formula in Appendix 14.2).

Null hypothesis

The null hypothesis is that the correlation is zero. The *t*-test therefore indicates only whether the correlation coefficient is *significantly different from zero*. Quite low coefficients can emerge as 'significant' if the sample is large enough.

SPSS and correlation

SPSS can be used to produce correlation coefficients between pairs of variables, as shown in Figure 14.18. The output is in the form of a symmetrical

Figure 14.18 Correlation matrix

SPSS procedures

1 Select **Statistics**.
2 Select **Correlate**.
3 Select **Bivariate**.
4 Select variables to be included.
5 Select **OK**.

SPSS output

```
          - -  Correlation Coefficients   - -
```

	INC	SPORT	THEATRE	NPARK	HOLS
INC	1.0000	-.4389	.4602	.0245	.9145
	(50)	(50)	(50)	(50)	(50)
	P= .	P= .001	P= .001	P= .866	P= .000
SPORT	-.4389	1.0000	-.6789	.2740	-.3684
	(50)	(50)	(50)	(50)	(50)
	P= .001	P= .	P= .000	P= .054	P= .008
THEATRE	.4602	-.6789	1.0000	-.2925	.3791
	(50)	(50)	(50)	(50)	(50)
	P= .001	P= .000	P= .	P= .039	P= .007
NPARK	.0245	.2740	-.2925	1.0000	.0581
	(50)	(50)	(50)	(50)	(50)
	P= .866	P= .054	P= .039	P= .	P= .688
HOLS	.9145	-.3684	.3791	.0581	1.0000
	(50)	(50)	(50)	(50)	(50)
	P= .000	P= .008	P= .007	P= .688	P= .

```
(Coefficient/Cases)/2-tailed Significance)
" . " is printed if a coefficient cannot be computed
```

matrix, so that, for example, the correlation between sport and income is the same as between income and sport. For each pair of variables, the output includes the correlation coefficient, the sample size (the number in brackets) and P, the probability related to the t-test. As with other tests, if the probability is below 0.05 we reject the null hypothesis: therefore only those correlations where the value of P is below 0.05 are significantly different from zero.

LINEAR REGRESSION

Introduction

Linear regression takes us one step further in this type of quantitative analysis – in the direction of 'prediction'. If the correlation between two variables is consistent enough, one variable can be used to 'predict' the other. In particular, easily measured variables (such as age or income) can be used to predict variables which are more difficult or costly to measure (such as participation in leisure activities). Examples of how knowledge of the relationship between variables might be used for prediction purposes are as follows; they suggest more sophisticated approaches to the analysis of Case studies 6.1 and 6.2.

1 Knowledge of the relationship between age and leisure participation can be used in planning leisure facilities for a community: the future age structure of the community can be relatively easily estimated and with this information demand for leisure activities can be estimated.
2 Relationships between income per head and amount of overseas air travel per head in different countries or over various time periods can be used to predict growth of air travel as incomes rise.

The procedures described here are just another format in which the relationships between variables of interest are examined. If the variables can be quantified, then the techniques enable the strength and nature of the relationship to be quantified also.

Regression model

To predict one variable on the basis of another a *model* or equation is needed, of the type:

Example 1: Leisure participation = *some number* times AGE
Example 2: Demand for overseas travel = *some number* times INCOME

Suppose leisure participation is measured in terms of the number of visits or days participation for some activity over the course of a year, and demand for travel is measured by the number of overseas trips in a year. Regression analysis produces an equation of the form:

Example 1: Days participation = $a + b$ times AGE
Example 2: Trips = $a + b$ times INCOME

The *beta coefficients* or *parameters a* and *b* are determined from examination of existing data, using regression analysis. The process of finding out the values of the parameters or coefficients is referred to as *calibration* of the model.

In general terms this is represented by the equation: $y = a + bx$, where y stands for participation or travel demand and x stands for age or income. Note that here *participation* and *travel demand* are the *dependent* variables and AGE and INCOME are the *independent* variables.

In visual terms this describes a 'regression line' fitted through the data, with 'intercept' or 'constant' of a and 'slope' of b, as shown in Figure 14.19. The regression procedure finds the 'line of best fit' by finding the line which minimises the sum of the (squared) differences between it and the data points, and specifies this line by giving values for a and b.

Figure 14.19 Regression line

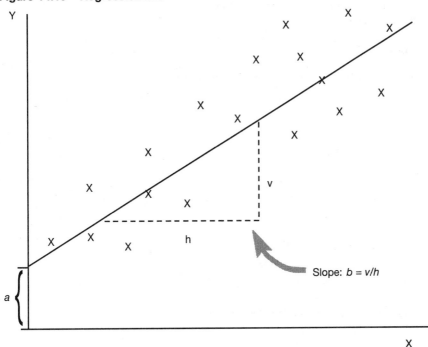

SPSS and regression

Examples of regression output from SPSS are shown in Figure 14.20. The SPSS program produces a large amount of output with which we are not concerned here: only the underlined items are discussed. However, the output illustrates the point that regression is an involved process. Only the broad outlines of regression are dealt with in this book. The output relates to *multiple* regression, which involves more than one independent variable, as discussed in the next section, but here we have only one independent variable, income.

The items we are interested in are the value of the regression coefficient (R, which is similar to the correlation coefficient) and its test of significance, and the beta coefficients listed under B. For Example 1, the relationship between income and holiday expenditure, the value of R is 0.915 and its probability (as measured by an F test) is shown as 0.000, which makes it highly significant. The *constant* (a) is −323.493 and the *coefficient* or *slope* (b) for income is 52.563. The regression equation is therefore:

Figure 14.20　Regression analysis

SPSS procedures

1 Select **Statistics**.
2 Select **Regression**.
3 Select **Linear**.
4 Select **dependent** and **independent** variables.
5 Select **OK**.

SPSS output

Example 1 Holiday expenditure and income

```
        * * * *   M U L T I P L E   R E G R E S S I O N   * * * *

Equation Number 1    Dependent Variable..   HOLS
Block Number    1    Method:  Enter         INC

Variable(s) Entered on Step Number   1..    INC        Income pa

Multiple R            .915    Analysis of Variance
R Square              .836                  DF    Sum of Squares   Mean Square
Adjusted R Square     .833    Regression     1    2679971          2679971
Standard Error      104.51    Residual      48    524283.2         10922.566

                             F =    245.361    Signif F =   .000

----------------- Variables in the Equation -----------------

Variable              B        SE B       Beta         T       Sig T
INC                52.563      3.356      .915       15.664     .000
(Constant)        -323.493    49.890                -6.484     .000
```

Example 2 Income and theatre-going

```
        * * * *   M U L T I P L E   R E G R E S S I O N   * * * *

Equation Number 1    Dependent Variable..   THEATRE
Block Number    1    Method:  Enter         INC

Variable(s) Entered on Step Number   1..    INC        Income pa

Multiple R          .46019    Analysis of Variance
R Square            .21178                  DF    Sum of Squares   Mean Square
Adjusted R Square   .19536    Regression     1    52.28355         52.28355
Standard Error     2.01348    Residual      48    194.59645         4.05409

                             F =    12.89648    Signif F =   .0008

----------------- Variables in the Equation -----------------

Variable              B        SE B       Beta         T       Sig T
INC               .232165     .064649    .460193     3.591     .0008
(Constant)        -.616742    .961162               -.642      .5241
```

Holiday expenditure (£ pa) = –323.493 + 52.563 × income (in £'000s pa)

This regression line can be plotted on to a graph, as shown in Figure 14.21. With this equation, if we knew a student's income we could estimate their level of holiday expenditure, either by reading it off the graph or calculating it. For example, for a student with an income of £10 000 a year:

Holiday expenditure (£ pa) =
–323.49 + 52.56 × 10 = –323.49 + 525.60 = £202.11

So we estimate that such a student would spend £202 on holidays in a year. Of course we are not saying that *every* student with income of £10 000 will spend this sum: the regression line/equation is a sort of average; it is not precise.

Figure 14.21   Regression line: holiday expenditure and income

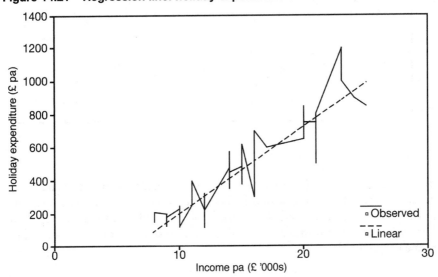

Note: This graphic is produced using the SPSS procedure **Curve Estimation** within **Regression**.

Example 2 in Figure 14.20 produces similar output for the relationship between theatre-going and income. In this case the resultant regression equation would be:

Theatre-going (times in three months) = –0.62 + 0.23 × income

Non-linear regression

In Figure 14.22 the relationship between the two variables, is *non-linear* – that is, the relationship indicated is curved, rather than being a straight line. The standard regression procedure would seek to fit a straight line to these data, which would not be an accurate reflection of the relationship. This emphasises the importance of examining the data *visually*, as done here, and not relying

Figure 14.22   Non-linear relationship

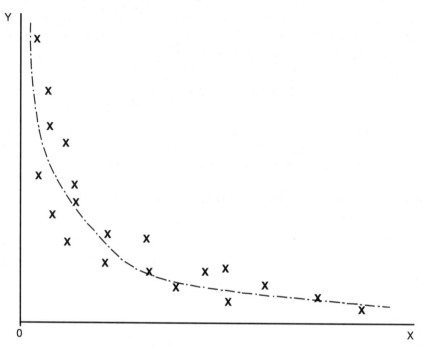

just on correlation coefficients. Where theory or observation of the data suggests that the relationship would be better represented by a *curved* line, *non-linear* methods may be used. These are available in SPSS and involve applying logarithms or other formulae to the data, but these techniques are beyond the scope of this book.

MULTIPLE REGRESSION

Multiple regression is linear regression involving more than one independent variable. For example, we might hypothesise that sports participation is dependent not just on income but also on age, or that overseas travel is dependent not just on income but also on the price of air fares. Thus our models, or regression equations, would be:

Example 1: Sports participation = $a + b \times$ income + $c \times$ age
Example 2: Travel = $a + b \times$ income + $c \times$ fares

In *linear* regression the procedure fits a straight line to the data – the line of *best fit*. In *multiple* regression the procedure fits a *surface* to the data – the surface of best fit. It is possible to visualise this in three dimensions (one dependent and two independent variables), with the axes forming a three-dimensional box, the observations suspended in space and the regression surface being a flat plane somewhere within the box. (SPSS offers a 3-D graphical option to represent this in the **Scattergram** procedure.) When additional variables are included then four, five or '*n*' dimensions are involved and it is not possible to visualise the process, but the mathematical principles used to establish the regression equation are the same.

An example, in which theatre-going is related to income and age, is shown in Figure 14.23. It will be noticed that the value of R has risen from 0.46 in the single variable case (Figure 14.20, Example 2) to 0.5799, indicating an improvement in the 'fit' of the data to the model. The model equation is now:

Theatre-going (per three months) = –3.49 + 0.056 × income + 0.0227 × age

Figure 14.23   Multiple regression

SPSS procedures

1 Select **Statistics**.
2 Select **Regression**.
3 Select **Linear**.
4 Select **dependent** and (more than one) **independent** variables.
5 Select **Enter** for all the selected variables to be included immediately, or **Stepwise** for the program to select and include variables in order of influence.
6 Select **OK**.

SPSS output

```
         * * * *   M U L T I P L E    R E G R E S S I O N   * * * *

Equation Number 1    Dependent Variable..   THEATRE

Block Number  1.  Method:  Enter      INC       AGE

Variable(s) Entered on Step Number  1..    AGE        Age
                                    2..    INC        Income pa


Multiple R          .57991   Analysis of Variance
R Square            .33629                DF    Sum of Squares   Mean Square
Adjusted R Square   .30805   Regression    2        83.02334       41.51167
Standard Error     1.86717   Residual     47       163.85666        3.48631

                     F =      11.90704     Signif F =   .0001


------------------ Variables in the Equation ------------------

Variable              B         SE B        Beta          T      Sig T

INC              .055873     .084373      .110751        .662    .5111
AGE              .226614     .076317      .496611       2.969    .0047
(Constant)     -3.493216    1.316375                   -2.654    .0108

End Block Number    1    All requested variables entered.
```

It is possible, in theory, to continue to add variables to the equation. This should, however, be done with caution, since it frequently involves 'multi-collinearity', where the independent variables are themselves inter-correlated. The 'independent' variables should be, as far as possible, just that: independent. Various tests exist to test for this phenomenon. Often, in leisure and tourism, a large number of variables is involved, many inter-correlated, but each contributing something to the leisure or tourist phenomenon under investigation. Multivariate analysis procedures, such as cluster and factor analysis, discussed below, are designed partly to overcome these problems.

FACTOR AND CLUSTER ANALYSIS

Introduction

Factor and cluster analysis are techniques which are available in SPSS and are used when the number of independent variables is large and there is a desire to group them in some way. The theoretical counterpart to this is that there are some complex phenomena which cannot be measured by one or two variables, but require a 'battery' of variables, each contributing some aspect to the make-up of the phenomenon. Examples are: a person's 'lifestyle' (made up of variables such as leisure and work patterns, income and expenditure, age and family situation); and a person's characteristics as a tourist – a 'tourist type' (made up of variables such as travel experience, expenditure patterns, products desired and satisfactions sought). Each of these is often researched using a large number of data items. For example, lifestyles have been measured by asking people as many as 300 questions about their attitudes to work, politics, morals, leisure, religion and so on.

Factor analysis

Factor analysis is based on the idea that certain variables 'go together', in that people with a high score on one variable also tend to have a high score on certain others, which might then form a group. For example, people who go to the theatre might also visit galleries; people with strong pro-environment views might be found to favour certain types of holiday. Analysis of this type of phenomenon can be approached using a simple, manual technique involving a correlation matrix of the variables, as illustrated in Figure 14.24. Groupings of variables can be produced by indicating which variables have their highest correlations with each other. In Figure 14.24 three groupings of variables is shown, where the arrows indicate the highest correlations.

This procedure only takes account of the highest correlation, with some use being made of the second highest, as indicated. But variables will have a range of lower-order relationships with each other which this method cannot take account of. A number of lower-order correlations may, cumulatively, be more significant than a single 'highest' correlation. Factor analysis is a mathematical

Figure 14.24   Simple manual factor analysis

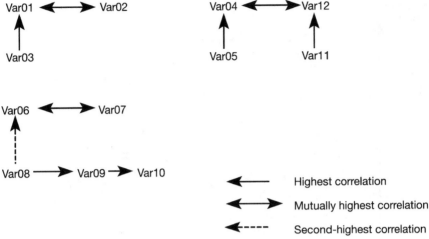

procedure which groups the variables taking account of *all* the correlations. The details of the method are, however, beyond the scope of this book.

Cluster analysis

Cluster analysis is another 'grouping' procedure, but it focuses on the individuals directly rather than the variables. Imagine a situation with two variables, age and some behavioural variable, and data points plotted in the usual way, as shown in Figure 14.25. It can be seen that there are three broad 'clusters' of respondents – two young clusters and one older cluster. Each of these clusters might form, for example, particular market segments. With just two variables and a few observations it is relatively simple to identify clusters visually. But with more variables and more cases this would not be possible.

Cluster analysis involves giving the computer a set of rules for building clusters. It first calculates the 'distances' between data points, in terms of a range of specified variables. Those points which are closest together are put into a first-round 'cluster' and a new 'point' half-way between the two is put in their place. The process is repeated to form a second round of clustering, and a third and fourth and so on, until there are only two 'points' left. The result is usually illustrated by a 'dendrogram', as shown in Figure 14.26.

IN CONCLUSION

Much leisure and tourism research, even of a quantitative nature, is conducted without the use of the techniques covered in this chapter. This is a reflection of the descriptive nature of much of the research in the field, as discussed in

Figure 14.25   Plots of 'clusters'

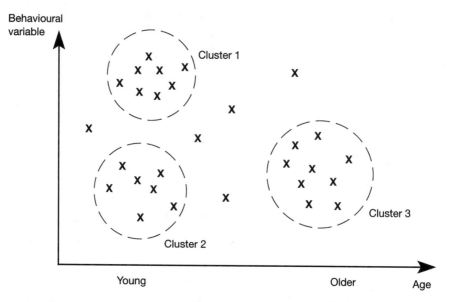

Figure 14.26   Dendrogram

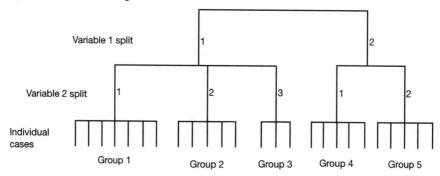

Chapter 1, the nature of the data involved and the needs of the audience or client for the research. Often in leisure and tourism the need is for 'broad brush' research findings: accuracy is required but a high level of precision is not. Contrast this with medical research, where precision is a matter of life or death. To some extent the level of use of statistical techniques is related to disciplinary traditions. Thus, for example, the use of statistical techniques in the American *Journal of Leisure Research* is quite common, as a result of the heavy involvement of psychologists in American leisure research, whereas in the British journal *Leisure Studies* statistical techniques are rarely deployed, reflecting the British tradition of qualitative sociology. In the tourism journals statistical techniques such as regression and correlation tend to arise fairly often because of the strong economic dimension of the research.

Many leisure or tourism researchers could therefore find that they rarely make use of the techniques presented in this chapter, but they should be able to interpret research reports which do make use of them, and they should be able to utilise them if called upon to do so.

As has been stressed throughout this book, data collection and analysis should be determined by a theoretical or evaluative framework. At the analysis stage the researcher should, ideally, not be wondering what to relate to what, and choosing variables and analyses in an *ad hoc* manner. While a certain amount of inductive exploration and even serendipity is inevitable, ideally there should be a basic analysis plan from the beginning. Key variables and the question of relationships between them should have been thought about in advance, for example as a result of an early 'concept mapping' exercise. Thus, while the examples given in this chapter may appear *ad hoc* and 'data driven', in a real research project the procedures used should be theory driven or problem or hypothesis driven.

QUESTIONS AND EXERCISES

It is suggested that the reader replicate the various analyses set out in this chapter, but using their own data set. This can be based on data which may have been collected for Chapter 13, but will involve adding a range of ratio variables to the questionnaire, similar to those listed in Appendix 14.1.

FURTHER READING

There are many excellent statistics textbooks available which cover the range of techniques included in this chapter, and, of course, much more. Texts vary in terms of the degree of familiarity with algebra that they assume on the part of the reader, so readers with limited mathematical knowledge should 'shop around' to find a text which deals with the topic in conceptual terms rather than in detailed mathematical terms. However, a certain amount of mathematical aptitude is, of course, essential. The SPSS handbook (Norusis, 1993) provides useful summaries of the techniques presented here, with worked examples. Examples of general research methods texts which include statistics are Ryan (1995) and Burns (1994); and a specialist text: Spatz and Johnston (1989).

For examples of the use of the techniques covered here, the reader should browse through *Journal of Leisure Research* and, to a lesser extent, *Leisure Sciences*.

APPENDIX 14.1
DETAILS OF EXAMPLE DATA FILE USED

Variable name	Variable label/description	Range of values	Data type
crse	Course enrolled in	1–4	Nominal
lib	Use of library	0–1	Nominal
cant	Use of canteen	0–1	Nominal
comp	Use of union computer services	0–1	Nominal
scs	Use of student counselling service	0–1	Nominal
rep	Rank importance of reputation	1–5	Ordinal
access	Rank importance of access	1–5	Ordinal
curr	Rank importance of curriculum	1–5	Ordinal
fees	Rank importance of fees	1–5	Ordinal
park	Rank importance of parking	1–5	Ordinal
cost	Expenditure on books	–	Ratio
text	Importance of textbook	1–3	Nominal
lect	Importance of knowledgeable lecturer	1–3	Nominal
assgn	Importance of easy assignments	1–1	Nominal
sug1	Suggestion for improvements	1–6	Nominal
sug2	Suggestion for improvements	1–6	Nominal
sug3	Suggestion for improvements	1–6	Nominal
age	Age	–	Ratio
gend	Gender	1–2	Nominal
inc	Annual income in £000s	–	Ratio
sport	Number of times played sport in last three months	–	Ratio
theatre	Number of times gone to theatre in last three months	–	Ratio
npark	Number of times visited national park in last three months	–	Ratio
meal	Number of times been out for a meal in last three months	–	Ratio
hols	Holiday expenditure, £ pa	–	Ratio
crser	Course recoded into: U/grad/Grad.dip./Masters	1–3	Nominal

APPENDIX 14.2
STATISTICAL FORMULAE

95 per cent confidence interval for normal distribution for percentage p

$$CI = 2 \sqrt{\frac{p(100-p)}{n-1}}$$

where n = sample size.

Chi-square

$$\chi^2 = \sqrt{\sum ((O-E)/E)^2}$$

t for difference between means

$$t = \sqrt{\frac{(\overline{x}_1 - \overline{x}_2)}{(s_1^2/n_1 + s_2^2/n_1)}}$$

Standard deviation

$$SD = \sqrt{\sum_n (x-\overline{x})^2}$$

Correlation coefficient

$$r = \frac{\sum ((x-\overline{x})(y-\overline{y}))^2}{(s_1^2/n_1 + s_2^2/n_1)}$$

Value of t for correlation coefficient

$$t = r\sqrt{(N-2)/(1-r^2)}$$

CHAPTER 15

Preparing a research report

INTRODUCTION

This chapter outlines key aspects of the preparation and presentation of written research reports, and discusses content, structure and layout. While much of the chapter is relevant to the writing of articles, in the main it focuses on the requirements of the consultancy report or monograph format.

The importance of the report

Written reports are a key element of the world of management and planning. Applied studies of the sort discussed in Chapter 1, namely feasibility studies, marketing plans, recreation needs studies, tourism development plans, market research studies and performance appraisals, all come in the form of written reports. The results of many academic studies are also produced in report, or monograph, format.

The medium is the message and in this case the medium is the written report. The ability to prepare a report, and the ability to recognise good quality and poor quality reports, should be seen as a key element in the skills of the manager. While form is no substitute for good content, a report which is poorly presented can undermine or even negate good content. While most of the researcher's attention should of course be focused on achieving high-quality substantive content, the general aspects raised in this chapter also merit serious attention.

Getting started

In discussing research proposals in Chapter 3 it was noted that researchers invariably leave too little time for report writing. Even when adequate time has been allocated in the timetable this is often whittled away and the writing of the report is delayed, leaving too little time. There is a tendency to put off report writing because it is difficult, and it is often felt that, with just a little more data analysis or a little more reading of the literature, the process of writing the report will become easier. This is rarely the case: it is always difficult!

A regrettably common practice is for writers of reports to spend a great deal of their depleted time, with the deadline looming, writing and preparing material which could have been attended to much earlier in the process. There are often large parts of any report which can be written before data analysis is complete, or even started. Such parts include the introduction, statement of objectives, outline of theoretical or evaluative framework, literature review and description of the methodology. In addition, time-consuming activities such as arranging for maps, illustrations and cover designs to be produced need not be left until the last minute.

CONTENT

Reports generally include some standard components, as shown in Figure 15.1, and these are discussed in turn below.

Cover

The cover should include minimal information, such as title, author(s) and publisher or sponsor. The lavishness and design content will vary with the context and the resources available. If the report is available for sale it should include an International Standard Book Number (ISBN) on the back cover. All publications in the western world have a 10-digit ISBN, the first digit '0' indicating the book is published in an English-speaking country, the second group identifying the publisher and the third group identifying the book (as can be seen on the back of this book, for example). ISBNs are allocated by national libraries, which receive free deposit copies of all publications in their country. The ISBN makes it easy to order publications through bookshops and ensures that the publication is catalogued in library systems around the world.

Title page

The title page is the first or second page inside the cover. (In some books the first page is a 'half-title' page, which contains an abbreviated title.) The title page may include much the same information as the cover or considerably more detail, as indicated in Figure 15.1. In some cases, as in commercially published books, some of the detail is provided on the reverse of the title page.

List of contents

Lists of contents can include just chapter titles or full details of sub-sections. An example of a contents page is shown in Figure 15.2. Modern word-processor packages include procedures for compiling tables of contents and lists, such as tables and figures.

Executive summary

An executive summary is sometimes thought of as the summary for the 'busy executive' who does not have time to read the whole report, but the term really refers to the idea that it should contain information necessary to take

Figure 15.1   Report components

● **Cover**	– Title of report
	– Author(s)
	– Institution or publisher (possibly on back cover or spine)
	– ISBN (back cover – *see* text)
● **Title page**	– Title of report
	– Author(s)
	– Institution or publisher, including address, phone numbers*
	– Sponsoring body (e.g. 'Report to the Tourism Commission')
	– Date of publication*
	– If the report is for sale: ISBN* (*see* text)
	(* sometimes on reverse of title page)
● **Contents page(s)**	– *See* Fig. 15.2 for example
● **Executive summary**	– Background, context and objectives
	– Methods and data sources
	– Main findings
	– Conclusions
	– Recommendations, where appropriate
● **Preface/Foreword**	
● **Acknowledgements**	– Funding organisations
	– Liaison officers of funding organisations
	– Members of steering committees
	– Organisations or individuals providing access to information etc.
	– Staff employed (e.g. including interviewers, coders, computer programmers, secretaries, wordprocessors)
	– Individuals (including academic supervisors) who have given advice, commented on report drafts, etc.
	– (Collectively) Individuals who responded to questionnaires etc.
● **Main body of the report**	
● **References**	
● **Appendices**	

Figure 15.2   Example of contents page

CONTENTS

Page

executive action on the basis of the report. An executive summary should contain a summary of *the whole report*, as indicated in Figure 15.1. It follows that the executive summary should be written *last*. A very approximate guide to length is as follows:

Report length	Executive summary length
Up to 20 pages	1–2 pages
Up to 50 pages	3–4 pages
Up to 100 pages	5–6 pages

Preface/foreword

Prefaces or Forewords are used for a variety of purposes. Usually they explain the origins of the study and outline any qualifications or limitations, and provide acknowledgements of assistance if there is no separate Acknowledgements section. Sometimes a significant individual is asked to write a Foreword, such as the director of an institution, a government minister or an eminent academic.

Acknowledgements

It is clearly a matter of courtesy to acknowledge any assistance received during the course of a research project. People and institutions who might be acknowledged are listed in Figure 15.1.

MAIN BODY OF THE REPORT – TECHNICAL ASPECTS

Section numbering

It is usual to number not only the major sections and chapters, but also subsections within chapters, as shown in the example in Figure 15.2.

Paragraph numbering

In some reports paragraphs are individually numbered. This can be useful for reference purposes when a report is being discussed in committees etc. Paragraphs can be numbered in a single series for the whole report or chapter by chapter: Chapter 1: paragraphs 1.1, 1.2, 1.3, etc.; Chapter 2: paragraphs 2.1, 2.2, 2.3 etc. and so on.

Page numbering

One problem in putting together long reports, especially when a number of authors are responsible for different sections, is to organise page numbering so that it follows on from chapter to chapter. This can be avoided by numbering each chapter separately, for example: Chapter 1: pages 1.1, 1.2, 1.3, etc.; Chapter 2: pages 2.1, 2.2, 2.3, etc. and so on.

Word processors can be made to produce page numbers in this form by using the header/footer and/or page-numbering facilities.

It is general practice for the title page, contents, acknowledgements and the executive summary to be numbered using roman numerals and for the report proper to start at page 1 with arabic numbers; again, most word processors will produce this.

Heading hierarchy

In the main body of the report a hierarchy of heading styles should be used, with the major chapter or section headings being in the most prominent style and with decreasing emphasis for sub-section headings. Such a convention helps readers to know where they are in a document. When a team is involved in writing a report it is clearly sensible to agree these heading styles in advance. With modern word-processor systems and printers a large hierarchy is available:

1. Chapter Titles

1.1 Section Headings

1.1.1 Sub-section Headings

Typing layout and spacing

Essays and books tend to use the convention of starting new paragraphs by indenting the first line. Report style is to separate paragraphs by a blank line and not to indent the first line. Report style also tends to have more headings. A document typed or word-processed in report style usually leaves wide margins, which raises the question as to whether it is necessary to print documents in 1.5 or double space format or whether single spacing is adequate (and more environmentally friendly!).

Tables and graphics

When presenting the results of quantitative research, an appropriate balance must be struck in the use of tables, graphics and text. In most cases, very complex tables are consigned to appendices and simplified versions are included in the body of the report. It may be appropriate to place *all* tables in appendices and provide only instantly readable graphics in the body of the report. The decision on which approach to use depends partly on the complexity of the data to be presented, but mainly on the type of audience.

Tables/graphics vs text

Tables, graphics and text each have a distinctive role to play in the presentation of the study findings. Tables provide information; graphics illustrate that information so that patterns can be seen in a visual way. The text should be telling a story or developing an argument and 'orchestrating' tables and graphics to support that task.

In Figure 15.3 Commentary A does little more than repeat what is in the table: it says nothing to the reader about the difference between men's and women's participation patterns, which is presumably the purpose of the exercise. Commentary B, on the other hand, is more informative, pointing out particular features of the data in the table.

Typically then, the text should be developing an argument and should make reference to the table or graphic to help the argument along or, if the text is primarily descriptive, the text should draw attention to notable features of the

Figure 15.3   Table and commentaries

Table X.X Participation in top five sports/physical activities, Great Britain, 1986		
	% participating in four weeks prior to interview (most popular quarter)	
Activity	Males	Females
Walking	21	18
Football	6	*
Snooker/billiards	17	3
Swimming – indoor	9	10
Darts	9	3
Keep fit/yoga	1	5

Source: General Household Survey, OPCS. * less than 0.05%.

Commentary A

The table indicates that the top five sports and physical recreation activities for men are walking (21%), snooker/billiards (17%), indoor swimming (9%), darts (9%) and football (6%), whereas for women the five most popular activities are walking (18%), indoor swimming (10%), keep fit/yoga (5%), snooker/billiards (3%) and darts (3%).

Commentary B

Men and women may have more in common in their patterns of leisure activity than is popularly imagined. The table indicates that four activities – walking, swimming, snooker/billiards and darts – are included in the top five most popular sport and physical recreation activities for both men and women. While in general men's participation levels are higher than those of women, the table shows that women's participation rate exceeds that of men for two of the activities, namely keep fit/yoga and swimming.

data presented in a table or graphic – the highest or lowest or the greatest contrast or the lack of contrast, and so on.

Presentation

Diagrams and tables should, as far as possible, be complete in themselves. That is, they should be fully labelled so that the reader can understand them without necessarily referring to the text. They should usually indicate the source of data – but where a report is based primarily on one primary data source, such as a survey, it is not necessary to indicate this on every table and diagram. (However, some consultants tend to provide this information so that if a user photocopies just one table or diagram then its source is indicated.)

MAIN BODY OF THE REPORT – STRUCTURE AND CONTENT

It could be said that the three most important aspects of a research report are: (1) structure, (2) structure and (3) structure! The *structure* of a report is of fundamental importance. It needs to be thoroughly discussed, particularly when a team is involved. While all reports have certain structural features in common, the important aspects concern the underlying argument and how that relates to the objectives of the study and any data collection and analysis involved. This is linked fundamentally to the research objectives, the theoretical or evaluative framework and the overall research strategy, as discussed in Chapter 3.

Before writing starts it can be useful to agree not only the report structure and format, but also target word-lengths for each chapter or section. While an agreed structure is a necessary starting point, it is also necessary to be flexible. As drafting gets going it may be found that what was originally conceived as one chapter needs to be divided into two or three chapters, or what was thought of as a separate chapter can be incorporated into another chapter or into an appendix. Throughout, consideration needs to be given to the overall length of the report, in terms of words or pages.

When a questionnaire survey is involved, there is a tendency to structure the presentation according to the sequence of questions in the questionnaire and, correspondingly, the sequence of tables as they are produced by the computer. This is not an appropriate way to proceed! Questionnaires are structured for ease of interview, for the convenience of interviewer and/or respondent: they do *not* provide a suitable sequence and structure for a report.

For an author to be clear in his or her own mind about structure is one thing; conveying this structure to the reader can be quite another. While the contents page and general organisation of a report should make the reader aware of the structure, this is rarely enough: it must be *explained*, often more than once. Thus it is good practice to provide an outline of the structure of the whole report in the introductory chapter, and outlines of each chapter in the introduction to each chapter. Summaries are useful at the end of each chapter and these can be revisited at the end of the report when drawing conclusions together. It is advisable to provide numerous references backwards and forwards, as reminders to the reader as to what stage they have reached in the overall 'story' of the report. When a list of 'factors', 'issues' or 'topics' is about to be discussed, one by one, it is useful to list the factors or issues to be discussed, and then summarise at the end of the section to indicate what the review of factors or issues has achieved.

Audiences and style

The style, format and length of a report are largely influenced by the type of audience at which it is aimed. Audiences may be:

- popular
- decision-makers
- experts

By popular is meant the general public who might read a report of research in a newspaper or magazine: full research reports are therefore not generally written for a popular readership. Decision-makers are groups such as elected members of councils, government ministers, members of boards of companies, or senior executives who may not have a detailed knowledge of a particular field. Experts are professionals and others who are familiar with the subject matter of the report. Clearly the amount of technical jargon used and the detail with which data are presented will be affected by this question of audience.

Functions

A report can be thought of in two ways: first, the report as narrative, and second, the report as record.

Narrative means that a report has to tell a *story* to the reader. The writer of the report therefore needs to think of the flow of the argument – the 'story' – in the same way that the writer of a novel has to consider the plot.

The report as *record* means that a report is often also a reference source where future readers may wish to look for information. For the report to be a good record it may need to include extensive detailed information which may interfere with the process of 'story telling'. The latter may call for presentation of only simplified factual information or key features of the data.

The narrative

The narrative of a research report usually develops as indicated in Figure 15.4. The items listed may emerge in a variety of chapter or section configurations. For example, sections A and B could be one chapter or section or three or four, depending on the complexity of the project.

Figure 15.4   Report narrative

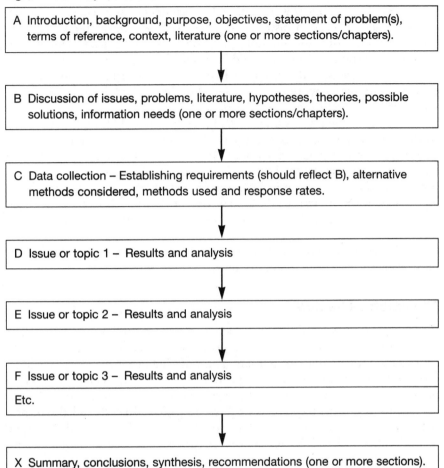

The introductory section, A, should reflect the considerations which emerged in the initial steps (1, 2 and 6 – *see* Figure 3.1 in Chapter 3) of the planning stages of the project. 'Context' includes reference to the environment in which the research is situated, including any initial literature review which may be involved. Section B should reflect steps 3–5 and 7–8 in the research planning process (*see* Figure 3.1) and may include further reference to the literature.

In sections B and C it is important that the relationship between data requirements and the research questions and theoretical or evaluative framework be explained, as discussed in Chapters 3 and 10. It should be clear from the discussion why the data are being collected, and how this relates to the planning, management or theoretical issues raised; how it was anticipated that the information collected would solve or shed light on the problems or issues raised, or aid decision-making.

In section C methodology should be described in detail; it should be clear why particular techniques were chosen, how samples or subjects were selected and what data-collection instruments were used. Where sample surveys are involved full information should be given on response rates and sample sizes obtained and some indication should be given of the consequences in terms of confidence intervals, as discussed in Chapter 12. These technical aspects of the results of any survey work can be included in the methodology section of the report or in the first of the results sections.

The results and analysis sections – D, E, F, etc. – should ideally be structured by the discussion in B, around issues, or elements of the research problem.

Sometimes conclusions are set out in the results and analysis section(s) and all that is required in the final section is to reiterate and draw them together. In other cases the final section includes the final stage of analysis and the drawing of conclusions. In writing the final section or chapter it is vital to refer back to the terms of reference and objectives to ensure that all objectives have been met.

Not all research reports include 'recommendations'. Recommendations are most likely to arise from evaluative research.

The report as 'record'

It is wise to think beyond the immediate use of a research report, and think of it also as the definitive record of the research conducted. It should therefore contain a summary of all the relevant data collected in a form which would be useful for any future user of the report. This means that, while data may be presented in the main body of the report in a highly condensed and summarised form in order to produce a readable narrative, they should also be presented in as much detail as possible, 'for the record'. Data included 'for the record' can be placed in appendices or, when large amounts of data are involved, in a separate statistical volume.

For example Table 6.1 in Chapter 6 in this book, on leisure participation, might be considered to be too complex for inclusion in the main body of a report so might be included in an appendix. In the main body of the report a simplified table could be included, giving details of just four or five of the fastest growing activities and the declining activities – in fact those activities which would be discussed in the text. Alternatively a graphic illustrating this limited amount of data could be presented.

In the case of questionnaire survey data it can be a good idea to provide a statistical appendix which includes tables from all the questions in the order they appear in the questionnaire, as discussed in Chapter 13. Any reader interested in a specific aspect of the data is then able to locate and use it. The main body of the report can then be structured around issues and not be constrained by the structure of the questionnaire.

In conclusion

Ultimately, the writing of a good research report is an art and a skill which develops with practice. Reports can be improved enormously as a result of comments from others – often because the writer has been 'too close' to the report for too long to be able to see glaring faults or omissions. The researcher or writer can also usually spot opportunities for improvement if he or she takes a short break and returns to the draft report with 'fresh eyes'. Finally, *checking and double checking the report for typing, spelling and typographical errors is well worth the laborious effort.*

OTHER MEDIA

While the written report is still the most common medium for the communication of research results, this is likely to change in future. In particular, within the next decade or so, multimedia presentations, using CD-ROM and other technology and combining sound and moving images, as well as the written word, will become commonplace. For the moment more mundane media are generally used as adjuncts to written reports. Often the researcher is required to present final or interim results of research in person and some sort of audiovisual aids are usually advisable, including: handouts; posters; overhead transparencies; slides; video clips; and computer-based 'slide-shows'.

A FINAL COMMENT

Research is a creative process which, in the words of Norbert Elias with which we began this text, aims to 'make known something previously unknown to human beings . . . to advance human knowledge, to make it more certain or better fitting. . . . The aim is . . . discovery'. It is hoped that this book will provide some assistance in that process of discovery and that the reader will enjoy some of the satisfactions and rewards which can come from worthwhile research.

QUESTIONS AND EXERCISES

No specific exercises are offered here. By now the reader should be capable of venturing into the world of research by carrying out a research project from beginning to end.

FURTHER READING

The best reading relevant to this chapter is the critical reading of research reports.

REFERENCES

Adler, P. A. and Adler, P. (1994) 'Observational techniques', in Denzin and Lincoln, *op. cit.*, pp. 377–92.

Age, *The* (1982) *The Age Lifestyle Study for the Eighties*, Melbourne: D. Syme & Co.

American Psychological Association (1983) *Publication Manual*, Washington, DC: APA.

Anderson, R. (1975) *Leisure: An Inappropriate Concept for Women?*, Canberra: AGPS.

Archer, B. H. (1994) 'Demand forecasting and estimation', ch. 10 of Ritchie and Goeldner, *op.cit.*, pp. 105–14.

Australian Bureau of Statistics (1994) *How Australians Use their Time*, (Cat. No. 4153.0) Canberra: ABS.

Australian Government Publishing Service (1994) *Style Manual for Authors, Editors and Printers*, Canberra: AGPS.

Bachman, J. G. and O'Malley, P. M. (1981) 'When four months equal a year: inconsistencies in student reports of drug use', *Public Opinion Quarterly*, Vol. 45, pp. 536–48.

Bailey, P. (1978) *Leisure and Class in Victorian England*, London: Routledge.

Bailey, P. (1989) 'Leisure, culture and the historian: reviewing the first generation of leisure historiography in Britain', *Leisure Studies*, Vol. 8, No. 2, pp. 107–28.

Baretje, R. (1964) *Bibliographie Touristique*, Aix-en-Provence: Centre d'Etudes du Tourisme.

Barnett, L. A. (ed.) (1988) *Research about Leisure: Past, Present and Future*, Champaign, IL.: Sagamore Publishing.

Barry, P. (1994) *The Rise and Rise of Kerry Packer*, Sydney: Bantam/ABC.

Barton, A. H. and Lazarsfield, P. (1969) 'Some functions of qualitative analysis of social research', in McCall and Simmons, *op. cit.*, pp. 163–95.

Barzun, J. and Graff, H. F. (1985) *The Modern Researcher*, 4th edn., San Diego, CA: Harcourt Brace Jovanovich.

Beauchamp, T. L. *et al.* (eds.) (1982) *Ethical Issues in Social Science Research*, Baltimore: Johns Hopkins University Press.

Bella, L. (1989) 'Women and leisure: beyond androcentrism', in E. L. Jackson and T. L. Burton (eds.) *Understanding Leisure and Recreation*, State College, PA: Venture, pp. 151–80.

Bennett, T. and Frow, J. (1991) *Art Galleries: Who Goes?* Redfern, NSW: Australia Council.

Bialeschki, M. D. and Henderson, K. (1986) 'Leisure in the common world of women', *Leisure Studies*, Vol. 5, No. 3, pp. 299–308.

Bickmore, D., Shaw, M. and Tulloch, T. (1980) 'Lifestyles on maps', *Geographical Magazine*, Vol. 52, No. 11, pp. 763–9.

Birenbaum, A. and Sagarin, E. (eds.) (1973) *People in Places: The Sociology of the Familiar*, London: Nelson.

Bitgood, S., Patterson, D. and Benefield, A. (1988) 'Exhibit design and visitor behaviour', *Environment and Behaviour*, Vol. 20, No. 4, pp. 474–91.

Bloch, C. and Lawsen, P. F. (1996) 'Play, sports and environment', *International Review for the Sociology of Sport*, Vol. 31, No. 2, pp. 205–15.

Boothby, J. (1987) 'Self-reported participation rates: further comment', *Leisure Studies*, Vol. 6, No. 1, pp. 99–104.

Borman, K. M., LeCompt, M. D. and Goetz, J. P. (1986) 'Ethnographic and qualitative research design and why it doesn't work', *American Behavioral Scientist*, Vol. 30, No. 1, pp. 42–57.

Botterill, T. D. (1989) 'Humanistic tourism? Personal constructions of a tourist: Sam visits Japan', *Leisure Studies*, Vol. 8, No. 3, pp. 281–94.

Bramham, P. and Henry, I. (1985) 'Political ideology and leisure policy in the United Kingdom', *Leisure Studies*, Vol. 4, No. 1, pp. 1–19.

Bramham, P., Henry, I., Mommaas, H. and Van Der Poel, H. (eds.) (1993) *Leisure Policies in Europe*, Wallingford, Oxon: CAB International.

Brandenburg, J., Greiner, W., Hamilton-Smith, H., Scholten, H., Senior, R. and Webb, J. (1982) 'A conceptual model of how people adopt recreation activities', *Leisure Studies*, Vol. 1, No. 3, pp. 263–76.

British Broadcasting Corporation (1978) *The People's Use of Time*, London: BBC.

Brown, P. (1995) 'Women, sport and the media: an historical perspective on sports coverage in the Sydney Morning Herald, 1890–1990', in C. Simpson and B. Gidlow (eds.) *Australian and New Zealand Association for Leisure Studies, Second Conference – Leisure Connexions*, Canterbury, New Zealand: Lincoln University, pp. 44–50.

Bryman, A. and Cramer, D. (1990) *Quantitative Data Analysis for Social Scientists*, London: Routledge.

BTA/Keele University (1967) *Pilot National Recreation Survey*, Keele, Staffs: University of Keele/British Travel Association.

Bulmer, M. (ed.) (1982) *Social Research Ethics*, London: Macmillan.

Burch, W. R. (1981) 'The ecology of metaphor: spacing regularities for humans and other primates in urban and wild habitats', *Leisure Sciences*, Vol. 4, No. 3, pp. 213–30.

Burch, W. R. Jr. (1964) *A New Look at an Old Friend – Observation as a Technique for Recreation Research*, Portland, OR: Pacific Northwest Forest and Range Experiment Station.

Burgess, R. G. (ed.) (1982) *Field Research: A Sourcebook and Field Manual*, London: Allen & Unwin.

Burkhardt, A., Toohey, K. and Veal, A. J. (1995) *The Olympic Games: A Bibliography*, Publication 15, Sydney: Centre for Leisure and Tourism Studies, University of Technology, Sydney.

Burkart, A. J. and Medlik, S. (1981) *Tourism: Past, Present and Future*, 2nd edn., London: Heinemann.

Burns, R. B. (1994) *Introduction to Research Methods*, 2nd edn., Melbourne: Longman Cheshire.

Burton, T. L. (1971) *Experiments in Recreation Research*, London: Allen & Unwin.

Buzan, T. (1995) *The Mind Map Book*, London: BBC Books.

Cairns, J., Jennet, N. and Sloane, P. J. (1986) 'The economics of professional team sports: a survey of theory and evidence', *Journal of Economic Studies*, Vol. 13, No. 1, pp. 3–80.

Calantone, R. J., Di Benedetto, C. A. and Bojanic, D. (1987) 'A comprehensive review of the tourism forecasting literature', *Journal of Travel Research*, Vol. 26, No. 2, pp. 28–39.

Calder, A. and Sheridan, D. (1984) *Speak for Yourself: A Mass Observation Anthology, 1937–49*, London: Jonathan Cape.

Calder, B. (1977) 'Focus groups and the nature of qualitative marketing research', *Journal of Marketing Research*, Vol. 14, Aug., pp. 353–64.

Campbell, F. L. (1970) 'Participant observation in outdoor recreation', *Journal of Leisure Research*, Vol. 2, No. 4, pp. 226–36.

Chadwick, R. A. (1994) 'Concepts, definitions, and measures used in travel and tourism research', ch. 7 of Ritchie and Goeldner, *op. cit.*, pp. 65–80.

Chase, D. R. and Godbey, G. C. (1983) 'The accuracy of self-reported participation rates', *Leisure Studies*, Vol. 2, No. 2, pp. 231–6.

Chase, D. and Harada, M. (1984) 'Response error in self-reported recreation participation', *Journal of Leisure Research*, Vol. 16, No. 4, pp. 322–9.

Child, E. (1983) 'Play and culture: a study of English and Asian children', *Leisure Studies*, Vol. 2, No. 2, pp. 169–86.

Chisnall, P. M. (1991) 'Market segmentation analysis', ch. 6 of *The Essence of Marketing Research*, New York: Prentice-Hall, pp. 76–91.

Christensen, J. E. (1980) 'A second look at the informal interview ...', *Journal of Leisure Research*, Vol. 12, No. 2, pp. 183–6.

Christensen, J. E. (1988) 'Statistical and methodological issues in leisure research', in Barnett, *op. cit.*, pp. 175–92.

Clarke, J. and Critcher, C. (1985) *The Devil Makes Work: Leisure in Capitalist Britain*, London: Macmillan.

Claxton, J. D. (1994) 'Conjoint analysis in travel research: a manager's guide', in Ritchie and Goeldner, *op. cit.*, pp. 513–22.

Coalter, F. (with Long, J. and Duffield, B.) (1988) *Recreational Welfare*, Aldershot: Avebury/Gower.

Coalter, F. (1990) 'Analysing leisure policy', in I. Henry (ed.) *Management and Planning in the Leisure Industries*, London: Macmillan, pp. 149–78.

Coalter, F. (1993) 'Sports participation: price or priorities?', *Leisure Studies*, Vol. 12, No. 3, pp. 171–82.

Cohen, E. (1972) 'Towards a sociology of international tourism', *Social Research*, Vol. 39, No. 1, pp. 164–82.

Cohen, E. (1984) 'The sociology of tourism: approaches, issues, and findings', *Annual Review of Sociology*, Vol. 10, pp. 373–92.

Cohen, E. (1988) 'Traditions in the qualitative sociology of tourism', *Annals of Tourism Research*, Vol. 15, No. 1, pp. 29–46.

Cohen, E. (1993) 'The study of touristic images of native people: mitigating the stereotype of a stereotype', in Pearce and Butler, *op. cit.*, pp. 36–69.

Coopers & Lybrand Associates (1981) *Service Provision and Pricing in Local Government*, London: HMSO.

Coppock, J. T. (1982) 'Geographical contributions to the study of leisure', *Leisure Studies*, Vol. 1, No. 1, pp. 1–28.

Coppock, J. T. and Duffield, B. S. (1975) *Recreation in the Countryside: A Spatial Analysis*, London: Macmillan.

Corley, J. (1982) 'Employment in the leisure industries in Britain 1960–80', *Leisure Studies*, Vol. 1, No. 1, pp. 109–11.

Cowling, D. *et al.* (1983) *Identifying the Market: Catchment Areas of Sports Centres and Swimming Pools*, Study 24, London: Sports Council.

Critcher, C. (1992) 'Is there anything on the box? Leisure studies and media studies', *Leisure Studies*, Vol. 11, No. 2, pp. 97–122.

Crouch, G. I. and Shaw, R. N. (1991) *International Tourism Demand: A Meta-Analytical Integration of Research Findings*, Management Paper No. 36, Melbourne: Graduate School of Management, Monash University.

Csikszentmihalyi, M. (1990) *Flow: The Psychology of Optimal Experience*, New York: Harper & Row.

Cumming, E. and Henry, W. (1961) *Growing Old: The Process of Disengagement*, New York: Praeger.

Cuneen, C., Findlay, M., Lynch, R. and Tupper, V. (1989) *Dynamics of Collective Conflict: Riots at the Bathurst 'Bike Races*, North Ryde, NSW: Law Book Co.

Cuneen, C. and Lynch, R. (1988) 'The social meaning of conflict in riots at the Australian Grand Prix motorcycle races', *Leisure Studies*, Vol. 7, No. 1, pp. 1–20.

Cunningham, H. (1980) *Leisure in the Industrial Revolution*, London: Croom Helm.

Cushman, G., Veal, A. J. and Zuzanek, J. (eds.) (1996) *World Leisure Participation: Free Time in the Global Village*, Wallingford, Oxon.: CAB International.

Dann, G., Nash, D. and Pearce, P. (1988) 'Special issue: methodological issues in tourism research', *Annals of Tourism Research*, Vol. 15, No. 1.

Dann, G. and Cohen, E. (1991) 'Sociology and tourism', *Annals of Tourism Research*, Vol. 18, No. 1, pp. 155–69.

Darcy, S. (1994) 'Australian leisure participation: the monthly data', *Australian Journal of Leisure and Recreation*, Vol. 4, No. 1, pp. 26–32.

Darcy, S. and Veal, A. J. (1996) 'Australia', ch. 2 of Cushman *et al.*, *op. cit.*, pp. 17–34.

Dare, B., Welton, G. and Coe, W. (1987) *Concepts of Leisure in Western Thought*, Dubuque, IA: Kendall Hunt.

DASETT – *see* Department of the Arts, Sport, the Environment, Tourism and Territories.

Deem, R. (1986) *All Work and No Play? The Sociology of Women and Leisure*, Milton Keynes: Open University Press.

Denzin, N. K. (1989) *The Research Act: A Theoretical Introduction to Sociological Methods*, 3rd edn., Englewood Cliffs, NJ: Prentice-Hall.

Denzin, N. K. and Lincoln, Y. S. (eds.) (1994) *Handbook of Qualitative Research*, Thousand Oaks, CA: Sage.

Department of the Arts, Sport, the Environment, Tourism and Territories (1988a) *The Economic Impact of Sport and Recreation – Household Expenditure*, Technical Paper No. 1, Canberra: AGPS.

Department of the Arts, Sport, the Environment, Tourism and Territories (1988b) *The Economic Impact of Sport and Recreation – Regular Physical Activity*, Technical Paper No. 2, Canberra: AGPS.

Department of the Arts, Sport, the Environment, Tourism and Territories (1989) *Ideas for Australian Recreation*, Canberra: AGPS.

Dillman, D. A. (1978) *Mail and Telephone Surveys: The Total Design Method*, New York: Wiley.

Driver, B. L., Brown, P. J. and Peterson, G. L. (eds.) (1991) *Benefits of Leisure*, State College, PA: Venture.

Duffield, B. S. *et al.* (1983) *A Digest of Sports Statistics*, 1st edn., Information Series 7, London: Sports Council.

During, S. (ed.) (1993) *The Cultural Studies Reader*, London: Routledge.

Dyer, R. (1993) 'Entertainment and utopia', ch. 18 of During, *op. cit.*, pp. 271–83.

Eadington, W. R. and Redman, M. (1991) 'Economics and tourism', *Annals of Tourism Research*, Vol. 18, No. 1, pp. 41–56.

Echtner, C. M. and Ritchie, J. R. B. (1993) 'The measurement of destination image: an empirical assessment', *Journal of Travel Research*, Vol. 21, pp. 3–13.

Edwards, A. (1991) 'The reliability of tourism statistics', *Economist Intelligence Unit: Travel and Tourism Analyst*, No. 1, pp. 62–75.

Elias, N. (1986) 'Introduction', in Elias and Dunning, *op. cit.*, pp. 19–62.

Elias, N. and Dunning, E. (1986) *Quest for Excitement: Sport and Leisure in the Civilizing Process*, Oxford: Basil Blackwell.

Ely, M. (1981) 'Systematic observation as a recreation research tool', ch. 4 of D. Mercer (ed.) *Outdoor Recreation: Australian Perspectives*, Malvern, Vic.: Sorrett, pp. 57–67.

Field, D. N. (1972) 'The telephone interview in leisure research', *Journal of Leisure Research*, Vol. 5, No. 1, pp. 51–9.

Fielding, N. G. and Lee, R. M. (eds.) (1991) *Using Computers in Qualitative Research*, London: Sage.

Fiske, J. (1983) 'Surfalism and sandiotics: the beach in Oz popular culture', *Australian Journal of Cultural Studies*, Vol. 1, No. 2, pp. 120–49.

Frank Small and Associates (1988) *Tourism Survey Kit*, Sydney: Tourism Commission of New South Wales.

Frechtling, D. C. (1994) 'Assessing the impacts of travel and tourism – measuring economic benefits', in Ritchie and Goeldner, *op. cit.*, pp. 367–91.

Giddens, A. (1993) *Sociology*, Cambridge: Polity Press.

Giddens, A. (ed.) (1974) *Positivism and Sociology*, London: Heinemann.

Glancy, M. (1986) 'Participant observation in the recreation setting', *Journal of Leisure Research*, Vol. 18, No. 2, pp. 59–80.

Glancy, M. (1993) 'Achieving intersubjectivity: the process of becoming the subject in leisure research', *Leisure Studies*, Vol. 12, No. 1, pp. 45–60.

Glaser, B. and Strauss, A. L. (1967) *The Discovery of Grounded Theory: Strategies for Qualitative Research*, Chicago: Aldine.

Glass, G. V., McGaw, B. and Smith, M. L. (1981) *Meta-Analysis in Social Research*, Beverly Hills, CA: Sage.

Glyptis, S. A. (1979) *Countryside Visitors: Site Use and Leisure Life-Style*, PhD thesis, University of Hull.

Glyptis, S. A. (1981a) 'People at play in the countryside', *Geography*, Vol. 66, pp. 277–85.

Glyptis, S. A. (1981b) 'Room to relax in the countryside', *The Planner*, Vol. 67, No. 5, pp. 120–2.

Godbey, G. and Scott, D. (1990) 'Reorienting leisure research – the case for qualitative methods', *Society and Leisure*, Vol. 13, No. 1, pp. 189–206.

Goeldner, C. R. (1994) 'Travel and tourism information sources', ch. 8 of Ritchie and Goeldner, *op. cit.*, pp. 81–90.

Goeldner, C. R. and Dicke, K. (1980) *Bibliography of Tourism and Travel Research*, 9 vols., Boulder, CO: University of Colorado.

Goffman, I. (1959) *The Presentation of Self in Everyday Life*, Garden City: Doubleday/Anchor.

Gold, S. M. (1972) 'The non-use of neighbourhood parks', *Journal of the American Institute of Planners*, November, pp. 369–78.

Graburn, N. H. H. and Jafari, J. (1991) 'Introduction: tourism social sciences', *Annals of Tourism Research*, Vol. 18, No. 1 (Special Issue: Tourism Social Sciences), pp. 1–11.

Graburn, N. H. H. and Moore, R. S. (1994) 'Anthropological research on tourism', in Ritchie and Goeldner, *op. cit.*, pp. 233–42.

Grant, D. (1984) 'Another look at the beach', *Australian Journal of Cultural Studies*, Vol. 2, No. 2, pp. 131–8.

Gratton, C. (1996) 'Great Britain', ch. 5 of Cushman *et al.*, *op. cit.*, pp. 113–30.

Gratton, C. and Taylor, P. (1995) 'From economic theory to leisure practice via empirics: the case of demand and price', *Leisure Studies*, Vol. 14, No. 4, pp. 245–62.

Gratton, C. and Tice, A. (1994) 'Trends in sports participation in Britain 1977–1987', *Leisure Studies*, Vol. 13, No. 1, pp. 49–66.

Green, E., Hebron, S. and Woodward, B. (1990) *Women's Leisure, What Leisure?*, London: Macmillan.

Green, H., Hunter, C. and Moore, B. (1990) 'Application of the delphi technique in tourism', *Annals of Tourism Research*, Vol. 17, pp. 270–9.

Grichting, W. L. and Caltabiano, M. L. (1986) 'Amount and direction of bias in survey interviewing', *Australian Psychologist*, Vol. 21, No. 1, pp. 69–78.

Griffin, C., Hobson, D., MacIntosh, S. and McCabe, T. (1982) 'Women and leisure', in J. Hargreaves (ed.) *Sport, Culture and Ideology*, London: Routledge, pp. 99–116.

Gunn, C. A. (1994) 'A perspective on the purpose and nature of tourism research methods', in Ritchie and Goeldner, *op. cit.*, pp. 3–12.

Gushiken, T. T. (1996) 'Recreation services and the Internet', paper presented to the World Leisure and Recreation Association Fourth World Congress, *Free Time and the Quality of Life for the 21st Century*, Cardiff, 15–19 July.

Hall, C. M. (1994) *Tourism and Politics: Policy, Power and Place*, Chichester: John Wiley.

Hall, S. and Jefferson, T. (eds.) (1976) *Resistance through Rituals: Youth Culture in Post-war Britain*, London: Hutchinson.

Hamilton-Smith, E. (ed.) (1994) 'Play: a reflection of society', theme issue of *Society and Leisure*, Vol. 17, No. 1.

Hantrais, L. and Kamphorst, T. J. (1987) *Trends in the Arts: A Multinational Perspective*, Amersfoot, Holland: Giordano Bruno.

Harper, J. A. and Balmer, K. R. (1989) 'The perceived benefits of public leisure services: an exploratory investigation', *Society and Leisure*, Vol. 12. No. 1, pp. 171–88.

Harper, W. and Hultsman, J. (1992) 'Interpreting leisure as text: the whole', *Leisure Studies*, Vol. 11, No. 3, pp. 233–42.

Harris, R. and Leiper, N. (eds.) (1995) *Sustainable Tourism: An Australian Perspective*, Melbourne: Butterworth-Heinemann.

Hatry, H. P. and Dunn, D. R. (1971) *Measuring the Effectiveness of Local Government Services: Recreation*, Washington, DC: The Urban Institute.

Havitz, M. E. and Sell, J. A. (1991) 'The experimental method and leisure/recreation research: promoting a more active role', *Society and Leisure*, Vol. 14, No. 1, pp. 47–68.

Heberlein, T. A. and Dunwiddie, P. (1979) 'Systematic observation of use levels, campsite selection and visitor characteristics at a High Mountain Lake', *Journal of Leisure Research*, Vol. 11, No. 4, pp. 307–16.

Hellevik, O. (1984) *Introduction to Causal Analysis: Exploring Survey Data by Crosstabulation*, London: Allen & Unwin.

Hemingway, J. (1995) 'Leisure studies and interpretive social inquiry', *Leisure Studies*, Vol. 14, No. 1, pp. 32–47.

Henderson, K. A. (1990) 'Reality comes through a prism: method choices in leisure research', *Society and Leisure*, Vol. 13, No. 1, pp. 169–88.

Henderson, K. A. (1991) *Dimensions of Choice: A Qualitative Approach to Recreation, Parks, and Leisure Research*, State College, PA: Venture.

Henderson, K. A. and Bialeschki, D. (1995) *Evaluating Leisure Services: Making Enlightened Decisions*, State College, PA: Venture.

Henderson, K. M., Bialeschki, D., Shaw, S. M. and Freysinger, V. J. (1989) *A Time of One's Own: A Feminist Perspective on Women's Leisure*, State College, PA: Venture.

Henley Centre for Forecasting (1986) *The Economic Impact and Importance of Sport in the United Kingdom*, London: Sports Council.

Henley Centre for Forecasting (quarterly) *Leisure Futures*, London: HCF.

Henry, I. P. (1993) *The Politics of Leisure Policy*, Basingstoke: Macmillan.

Henry, I. and Spink, J. (1990) 'Planning for leisure: the commercial and public sectors', in I. P. Henry (ed.) *Management and Planning in the Leisure Industries*, London: Macmillan, pp. 33–69.

Hodder, I. (1994) 'The interpretation of documents and material culture', ch. 24 of Denzin and Lincoln, *op. cit.*, pp. 393–402.

Hoinville, G. and Jowell, R. (1978) *Survey Research Practice*, London: Heinemann.

Hollands, R. G. (1985) 'Working class youth, leisure and the search for work', in S. R. Parker and A. J. Veal (eds.) *Work, Non-work and Leisure*, London: Leisure Studies Association, pp. 3–29.

Hornery, A. (1996) 'Market researchers facing major hurdles', *Sydney Morning Herald*, 11 April, p. 26.

Howard, D. R. and Crompton, J. L. (1980) *Financing, Managing and Marketing Recreation and Park Resources*, Dubuque, IA: Wm. C. Brown.

Howard, K. and Sharp, J. A. (1983) *The Management of a Student Research Project*, Aldershot, Hants.: Gower.

Howe, C. Z. (1991) 'Considerations when using phenomenology in leisure inquiry: beliefs, methods and analysis in naturalistic research', *Leisure Studies*, Vol. 10, No. 1, pp. 49–62.

Howell, S. and Badmin, P. (1996) *Performance, Monitoring and Evaluation in Leisure Management*, London: Pitman.

Huberman, A. M. and Miles, M. B. (1994) 'Data management and analysis methods', in Denzin and Lincoln, *op. cit.*, pp. 428–44.

Hudson, S. (1988) *How to Conduct Community Needs Assessment Surveys in Public Parks and Recreation*, Columbus, OH: Publishing Horizons.

Huizinga, J. (1955) *Homo Ludens: A Study of the Play Element in Culture*, Boston: Beacon Press.

Hultsman, J. and Harper, W. (1992) 'Interpreting leisure as text: the part', *Leisure Studies*, Vol. 11, No. 2, pp. 135–46.

Hurst, F. (1994) 'Enroute surveys', ch. 33 of Ritchie and Goeldner, *op. cit.*, pp. 453–72.

Ingham, R. (1986) 'Psychological contributions to the study of leisure – Part One', *Leisure Studies*, Vol. 5, No. 3, pp. 255–80.

Ingham, R. (1987) 'Psychological contributions to the study of leisure – Part Two', *Leisure Studies*, Vol. 6, No. 1, pp. 1–14.

Iso-Ahola, S. E. (1980) *The Social Psychology of Leisure and Recreation*, Dubuque, IA: Wm. C. Brown.

Jackson, E. L. and Burton, T. L. (eds.) (1989) *Understanding Leisure and Recreation: Mapping the Past and Charting the Future*, State College, PA: Venture.

Jafari, J. and Aaser, D. (1988) 'Tourism as the subject of doctoral dissertations', *Annals of Tourism Research*, Vol. 15, No. 3, pp. 407–29.

Jarvie, G. and Maguire, J. (1994) *Sport and Leisure in Social Thought*, London: Routledge.

Kamphorst, T. J. and Roberts, K. (eds.) (1989) *Trends in Sports: A Multinational Perspective*, Culemborg, Holland: Giordano Bruno.

Kamphorst, T. J., Tibori, T. T. and Giljam, M. J. (1984) 'Quantitative and qualitative research: shall the twain ever meet?' *World Leisure & Recreation*, Vol. 26, Dec., pp. 25–7.

Kellehear, A. (1993) *The Unobtrusive Researcher: A Guide to Methods*, Sydney: Allen & Unwin.

Kelly, G. A. (1955) *The Psychology of Personal Constructs*, New York: Norton.

Kelly, J. R. (1980) 'Leisure and quality: beyond the quantitative barrier in research', ch. 23 of T. L. Goodale and P. A. Witt (eds.) *Recreation and Leisure: Issues in an Era of Change*, State College, PA: Venture, pp. 300–14.

Kelly, J. R. (1982) *Leisure*, Englewood Cliffs, NJ: Prentice-Hall.

Kelly, J. R. (1983) *Leisure Identities and Interactions*, London: Allen & Unwin.

Kelly, J. R. (1987a) *Freedom to Be: A New Sociology of Leisure*, New York: Macmillan.

Kelly, J. R. (1987b) *Recreation Trends – Toward the Year 2000*, Champaign, IL: Management Learning Laboratories.

Kelly, J. R. (1994) 'The symbolic interaction metaphor and leisure: critical challenges', *Leisure Studies*, Vol. 13, No. 2, pp. 81–96.

Kelly, J. R. and Godbey, G. (1992) *The Sociology of Leisure*, State College, PA: Venture.

Kelsey, C. and Gray, H. (1986a) *The Citizen Survey Process in Parks and Recreation*, Reston, VA: American Alliance for Health, P.E., Recreation and Dance.

Kelsey, C. and Gray, H. (1986b) *The Feasibility Study Process for Parks and Recreation*, Reston, VA: American Alliance for Health, P.E., Recreation and Dance.

Kidder, L. H. (1981) *Selltiz, Wrightsman and Cook's Research Methods in Social Relations*, New York: Holt, Rinehart & Winston.

Kimmel, A. J. (1988) *Ethics and Values in Applied Social Research*, Newbury Park, CA: Sage.

Klugman, K., Kuenz, J., Waldrop, S. and Willis, S. (1995) *Inside the Mouse: The Project on Disney*, Durham, NC: Duke University Press.

Kraus, R. and Allen, L. (1987) *Research and Evaluation in Recreation, Parks, and Leisure Studies*, Columbus, OH: Publishing Horizons.

Krenz, C. and Sax, G. (1986) 'What quantitative research is and why it doesn't work', *American Behavioral Scientist*, Vol. 30, No. 1, pp. 58–69.

Krippendorf, J. (1987) *The Holiday Makers: Understanding the Impact of Leisure and Travel*, Oxford: Heinemann.

Krueger, R. A. (1988) *Focus Groups: A Practical Guide for Applied Research*, Newbury Park, CA: Sage.

Labovitz, S. and Hagedorn, R. (1971) *Introduction to Social Research*, New York: McGraw-Hill.

LaPage, W. F. (1981) 'A further look at the informal interview', *Journal of Leisure Research*, Vol. 13, No. 2, pp. 174–6.

LaPage, W. F. (1994) 'Using panels for tourism and travel research', ch. 40 of Ritchie and Goeldner, *op. cit.*, pp. 481–6.

Lavrakas, P. K. (1993) *Telephone Survey Methods: Sampling, Selection and Supervision*, 2nd edn. Newbury Park, CA: Sage.

Leiper, N. (1995) *Tourism Management*, Collingwood, Vic.: RMIT Press/TAFE Publications.

Lofland, J. and Lofland, L. H. (1984) *Analyzing Social Settings: A Guide to Qualitative Observation and Analysis*, 2nd edn., Belmont, CA: Wadsworth.

Loomis, R. J. (1987) *Museum Visitor Evaluation: New Tool for Management*, Nashville, TN: American Association for State and Local History.

Lucas, R. C. (1970) *User Evaluation of Campgrounds*, St. Paul, MN: US Forest Service.

Lynch, R. and Veal, A. J. (1996) *Australian Leisure*, Melbourne: Longman Australia.

McCall, G. J. and Simmons, J. L. (eds.) (1969) *Issues in Participant Observation*, Reading, MA: Addison-Wesley.

MacCannell, D. (1976) *The Tourist: A New Theory of the Leisure Class*, London: Macmillan.

MacCannell, D. (1993) *The Empty Meeting Grounds*, London: Routledge.

McFee, M. (1992) *LSA Publications Index Book*, Eastbourne: Leisure Studies Association.

McRobbie, A. (1994) *Postmodernism and Popular Culture*, London: Routledge.

Maguire, J. (1988) 'Doing figurational sociology: some preliminary observations on methodological issues and sensitizing concepts', *Leisure Studies*, Vol. 7, No. 2, pp. 187–94.

Mallon, B. (1984) *The Olympics: A Bibliography*, New York: Garland.

Marans, R. W. and Mohai, P. (1991) 'Leisure resources, recreation activity, and the quality of life', in Driver *et al.*, *op. cit.*, pp. 351–64.

Marriott, K. (1987) *Recreation Planning: A Manual for Local Government*, Adelaide: Dept. of Recreation and Sport, South Australia.

Marsh, P. *et al.* (1978) *The Rules of Disorder*, London: Routledge.

Martilla, J. A. and James, J. C. (1977) 'Importance-performance analysis', *Journal of Marketing*, Vol. 41, No. 1, pp. 77–9.

Martin, S. and Mason, W. (annual) *The UK Sports, Entertainment etc. Market*, Sudbury, Suffolk: Leisure Consultants.

Matthews, H. G. and Richter, L. (1991) 'Political science and tourism', *Annals of Tourism Research*, Vol. 18, No. 1, pp. 120–35.

Mitchell, A. (1985) *The Nine American Lifestyles*, New York: Collier Macmillan.

Mitchell, L. S. (1994) 'Research on the geography of tourism', ch. 17 of Ritchie and Goeldner, *op. cit.*, pp. 197–208.

Mitchell, L. S. and Murphy, P. E. (1991) 'Geography and tourism', *Annals of Tourism Research*, Vol. 18, No. 1, pp. 57–70.

Moeller, G. H. *et al.* (1980a) 'The informal interview as a technique for recreation research', *Journal of Leisure Research*, Vol. 12, No. 2, pp. 174–82.

Moeller, G. H. *et al.* (1980b) 'A response to "A second look at the informal interview"', *Journal of Leisure Research*, Vol. 12, No. 2, pp. 187–8.

Moeller, G. H. and Shafer, E. L. (1994) 'The Delphi technique: a tool for long-range tourism and travel planning', ch. 39 of Ritchie and Goeldner, *op. cit.*, pp. 473–80.

Moorhouse, H. F. (1989) 'Models of work, models of leisure', in C. Rojek (ed.) *Leisure for Leisure*, London: Macmillan, pp. 15–35.

Morgan, D. (1994) 'It began with the piton: the challenge to British rock climbing in a post-modernist framework', in I. Henry (ed.) *Leisure: Modernity, Postmodernity and Lifestyles*, Eastbourne, Sussex: Leisure Studies Association, pp. 341–54.

Morgan, D. L. (ed.) (1993) *Successful Focus Groups: Advancing the State of the Art*, Newbury Park, CA: Sage.

Murphy, J. F. (ed.) (1974) *Concepts of Leisure: Philosophical Implications*, Englewood Cliffs, NJ: Prentice-Hall.

Murphy, P. (1991) 'Data gathering for community-oriented tourism planning: a case study of Vancouver Island, British Columbia', *Leisure Studies*, Vol. 10, No. 1, pp. 65–80.

Myerscough, J. (1988) *The Economic Importance of the Arts in Britain*, London: Policy Studies Institute.

Nash, D. and Smith, V. L. (1991) 'Anthropology and tourism', *Annals of Tourism Research*, Vol. 18, No. 1, pp. 170–7.

Norusis, M. J. (1993) *SPSS for Windows, Base System User's Guide: Release 6.0*, Chicago: SPSS Inc.

O'Brien, S. and Ford, R. (1988) 'Can we at last say goodbye to social class? An examination of the usefulness and stability of some alternative methods of measurement', *Journal of the Market Research Society*, Vol. 30, No. 3, pp. 289–332.

O'Connor, B. and Boyle, R. (1993) 'Dallas with balls: televized sport, soap opera and male and female pleasures', *Leisure Studies*, Vol. 12, No. 2, pp. 107–20.

OECD – Organisation for Economic Co-operation and Development (annual) *International Tourism and Tourism Policies in OECD Member Countries*, Paris: OECD.

Office of Population Censuses and Surveys (1987) *General Household Survey*, London: HMSO.

Office of Population Censuses and Surveys (annual) *General Household Survey*, London: HMSO.

Oppenheim, A. N. (1992) *Questionnaire Design, Interviewing and Attitude Measurement*, London: Pinter.

Parker, S. (1971) *The Future of Work and Leisure*, London: Palladin.

Parker, S. R. (1976) *The Sociology of Leisure*, London: George Allen & Unwin.

Parry, N. C. A. (1983) 'Sociological contributions to the study of leisure', *Leisure Studies*, Vol. 2, No. 1, pp. 57–82.

Patmore, A. (1983) *Recreation and Resources*, Oxford: Basil Blackwell.

Pearce, D. (1987) *Tourism Today: A Geographical Analysis*, Harlow: Longman.

Pearce, D. G. and Butler, R. W. (eds.) (1993) *Tourism Research: Critiques and Challenges*, London: Routledge.

Pearce, P. L. (1982) *The Social Psychology of Tourist Behaviour*, Oxford: Pergamon.

Pearce, P. L. (1988) *The Ulysses Factor: Evaluating Visitors in Tourist Settings*, New York: Springer-Verlag.

Pearce, P. L. and Stringer, P. F. (1991) 'Psychology and tourism', *Annals of Tourism Research*, Vol. 18, No. 1, pp. 136–54.

Peine, J. D. (1984) *Proceedings of a Workshop on Unobtrusive Techniques to Study Social Behavior in Parks*, Atlanta, GA: National Park Service, Southeast Regional Office.

Perdue, R. R. and Botkin, M. R. (1988) 'Visitor survey versus conversion study', *Annals of Tourism Research*, Vol. 15, No. 1, pp. 76–87.

Perkins, H. C. and Cushman, G. (eds.) (1993) *Leisure, Recreation and Tourism*, Auckland: Longman Paul.

Peterson, K. I. (1994) 'Qualitative research methods for the travel and tourism industry', ch. 41 of Ritchie and Goeldner, *op. cit.*, pp. 487–92.

Pigram, J. (1983) *Outdoor Recreation and Resource Management*, London: Croom Helm.

Pizam, A. (1994) 'Planning a tourism research investigation', ch. 9 of Ritchie and Goeldner, *op. cit.*, pp. 91–104.

Plog, S. C. (1994) 'Developing and using psychographics in tourism research', ch. 19 of Ritchie and Goeldner, *op. cit.*, pp. 209–18.

Pollard, W. E. (1987) 'Decision making and the use of evaluation research', *American Behavioral Scientist*, Vol. 30, No. 6, pp. 661–76.

Punch, M. (1994) 'Politics and ethics in qualitative research', in Denzin and Lincoln, *op. cit.*, pp. 83–98.

Rapoport, R. and Rapoport, R. N. (1975) *Leisure and the Family Life Cycle*, London: Routledge.

Ravenscroft, N. (1993) 'Public leisure provision and the good citizen', *Leisure Studies*, Vol. 12, No. 1, pp. 33–44.

Reynolds, F. and Johnson, D. (1978) 'Validity of focus group findings', *Journal of Advertising Research*, pp. 3–24.

Richards, T. J. and Richards, L. (1994) 'Using computers in qualitative research', ch. 28 of Denzin and Lincoln, *op. cit.*, pp. 445–62.

Richter, L. K. (1994) 'The political dimensions of tourism', ch. 19 of Ritchie and Goeldner, *op. cit.*, pp. 219–32.

Ritchie, J. R. B. and Goeldner, C. R. (eds.) (1994) *Travel, Tourism and Hospitality Research*, 2nd edn., New York: John Wiley.

Roberts, K. (1978) *Contemporary Society and the Growth of Leisure*, London: Longman.

Roberts, K. (1983) *Youth and Leisure*, London: Allen & Unwin.

Robertson, R. W. and Veal, A. J. (1987) *Port Hacking Visitor Use Study*, Sydney: Centre for Leisure and Tourism Studies, UTS.

Rojek, C. (1985) *Capitalism and Leisure Theory*, London: Tavistock.

Rojek, C. (1989) 'Leisure and recreation theory', in Jackson and Burton, *op. cit.*, pp. 69–88.

Rojek, C. (1990) 'Baudrillard and leisure', *Leisure Studies*, Vol. 9, No. 1, pp. 7–20.

Rojek, C. (1993) 'Disney culture', *Leisure Studies*, Vol. 12, No. 2, pp. 121–36.

Rojek, C. (1995) *Decentring Leisure: Rethinking Leisure Theory*, London: Sage.

Rowe, D. (1995) *Popular Cultures: Rock Music, Sport and the Politics of Pleasure*, London: Sage.

Rowe, D. and Brown, P. (1994) 'Promoting women's sport: theory, policy and practice', *Leisure Studies*, Vol. 13, No. 2, pp. 97–110.

Ruddell, E. J. and Hammit, W. E. (1987) 'Prospect refuge theory: a psychological orientation for edge effect in recreation environments', *Journal of Leisure Research*, Vol. 19, No. 4, pp. 249–60.

Ruskin, H. and Sivan, A. (eds.) (1995) *Leisure Education: Towards the 21st Century*, Proceedings of the International Seminar of the World Leisure and Recreation Commission on Education, Jerusalem, August, 1993, Provo, Utah: Brigham Young University Press.

Russell, B. (1935) *In Praise of Idleness and Other Essays*, London: Allen & Unwin.

Ryan, C. (1991) *Recreational Tourism: A Social Science Perspective*, London: Routledge.

Ryan, C. (1995) *Researching Tourist Satisfaction: Issues, Concepts, Problems*, London: Routledge.

Saunders, D. M. and Turner, D. E. (1987) 'Gambling and leisure: the case of racing', *Leisure Studies*, Vol. 6, No. 3, pp. 281–300.

Sahlins, M. (1972) *Stone Age Economics*, New York: Aldine.

Scraton, S. (1994) 'The changing world of women and leisure: feminism, "post-feminism" and leisure', *Leisure Studies*, Vol. 13, No. 4, pp. 249–61.

Seaton, A. V. (1994) 'Intimations of modernity: the cocktail cult between the wars', in I. Henry (ed.) *Leisure: Modernity, Postmodernity and Lifestyles*, Eastbourne, Sussex: Leisure Studies Association, pp. 323–40.

Settle, J. G. (1977) *Leisure in the North West: A Tool for Forecasting*, London: Sports Council.

Shadish, W. R. Jr., Cook, T. D. and Leviton, L. C. (1991) *Foundations of Program Evaluation: Theories of Practice*, Newbury Park, CA: Sage.

Shaw, M. (1984) *Sport and Leisure Participation and Life-styles in Different Residential Neighbourhoods*, London: Sports Council/SSRC.

Shih, D. (1986) 'VALS as a tool of tourism marketing research', *Journal of Travel Research*, Spring, pp. 2–11.

Sieber, J. E. (1992) *Planning Ethically Responsible Research*, Newbury Park, CA: Sage.

Sillitoe, K. K. (1969) *Planning for Leisure*, London: HMSO.

Silverman, D. (1993) *Interpreting Qualitative Data: Methods for Analysing Talk, Text and Interaction*, London: Sage.

Smith, M. (1985) 'A participant observer study of a "rough" working class pub', *Leisure Studies*, Vol. 4, No. 3, pp. 293–306.

Smith, S. L. J. (1983) *Recreation Geography*, Harlow: Longman.

Smith, S. L. J. (1989) *Tourism Analysis: A Handbook*, Harlow: Longman.

Sönmez, S., Shinew, K., Marchese, L., Veldkamp, C. and Burnett, G. W. (1993) 'Leisure corrupted: an artist's portrait of leisure in a changing society', *Leisure Studies*, Vol. 12, No. 4, pp. 266–76.

Spatz, C. and Johnston, J. O. (1989) *Basic Statistics: Tales of Distribution*, 4th edn., Pacific Grove, CA: Brooks/Cole Publishing.

Sports Council (1982) *Sport in the Community: The Next Ten Years*, London: Sports Council.

Stake, R. E. (1994) 'Case studies', ch. 14 of Denzin and Lincoln, *op. cit.*, pp. 236–47.

Stebbins, R. (1992) *Amateurs, Professionals and Serious Leisure*, Montreal: McGill-Queen's University Press.

Stewart, D. W. and Shamdasani, P. N. (1990) *Focus Groups: Theory and Practice*, Newbury Park, CA: Sage.

Stockdale, J. (1984) 'People's conceptions of leisure', in A. Tomlinson (ed.) *Leisure: Politics, Planning and People*, London: Leisure Studies Association, pp. 86–115.

Strauss, A. L. (1987) *Qualitative Analysis for Social Scientists*, Cambridge: Cambridge University Press.

Strauss, A. and Corbin, J. (1994) 'Grounded theory methodology', in Denzin and Lincoln, *op. cit.*, pp. 273–85.

Straw, W. (1993) 'Characterising rock music culture: the case of heavy metal', ch. 24 of During, *op. cit.*, pp. 368–81.

Sydney Morning Herald (1996) 'Our green future', 7 June, p. 12.

Szalai, A. (ed.) (1972) *The Use of Time: Daily Activities of Urban and Suburban Populations in Twelve Countries*, The Hague: Mouton.

Tomlinson, A. (ed.) (1990) *Consumption, Identity, and Style; Marketing, Meanings, and the Packaging of Pleasure*, London: Comedia/Routledge.

Toohey, K. (1990) 'A content analysis of the Australian television coverage of the 1988 Seoul Olympics', paper to the *Commonwealth and International Conference of Physical Education, Sport, Health, Dance, Recreation and Leisure*, January, Auckland.

Torkildsen, G. (1983) *Leisure and Recreation Management*, London: Spon.

Torkildsen, G. (1993) *Torkildsen's Guides to Leisure Management*, Harlow, Essex: Longman.

Tourism and Recreation Research Unit (TRRU) (1983) *Recreation Site Survey Manual: Methods and Techniques for Conducting Visitor Surveys*, London: Spon.

Towner, J. and Wall, G. (1991) 'History and tourism', *Annals of Tourism Research*, Vol. 18, No. 1, pp. 71–84.

Tyre, G. L. and Siderelis, C. D. (1978) 'Instant-count sampling – a technique for estimating recreation use in municipal settings', *Journal of Leisure Research*, Vol. 10, No. 2, pp. 173–80.

Urry, J. (1990) *The Tourist Gaze: Leisure and Travel in Contemporary Societies*, London: Sage.

Urry, J. (1994) 'Cultural change and contemporary tourism', *Leisure Studies*, Vol. 13, No. 4, pp. 233–8.

Van der Zande, A. N. (1985) 'Distribution patterns of visitors in large areas: a problem of measurement and analysis', *Leisure Studies*, Vol. 4, No. 1, pp. 85–100.

Van Doren, C. S. and Solan, D. S. (1979) 'Listing of dissertations and theses in leisure and recreation: August 1975 to August 1977', *Journal of Leisure Research*, Vol. 10, No. 3, pp. 219–44.

Van Doren, C. S. and Stubbles, R. (1976) 'Listing of dissertations and theses in leisure and recreation', *Journal of Leisure Research*, Vol. 7, No. 1, pp. 69–80.

Veal, A. J. (1984) 'Leisure in England and Wales', *Leisure Studies*, Vol. 3, No. 2, pp. 221–30.

Veal, A. J. (1987) 'The leisure forecasting tradition', ch. 7 of *Leisure and the Future*, London: Allen & Unwin, pp. 125–56.

Veal, A. J. (1988) 'Are user surveys useful?' in J. and N. Parry (eds.) *Leisure, The Arts and the Community*, Conference papers No. 30, Eastbourne, UK: Leisure Studies Association, pp. 20–7.

Veal, A. J. (1989a) 'Leisure, lifestyle and status: a pluralistic framework for analysis', *Leisure Studies*, Vol. 8, No. 2, pp. 141–54.

Veal, A. J. (1989b) 'The doubtful contribution of economics to leisure management', *Society and Leisure*, Vol. 12, No. 2, pp. 147–56.

Veal, A. J. (1990) *Joint Provision and Dual Use of Leisure Facilities*, London: Polytechnic of North London.

Veal, A. J. (1993a) 'The concept of lifestyle: a review', *Leisure Studies*, Vol. 12, No. 4, pp. 233–52.

Veal, A. J. (1993b) 'Leisure participation in Australia, 1985–1991: a note on the data', *Australian Journal of Leisure and Recreation*, Vol. 3, No. 1, pp. 37–43.

Veal, A. J. (1993c) 'Leisure surveys in Australia', *ANZALS Leisure Research Series*, Vol. 1, pp. 197–210.

Veal, A. J. (1993d) 'Lifestyle, leisure and neighbourhood' and 'National Leisure surveys: the British experience', in A. J. Veal, G. Cushman and P. Jonson (eds.) *Leisure & Tourism: Social & Environmental Change World Congress*, Sydney: World Leisure & Recreation Assn/University of Technology, pp. 404–17.

Veal, A. J. (1994a) *Leisure Policy and Planning*, Harlow: Longman/Pitman.

Veal, A. J. (1994b) 'Intersubjectivity and the transatlantic divide: a comment on Glancy (and Ragheb and Tate)', *Leisure Studies*, Vol. 13, No. 3, pp. 211–16.

Veal, A. J. (1995) 'Leisure studies: frameworks for analysis', in Ruskin and Sivan, *op. cit.*, pp. 124–36.

Vickerman, R. W. (1983) 'The contribution of economics to the study of leisure', *Leisure Studies*, Vol. 2, No. 3, pp. 345–64.

Walker J. C. (1988) *Louts and Legends*, Sydney: Allen & Unwin.

Weiler, B. and Hall, C. M. (eds.) (1992) *Special Interest Tourism*, London: Belhaven.

Wells, W. D. (ed.) (1974) *Life Style and Psychographics*, Chicago: American Marketing Assn.

Whyte, W. F. (1955) *Street Corner Society*, Chicago: Univ. Chicago Press.

Whyte, W. F. (1982) 'Interviewing in field research', in R. G. Burgess (ed.) *Field Research: A Sourcebook and Field Manual*, London: Allen & Unwin, pp. 111–22.

Williams, A. M. and Shaw, G. (1988) *Tourism and Economic Development: Western European Experience*, London: Belhaven.

Williams, E. A., Jenkins, C. and Neville, A. M. (1988) 'Social area influences on leisure activity – an exploration of the ACORN classification with reference to sport', *Leisure Studies*, Vol. 7, No. 1, pp. 81–95.

Williams, S. (1995) *Outdoor Recreation and the Urban Environment*, London: Routledge.

Williamson, J. B., Barry, S. T. and Dorr, R. S. (1982) *The Research Craft*, Boston: Little, Brown.

Wilson, J. (1988) *Politics and Leisure*, London: Allen & Unwin.

Wilson, K. (1995) 'Olympians or lemmings? The postmodernist fun run', *Leisure Studies*, Vol. 14, No. 3, pp. 174–85.

Wilson, M. J. *et al.* (1979) 'Styles of research in social science', in *Variety in Social Science Research* (Block 1, Part 1 of Course DE303: Research Methods in Education and Social Science), Milton Keynes: Open University Press, pp. 11–24.

Wimbush, E. and Talbot, M. (eds.) (1988) *Relative Freedoms: Women and Leisure*, Milton Keynes: Open University Press.

Witt, C. A. and Wright, P. L. (1992) 'Tourist motivation: life after Maslow', in P. Johnston and B. Thomas (eds.) *Choice and Demand in Tourism*, London: Mansell, pp. 33–55.

Woodside, A. G. and Ronkainen, I. A. (1994) 'Improving advertising conversion studies', ch. 47 of Ritchie and Goeldner, *op. cit.*, pp. 481–7.

World Tourism Organisation (annual) *Yearbook of Tourism Statistics*, Madrid: WTO.

Wynne, D. (1986) 'Living on "The Heath"', *Leisure Studies*, Vol. 5, No. 1, pp. 109–16.

Young, M. and Willmott, P. (1973) *The Symmetrical Family*, London: Routledge.

Zukin, S. (1990) 'Socio-spatial prototypes of a new organization of consumption: the role of real cultural capital', *Sociology*, Vol. 24, No. 1, pp. 37–55.

INDEX